CW01476736

PARTICIPATION AS PROCESS - PROCESS AS GROWTH

THE MAL-DEVELOPMENT MODEL:
A DOWNPAYMENT ON DISASTER

...*The model is costly. It neglects resources that the local environment could provide and the skills that local people could supply, counting rather on imports, at escalating prices. It neglects not only peasants but anyone who does not belong to a thin layer at the top of society, identified as the "modernizing" elements. They will be the targets of development, and their wealth and consequent investments are expected to provide the motor for further growth. Eventually--it is not clear when--everyone in the society will benefit through the "trickle-down" process. "Modernization", like "development" itself, is a myth-word in whose name any destruction, and any expenditure, may be undertaken with impunity.*

SUSAN GEORGE
IN "A FATE WORSE THAN DEBT"

PARTICIPATION
AS PROCESS
- PROCESS
AS GROWTH

- what
we can learn
from Grameen Bank
Bangladesh

ANDREAS FUGLESANG
DALE CHANDLER
in collaboration with Daya Akuretiyagama

Published by
Grameen Trust
Mirpur Two, Dhaka 1216
Bangladesh

First Published
December , 1993

Copyright ©
Grameen Trust

Cover Designed by
Authors

Printing Supervised by
Aminur Rahman Nasim

Printed by
Graphtone Printers
55/1, Purana Paltan
Dhaka 1000
Bangladesh

ISBN : 984-05-1238-2

Photos by M. Salahuddin Azizee. Vignettes and drawings by children in the centre schools, Tapan Kumar Debnath and Andreas Fuglesang. The views and ideas expressed in this book are of the authors and do not necessarily reflect those of Grameen Bank or any of its sister organizations.

Price
Taka 150.00
US $ 15.00

FIRST BANK WORKER:
I remember the 50 taka loan
to the first loanee.
Sophia Khatoon hid her face
as she made her thumbprint.
When she extended her hand
for the money, it was trembling.

TO ALL BANK WORKERS
for the millions of hands
no longer trembling

PREFACE

This book is a revised and updated version of *Participation as Process* which was published jointly by the Norwegian Ministry of Development Cooperation (Norad) and Grameen Bank in 1986.

Considering the many developments since then, and the demand for the book in information and training, Professor Muhammad Yunus invited us to review both the Bank and the book. We are grateful to him and the Grameen Trust for making the undertaking possible in November 1992. We asked Daya Akuretiyagama to help us on the mission. Zubaida Nazneen joined our team as interpreter. Our deep appreciation to them both.

It should be clear to the readers that the function of banking is a highly-skilled craft. When the craft unites with organizational talent and an unwavering commitment to reach the poor, a successful replication may be on its way. Our intention in reworking the book has been to make Grameen Bank and its family of organizations as a whole, accessible to the reader. Our hope is that this has been achieved.

July 1993

Andreas Fuglesang
Dale Chandler

CONTENTS

ABOUT SEEING AND DESCRIBING   1

DAILY LIFE OF LITTLE PEOPLE   13
The issue of self-image   15
Skills and assets of poverty   16
Human manipulation   19
Social discontinuity   22
The social negation of women   24

PEOPLE'S BANK PEOPLE'S MOVEMENT   31
Conflict or process   31
Critical fit   35
Some organizational modes of thought   37
A socio-economic formation   39
Many interacting functions   41
Centre functions   42
Development facilitation functions   50
Service functions   61
The SIDE programme   71
Training   74
Growth and shedding of functions   80
The discipline of accountability   83

ix

PROGRAMMES AND PROCESSES   87
The process of group formation   90
The loan procedures   94
The power of standing and moving together   100

ECONOMIC DEVELOPMENT PROGRAMME   103
Group fund   103
Emergency fund   106
Special savings fund   107
Children's welfare fund   107
Types of loans   108

SOCIAL DEVELOPMENT PROGRAMME   119
Workshop programme   120
Centre school programme   128
Supplies and skill-training   129

Process in workshops   131
Process through the journal Uddog   143
Process in joint enterprises   149
Process and women   152
Process through other organizations   157
Process in just another centre meeting   160
Process from the centre to the boardroom   163

NATURAL DISASTERS - INTENSIVE CARE   165
Rangpur: special rehabilitation programme   168

CONGLOMERATE GROWTH
- GRAMEEN FAMILY OF ORGANIZATIONS   177
Krishi foundation   178
    The primary farm - a basic concept   183
Fisheries foundation   191
Grameen trust   198
Other foundations   201
Conglomerate growth   203

THE BANK'S GROWTH SPURT
- EFFECTS AND CONSEQUENCES   205
A showcase on microlevel   205
Towards the macrolevel effect   209
Organizational growing pains   217
The "firefighting" programme   221
Organizational life cycle   225
Growth of children   228
The donor dilemma   233
Interaction with mainstream economy   235
Towards a new polity?   238
What can we learn?   239

REFERENCES   245

ANNEXES   253

Annex 1
English Version of Bidhimala (Constitution)   255

Annex 2
Grameen Bank Ordinance   263

Annex 3
Head Office Organizational Chart   264

Annex 4
List of Periodical Statements
Monitoring and Evaluation Department   265

Annex 5
Duties of Group Chairperson   271

Annex 6
Duties of Centre Chief   272

Annex 7
Training Manual for Women's Workshops   274

ABOUT SEEING
AND DESCRIBING

We are creating
a counterculture.
Grameen Bank is
a lot of defiance.
MUHAMMAD YUNUS

WHAT DO WE SEE?

We shall start our description of Grameen Bank by pointing to a peculiarity in human perception of reality of which people frequently are not aware. The mental process of focusing attention on something is, by its very nature, also a process by which we exclude many other things from our attention. Our perception is selective. The philosopher Ludwig Wittgenstein was fond of the following figure to demonstrate the point:

You may perceive this as a duck, but if you study some more of the visual clues you may, after a while, see it as a rabbit. The point is that when we are mentally attentive to the "duck-seeing" aspect, we see only the duck. There is a resistance to seeing the rabbit--or vice-versa. Yet, we cannot dispute that it is both. It is a "duck-rabbit". Similarly, the following figure can be seen in more ways than two, depending from which angle we are looking at it.

1

Is it a cowboy hat, a man in a barbershop, a clown or one with a turban?

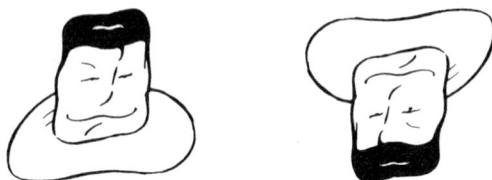

We do not see and observe reality only with our eyes, but with our attitudes, with the faith or values we hold and not the least with the particular conceptual skeleton we were born with as academics. While scientific capacity for deduction and analysis seems boundless, the human capability of perceiving the whole, of synthesizing, seems to be of a more limited nature. Economists will tend to see Grameen Bank basically as a bank, or at most, a credit system with some characteristic money-processing features. The reader should not doubt that it is a banking business but it is also much more than that. Certainly it is not a lame duck and there may be a rabbit in the hat.

For a long time we suffered from the visual delusion that the Bank's emblem was a house until somebody told us it is actually an arrow with the colours of the Bangladesh flag, dark green and red, pointing upwards, a symbol of people's upliftment and progress. We would strongly argue for the perception of it as a people's movement, a socio-economic formation, and the first in the world that has managed to make itself almost self-sustainable within a national economy extremely hostile to the poor. It is an arrow up, a rock of honesty and efficiency in a swamp of corruption and deceit. Bangladesh receives 1.6 billion US dollars a year in foreign aid from principal donors and has little to show for it among its 60 million poor. The money is spirited away by a supreme and greedy establishment of government bureaucrats, politicians, businessmen and landowning elite. The Bengali are a remarkable people. The counterculture of Grameen Bank grows out of a deep sense of human rights, shame, hurt and daredevil defiance: We are not a basket case, we shall show ourselves and the world that development can also be done right! Seeing Grameen as a bank only is an incomplete, defective perception. It is best described in an interdisciplinary manner, in which economics is not considered more essential than any other aspect.

2

SOCIAL PSYCHOLOGY   POLITICAL SCIENCE   ORGANIZATION DEVELOPMENT   DEVELOPMENT PLANNING   SOCIOLOGY   ECONOMICS   HUMAN RIGHTS

It would be a great mistake to assume that Grameen Bank has succeeded just because it has succeeded to be profitable economically. In our description of it, we will endeavour to include viewpoints from most of these subject areas.

HUMAN VALUE ECONOMICS

The Bank endeavours to practice a type of economics that has yet to be described theoretically. The fundamental value in conventional economics is profit maximation, a maximum return to the owner of the capital for his consumption or further investment. Grameen accepts this economic credo but it adds: there is a second value to be included: the social imperative of poverty alleviation, the human right to credit. The Bank thereby introduces a two value paradigm in economics. It is both a financial system and a system of social values. Rather than talking about profit maximation, it talks about profit optimation for the benefit of the poor. The monetarists are wrong, people do not produce only for the monies, but for the feeling of dignity. Although the viability of this paradigm has been proven in practice, its theory is as yet only sketchily described by Yunus who points out: "In economic literature there are only categories like "labour" or "entrepreneurs". It does not talk about "people" or least of all about "children". Neo-classical economics may be better described as a business science, than as a genuine social science. The trickle down theory does not work. Many smart people tell us that poverty alleviation is a non-issue. They tell us that if we concentrate on the growth of the economy the problem of poverty will take care of itself. Don't get brow-beaten by these smart people. Instead of waiting for poverty to disappear at the end of a hot pursuit of economic growth (by that time poverty usually gets worse!), a safer strategy will be to achieve growth through concentrating on elimination of poverty. Resource-poor nations with high incidence of poverty, waste away enormous human capability each day by denying poor people the use of their energy and ingenuity. If they could have been made economically active, not only they could have contributed in the national production, they would have helped expand the domestic market for the products produced. The poor can be transformed into the engine of growth, if we only allow them to

3

unleash their capacity." And Yunus adds: "We cannot be at peace with ourselves if we know there is a human being who lives without dignity. If we cannot ensure dignity for others, our own dignity becomes an empty pretence". To understand Grameen Bank the reader must understand this profound attitude to and belief in people. This is the mindset that inspires its leadership and staff members and explains their thinking, decision making and actions. Economics is an important social science, but when the issue is to make society a better place for everybody, it is much less scientific than economists think.

A WORM'S-EYE PLANNING HORIZON
With such a starting point the Bank does not revel in macro-economic visions and leaps of capital-intensive technological developments. Although they do not at all disdain such a bird's-eye overview, the leaders of the Bank prefer their own perception of the need for the worm's-eye perspective. They move with their nose close to the micro ground. Characteristic for their operational and strategic thinking, is a continuously rolling planning horizon, based on an incredible grasp and command of detail. Rather than setting hard and fast objectives, they have a strong feeling of direction and focus on analyzing constraints and identifying opportunities for action towards their goals.

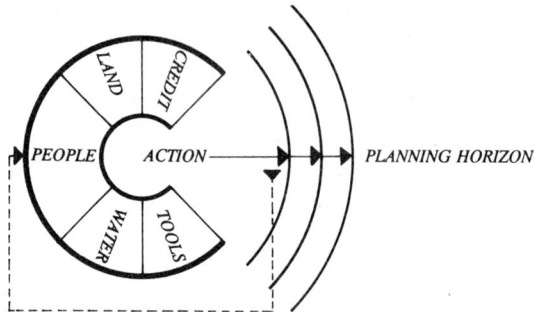

This is a helpful way of seeing the wholeness of the development effort now emerging from Grameen Bank. Bangladesh abounds in people, land and water. Particularly people and land are interrelated--the more people, the less land there is for each person. These are the basic resources the Bank's planning evolves around. It draws its 12 000 or more staff members from the educated unemployed youth of the country and uses their capabilities to stimulate productivity and progress among the nationally neglected poor. It has also started drawing more heavily on the underutilized human resources at government research institutions. In the same pragmatic spirit, it now steps up the exploitation of land and water resources by including programmes for redemption of fallow fields, crop diversification and restoration of idle water pumps and irrigation systems. Credit is another major input resource and, naturally, tools and equipment. The endeavour is, however, to limit the input of technology to what is strictly appropriate to the work situation of the poor. As the reader shall see later, credit and banking are only a small part of what is happening. The development activities now emerging from Grameen amount to a comprehensive, all out and defiant attack on poverty in Bangladesh.

ORGANIZATIONAL DEVELOPMENT

It is the starting point for Grameen as a counterculture that it considers government institutions ineffective and incapable of solving the problem of poverty in Bangladesh. It is therefore imperative to build institutions which are more capable. Grameen Bank itself is an attempt at that and, for the same reason, has become more than and something different from an institution in a conventional sense. The process that takes place in the Bank is better characterized as organizational development for participation. Yunus has expressed this view succinctly. "The most essential element I would emphasize in any development strategy is its focus on the human being. It should not aim at any physical accumulations and achievements. An integral part of that focus would be particular attention to the structure of institutions and organizations and the processes keeping these operational. I would modify or discard institutions and organizations which restrict people's initiative and enterprise. I would promote organizational forms which help people achieve their potentials. In doing so I would focus particularly on the poorest, the bottom 50% of the population. The upper 50% are usually the beneficiaries of the existing institutions, practices and processes. Creation of new institutions will either take some benefits away from the upper half or they will not see any new benefit in them.

I would lay emphasis on creating local self-government institutions at the village level. The smaller the local government territory is, the better the chance is for the poor to participate in decision making. I would be opposed to all kinds of hand-me-down resource transfers. No giveaways, no hand-outs. I would be tough in negotiating "prices" each community should pay before they receive anything from me. These payments are not meant for me. People would be required to pay to themselves for a better future"

This basic philosophy of organizational development will explain to the reader much of the events and processes inside and around Grameen Bank to be described in this book. Since the first loanee, Sophia Khatoon, took her loan

5

of taka 50 in August 1976, the Bank has expanded at an exceptional yearly rate. It now has more than 1.5 million members and disburses yearly about 2500 million taka in loans through 1 000 branch offices. It was officially recognized as a Bank in 1983. This process of organizational growth and development has some basic features the reader should be familiar with from the outset. Firstly, the leaders talk about the difference between *induced* and *acquired growth*. An enterprise of this nature with heavy staff costs needs to reach a high loan volume quickly in order to break even and become economically viable and perform effectively. To induce such growth by pushing for it through various types of costly promotion efforts would not be economically effective. From an organizational development point of view, the issue was to acquire at the outset a self-generated accelerating growth capacity. The demand for loans was there. The staff candidates could readily be selected from among the unemployed well-educated youth of the country.

This acquired growth potential and the driving force in Grameen Bank's spectacular, almost exponential, growth, has been its approach to staff training. Acting on the premise that experience is the best teacher, the trainees spend 80% of their training time working in the branch offices among experienced staff. Staffing average at these offices is 9, of whom 5 are usually trainees. They contribute essential labour in the loan processing of the branch. After 6 months they can be transferred to work in new branches. With a starting point of 50 branches these would, after 6 months, have 250 bank assistants available for new branches. After 12 months, there would be 100 branches producing 500 bank assistants and after 18 months 200 branches producing 1000 bank assistants. In practice many factors would modify this acquired growth potential, but this is essentially what has happened.

Secondly, the staff in the Bank more and more use the concepts of *horizontal* and *vertical growth*.

Horizontal growth characterizes what has happened up till now. The original and tested model of the banking operation has remained mainly unchanged, but its application has been expanded to a larger and larger population. The Bank is now servicing, with one or two exceptions, all districts in Bangladesh. This has been what could well be described as a horizontal cloning process, growing in size through decentralization and shedding of functions and responsibility from the centre towards the periphery. Leadership and staff members have various opinions about where the optimal limit for this process is. Some say at the level of 1000 branches; others say 1100 or 1200. That might imply up to 2 million members. Beyond that, the thinking is in terms of other, additional Grameen Banks, possibly joined in a federation. There is room enough for an almost infinite horizontal expansion of such loan services among the 50 million poor in Bangladesh.

Consequently, more and more people in the Bank are focusing now on the idea of vertical growth. By that they mean precisely what their emblem stands for: upliftment, organizational progress towards a higher and better quality of performance, a better and more appropriate package of loan products to offer the clients, more effective procedures for processing loans, better utilization of staff time, improved staff relations, rationalization of organizational structure, administration, management--in short doing what they do, but doing it much better and going further.

EXPANDING BEYOND

In its all-out, direct and dynamic attack on structural poverty, the Bank's leadership recognized early that the credit operation itself would be limited in its effect. But since it had thoroughly proven its worth, the Bank's approach should not be altered. Rather, one should seize at given opportunities and create new, additional organizations streamlined for their particular purpose. This process of institution building for the benefit of the poor has proceeded rapidly. Not the least haphazard, it is a carefully-directed process in thoughtful response to the practical needs of the poor as these have manifested themselves in the daily work of the Bank. Some of the ideas emerged during the original action research in Jobra in 1976, such as the 3-share cropping system. For the reader's preliminary overview, we outline this process of expanding beyond. Denser description follows later in the book.

THE FIRST STALK OF RICE

The Bank, registered 1983, is the first idea to come to fruition in the Grameen endeavour to eradicate poverty. The experience of developing it organizationally has exposed a wider array of structural oppression to be addressed. For this, building of other institutions is required, which can develop and support specialist competence not available within the Bank itself - and organize and integrate this with the practical skills and ingenuity of the poor themselves.

MORE EFFECTIVE AGRICULTURE

Inequity in the social and economic structure of Bangladesh is the underlying direct cause of the inefficiency in national food production and distribution. Much land is laying fallow, water resources are underutilized, government agricultural extension services and specialist knowledge in research institutions are not applied, available technology is malfunctioning or idle, rural credit systems have collapsed in moral and financial bankruptcy. Grameen Krishi Foundation was registered in 1991 as a separate legal entity to take on the gigantic task of development within agriculture and related fields. It has financial support from several of the major donor agencies.

9

DIALOGUE THROUGH TRUST

Through its fundamental trust in people, Grameen continually identifies opportunities and potentials for attacking poverty by responding to those who have talent, motivation, practical or specialist skills and will to act. Grameen Trust--it could not have a more befitting name--was registered in 1989. It has donor support, publishes the newsletter, *Grameen Dialogue*, and organizes the international *Dialogue training programmes*. The purpose is to spread the Grameen ideas and provide support to poverty eradication through replications of the Grameen credit approach in other countries as well as in Bangladesh. It provides consultant services, training and seed capital, and also undertakes the legal trusteeship of development projects for the benefit of the poor.

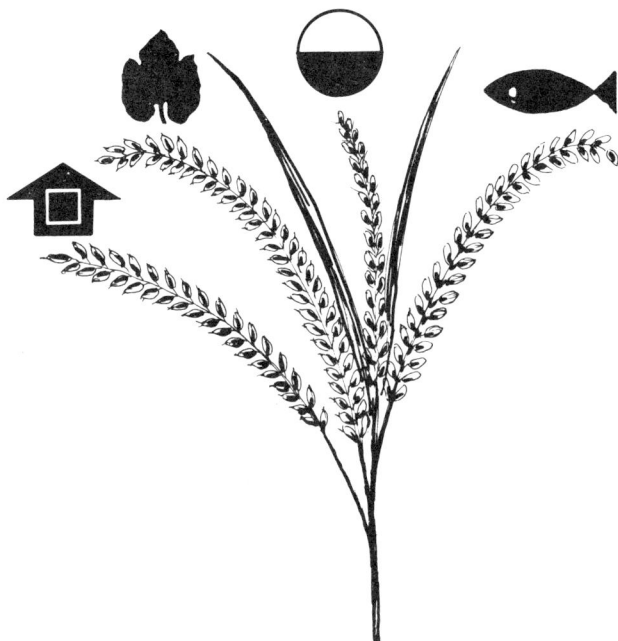

FINGERLINGS AND FISH PONDS

Aquaculture properly undertaken is a highly profitable way of exploiting the water resources of Bangladesh. Grameen has gained experience through the management of the Joysagar scheme and is now gradually expanding this area of action under the auspices of the Grameen Krishi Foundation. The first focus is to bring into effective production the many idle or neglected ponds. Hatcheries for fingerlings are already in operation. Staff are being trained and an effective share-cropping system is developed. When time is ripe there is the intention to rationalize this operation by transferring it to a special Fisheries Foundation.

11

THE FUTURE VISION OF THE GRAMEEN MOVEMENT

The Trust is exploring several other opportunities for attacking poverty directly within Bangladesh. Grameen is concerned with the generally bad health status of the poor and hopes to involve medical professionals in setting up services. A specialized Health Foundation may provide an appropriate institutional context. So far the Bank's services have been limited to rural areas. The leadership is now starting to focus on the situation of the urban poor. When enough experience is gained this may lead to the creation of an urban foundation. One can already now see the outline of the Grameen family of organizations within which Grameen Bank is the pater familias. And--the organizational soil being so fertile--one should not exclude that even more stalks will sprout from it in the future!

DAILY LIFE OF LITTLE PEOPLE

VISITOR:
Do you know Grameen?
DHAKA SHOPKEEPER:
Oh yes, the Bank for
the little people.

And little they are--the men and particularly the women of the rice fields of Bangladesh, underpaid, underfed and underrated, with backs bent and muddy feet, always belittled by the mighty. Yunus is quite explicit on this point of the Grameen ideology: "Poverty is the consequence of the institutional arrangements created by the powerful. It is not the consequence of the failing ability of the poor to cope for themselves. These arrangements damage people's creativity and initiative. Institutions should rather create an enabling environment so that the poor can benefit economically from the skills they already have." It could not be more clearly stated.

THE MIRRORS IN SOCIAL REALITY
Travel for foreigners in rural Bangladesh is fraught with dangers, but not from robbery, hunger or thirst. Hospitality is a national virtue, rice is healthy food, and strong tea with milk and cardamom is a delight after a long walk. The dangers are in our own way of seeing and thinking about people who happen to be poor. The Bengali poet Lalon Shah says: *"Close to my home is the city of Mirrors where my neighbour lives, but even for a day I didn't see him yet"*. Our problem is not seeing the tangible reality of poverty. The real problem lies in the mirrors hidden in our assumptions about poverty which control our way of seeing and thinking about it.

What makes us give priority to the marginalization or disadvantages of the poor

13

at the expense of recognizing the value and distinctiveness of their own culture? All cultures develop special skills in people, so does the culture of poverty. It is, in a very literal sense of the word, a sub-culture. When we assume that people are disadvantaged, we rush to create a development programme to deal with their disadvantages, instead of a programme based on the skills people have at their fingertips. Some social analysts would react negatively to the characterization of poverty as a culture. We very deliberately spite that reaction.

Common assumptions. The poor have always been researched, described and interpreted by the rich and the educated, never by themselves. Still today, development literature largely assumes that poor people must change their attitude and behaviour before they can take the first step out of poverty. Surely the inference is that poverty is a self-inflicted, self-generating phenomenon? The focus then is placed on what the poor are doing to themselves, rather than on what an oppressive economic system is doing to the poor. It is time the social sciences seriously question the assumptions behind the models of attitude and behaviour modification. These have splintered poverty into myths that are quite damaging in their attributions about the poor: The poor lack innovativeness, surrender to mutual distrust, have no empathy, are apathetic. They do not have quite the same feelings as "us", lack aspirations and motivation, are intransigent and unwilling to take risks, cannot conceptualize progress, and, finally, are handicapped by not understanding the larger political context. In other words, the poor are mentally stunted and ignorant. They have no skills and are inept problem solvers. They must be the recipients of new knowledge, through more and more effective communication programmes, develop skills and be conscientized according to the most recent and fashionable set of development assumptions.

The Judeo-Christian Western tradition of the free-willed and autonomous individual has concealed to us the social nature of knowledge. It has led us into the delusion that knowledge is produced by the spirit in us. Or it is the product of the intellectual and "scientific" performance of individuals rather than the product of a communal process. In addition, the technology of writing, the act of writing or reading, because it reinforces an individual-centred, linear interpretation of knowledge, isolates a person from others in the pursuit of learning.

Interviewing the poorest among the poor in Bangladesh leaves little room to romanticize their situation. The mental and physical impact of hard labour in combination with chronic malnutrition can never quite be understood by the

14

well-fed intellectual. It confirmed our long-held suspicion though, that conscientization of the poor as a precondition for their socio-economic development is a concept increasingly in need of reassessment. We shall return to that later.

Poor people we have met in Bangladesh or elsewhere are not as apathetic, lethargic or limited in their horizon as often described. On the contrary, people are able to understand very well the larger socio-economic context of their poverty. People learn and understand very quickly what they may not know. It can be said that poor people are often very tired, yes. But it is very unfair to say that they are mentally stunted or unable to conceptualize. If anything, people are stunned to silence by the irrelevance of some of the questions asked by researchers. Other questionable assumptions nurtured about the culture of poverty have sprung out of the economic bias of development theory. First there is the primary assumption that the poor do not contribute to the national economy. From this derives a secondary set of attitudes which pre-emptorily concludes the poor are not really productive, not capable of looking after money, cannot utilize investment capital profitably, do not know how to economize with resources and, in general, are economically irrational. Development literature, therefore, talks about the needs, wants and liabilities of the poor. The poor are poor in everything. Poverty equals nothing. Worse, it denies dignity.

THE ISSUE OF SELF IMAGE
Yet, there is the issue that economic marginality sometimes is accompanied by marginality in human relationships. Parents do not always have the surplus of mental energy to interact in a positive manner with their children. Once trapped in an oppressive social structure, the marginal community in a sense keeps on marginalizing itself. Poverty reproduces poverty. Children of the poorest families do not enter school and those who do frequently drop out by Grade 3 or 4 when they are old enough to contribute labour for the family. Drug abuse, wife battering and child molestation are, worldwide, the very manifestations of poverty. Against its own volition, the very poor child develops a poor self-image, a poor vocabulary, a poor imagination and is in poor contact with its own feelings. In time, as parent, it transfers this negative self-image to its own children which results in a lack of self-esteem and feeling of agency. Children have an urge to be competent and feel competent through approval from significant adults. They have a desire to be like them and to participate in their activities. The rousing feeling of agency: *I* can do! *I* can manage! emerges from the achievement of self-generated goals and from the associated appreciation of significant others. Equally, adults have a need for

15

feelings of accomplishment and mastery in what they are doing through admiration or praise from family members, neighbours or the larger community, however tacitly or indirectly it be expressed. It appears the belittlement of the poor is a deep hurt in their hearts. Development of self-esteem and feelings of agency is at the core of the issue of poverty eradication. We should start by focusing on people's accomplishments.

SKILLS AND ASSETS OF POVERTY

Poverty is a culture. It cannot be a culture void of everything, so we should attempt to find out what it is, rather than what it isn't. We should start an appraisal of the culture of poverty based on the assets, resources and skills people have.

Listening skills. In the South, the culture of poverty is oral in the sense that the technology of writing is used only by a few. Oral cultures develop two very important skills in people. Listening is taken so much for granted that it is rarely considered a skill. Yet, it is a perceptual and conceptual ability or capacity to "read" reality through the ear. People develop this capacity acutely when they rely exclusively on oral communication. It extends beyond reading the sounds of the natural environment and into the skills of social intelligence, the ability to perceive and interpret social situations. (1) In daily life, it means applying the spoken word deftly to participate and survive in the community. An oral culture is a communal culture in a very special sense: It does not survive without the spirit of the community.

Memory skills. When people have no other means of storing information and knowledge, they develop an excellent memory. As a skill, this is glibly overlooked. The folklore of puns, euphemisms, colloquialisms, proverbs, songs and stories is more than folksy fun. These various and entertaining forms have special functions in an oral society. Eloquence and subtlety are valued; a well-phrased statement is remembered. The price paid for acquiring the skills demanded by the technology of writing is the deterioration of listening and remembering skills.

Survival skills. A particular skill acquired by the poor is the ability to economize the use of their own energy, i.e. work economy. This skill extends into qualities such as patience and perseverance. The culture of poverty is a little-by-little culture, not by choice but by necessity. The relationship between food intake and labour output is finely balanced., Sometimes we assume wrongly that people are lazy when, in fact, they are just applying a skilled economic judgement. People do not work more or harder, because they know

16

that the benefit of higher labour input may be marginal. This economy can be observed in the labour involved in subsistence agriculture. Observe also the porter, the cart or rickshaw puller, how their modes of movement, use of body weight and work tempo are tuned to achieve a minimal expenditure of body energy. People are quick to exert themselves in hard labour if the benefit from it is substantial enough in the short- or long-term.

Resource utilization. Every source of energy, every material object, every resource available, is explored for its particular qualities and applications. Always, an available resource is utilized in a remarkable variety of ways and combinations to maximize its potential. The evidence of this endeavour is everywhere in the culture of poverty: utilization of land, water, crops or building materials. Observers from affluent societies have reason to feel deeply ashamed of their incompetence in the skill of resource utilization. Certainly the slum dweller's shelter of rusty iron flakes, cardboard boxes, newsprint and plastic sheets is a heap of leftovers. It can also abe seen as a masterpiece of resource utilization. Saying this does not deny that development is necessary and urgent. The point is: the poor are very capable of making appropriate use of resources made available to them in appropriate ways. (2)

Occupation skills. Often the culture of poverty has a high degree of labour division. Some people engage in agriculture or process agricultural products, some provide transport services; some undertake distribution of products through trade; some are involved in crafts. In Bangladesh, the division of labour seems infinite: rice growing, pulse husking, betel nut processing, lime making, spice processing, rickshaw or cart pulling, buffalo carting, ferry services, vegetable trading, mustard oil manufacture and trading, hide and skin preparation, cattle fattening and selling, bamboo work, shoe making, pottery making, carpentry, broom making, weaving, preparation of special sweets, fire cracker making among many others. Human ingenuity in the endeavour to survive appears inexhaustible. Often people command several of these skills. Common to them all is the competence involved if they are to make a living from it. Our emphasis on the many skills of the poor does not mean training in new skills or upgrading others is unnecessary. People acquire a new skill willingly and easily when they recognize its benefit. The point is simple: a self-reliant, endogenous development can be generated only from the skill resource base people already have. Training in new skills is part of the ongoing process once it has started. People gain self-confidence and self-esteem by using the skills they master. All too often we overlook how much people enjoy using their skills.

17

The economy of poverty. The culture of poverty is also an economy of poverty, an isolated but oppressed economic sub-system that leads its own life below the life of the national economy. The economy of poverty caters for itself on its own. Its exploited labour serves to sustain the national economy, yet, its productivity is not reflected in the national accounts. For a variety of reasons, the economy of poverty is at the losing end of the rope despite its labour and skills. Its resource base is too narrow. Poverty is poverty because it cannot on its own overcome the inherent and chronic gap between production and consumption. Much less can it start and sustain the process of accumulation that is a premise for progress. The poor have no land or a very limited access to land. They have no access to credit or an access to credit which is highly exploitative. They are underpaid for their work; and this cycle of degradation is compounded by the inadequacy of food intake which depletes their only remaining resource, their labour. Calorie intake is far short of requirement, protein intake is grossly deficient, and vitamin and mineral deficiencies are common.

ECONOMY AND NUTRITION

The dietary situation of the poor is further complicated by agro-economic developments. With the introduction of seed-water-fertilizer technology the cropping pattern in Bangladesh has changed. Previously, pulse was an essential diet component. The saying was, *"Daal Bhate Bangalee"*, a Bengali is made of pulse and rice. It is factually underscored because the amino acid content of pulses complements the low quality protein in rice. But the new technology is not favourable for pulse cultivation and it has decreased considerably. Exactly the same has happened to cultivation of oilseeds. Studies show that this negative change in cropping pattern and concomitant dietary pattern has aggravated the widespread protein and fat deficiency among the poor. (3) In such a situation, when the dietary needs of women and growing children are not recognized at all, their situation in disastrous. It is generally accepted, moreover, that the nutritional status of the children is directly related to the income level of the households.

Perhaps in the economy of poverty the economic laws do not quite apply? The level of consumption is so low that any small increase in income leads to the excess being spent on increased consumption rather than on accumulation? Are the economic parameters of supply and demand inadequate to explain economic behaviour among the poor? Prices, profits, wages, interest rates, shortages or famines are not functions of quantifiable economic variables, but results of a complex and powerful social process which can be described better in qualitative terms. Free choice dynamics is also a delusion in circumstances

18

where nature intervenes frequently and erratically in the economic system. The economy of poverty is ravaged by an aggregate of forces which are largely outside its control. Natural disaster are major contributory factors, but these are not the sole explanation. Socio-economic forces are interacting with the disaster situations in a way that aggravates the distress enormously. In the following we attempt to describe this aggregate of forces, basing our description only in part on our own experiences and drawing heavily on studies published by BRAC. (4)

HUMAN MANIPULATION

Year after year enormous amounts of resources are poured into famine relief. On the part of governments or donors, the problem is perceived as a chronic reality demanding programmes which deal with food availability, storage, medical supplies, transport, distribution and overall logistics. Due to the urgency of the situation, it is understandable, but regrettable that the poor are not consulted about how to cope with it. No one sees the need to ask the recipients, those who suffer the famine, about their perception of the problem or their opinions and ideas for solving it. Leaping from emergency to emergency, we will never be able to alter the conditions in the long term. What is necessary is to understand the structural cause of famine as people themselves perceive them. Once more, governments and aid agencies are the victims of their own false assumptions about poor people's competence and intellectual capacity.

Although famine is triggered by events beyond human control, this does not explain entirely the severity or delay in food distribution. Natural factors that may cause a famine situation are timing of the rains or no rains, pest infestations of a crop which reduce yields, and tidal waves or river flooding. Any of these might disturb the complex and intense cropping cycle which, in some areas of Bangladesh, includes up to three harvests a year. These are, the *boro* harvest in April-June, the *aus* harvest in July-August and the *aman* harvest in November-December. Yet, crop yields are generally too low to meet domestic needs. In years of poor harvests, Bangladesh has had to import up to 1.5 million tons of rice. The slightest imbalance may create local or widespread food shortages. Famine becomes a fact until the tenuous balance is re-established. However, the poor are quite aware of the socio-economic factors at work which determine the severity of their suffering. No external conscientizing process is required. A human manipulation exists which aggravates the famine. The social structure in the villages prevents the sufferings of the famine to be borne equitably by all community members. It serves to intensify the polarization between those who are influential and wealthy and those who are dependent and poor, to the benefit of the former.

As the BRAC report documents, the poor can explain how food shortages are aggravated by stockpiling. The larger landowners tend to act in concert and maintain an informal monopoly control of the food supply. As the impending shortage becomes apparent, they divert more and more of their supplies into storage and wait for the prices to start rising. A second blow hits the poor with the fall in agricultural production. The need for their work in the fields also falls. Labour, the only resource the poor have to offer, is immediately in a situation of excess supply, forcing the wage rate to drop drastically. The economic effect is much less money available to buy much more expensive food. In times of famine, it is not uncommon that the price of a family's daily rice supply is five to six times higher than the daily wage rate of a labourer.

MONEYLENDING
Faced with desperation, the only recourse for the poor is to pawn or sell the minuscule piece of land they might possess. Other meagre possessions such as household utensils, pieces of furniture or a treasured ring or bracelet soon line the coffers of the *mohajan*, the village moneylender. Usually people start pawning the smallest and most dispensable item. Here again the poor run headlong into a set of socio-economic forces.

Their acute need for cash to buy food for the family forces the poor to borrow from the rich landlords who are often the moneylenders. Pawning or loaning is the preferred transaction between the two parties. It allows the poor to retain the hope that the object will be recovered one day through payment, a reality that rarely occurs. It allows the moneylender to reinforce a relationship of dependency which is the phycological basis for his business. Taking full advantage of the situation, the moneylender attempts to ensure that repayment is impossible, creating an ongoing condition of dependence. The moneylender has the sovereign power to set the price for the item being pawned. Usually it is adjusted to half or one-third of the item's market value. The interest charged can be anything up to 300 to 400% annually. Nevertheless, the poor gladly accept the terms; their situation is too desperate for argument. BRAC cites the case of "One woman in Roumari who became simply unable to stand the cries of her hungry children and, leaving them uncared, hanged herself." It is likely that the informal source of credit available through the *mohajans* meets 80% of the need for credit in rural Bangladesh. In spite of several attempts, institutional credit has had little impact, especially on the situation of the poorest.

With the crippling interest rates, the poor have virtually no chance of repaying the principal of the loan in the allotted time. The moneylender gets the upper hand both ways. In case of default he has the item, but that's not his primary objective. He prefers a situation of continued dependence with the regular income in the form of interest payments. The poor dread a situation of default, partly out of deference to superiority and partly because they know they will need recourse to a loan next time the squeeze is on. A host of social norms come to play in the relationship. The borrower feels obligated and subservient to the lender who, on his part, is expected to play the role of "benefactor" or "protector" the next time around. Social norms prescribe the forms of honourable behaviour expected of both roles. The borrower is expected to display reticence and politeness considered appropriate for a person under obligation. Arrogant behaviour might jeopardize future chances for a loan. The loan transaction becomes a means of establishing a social as well as an economic relationship. The conversation between the two parties is a means of establishing a particular set of social attitudes rather than a strictly economic evaluation of a loan proposal. This is a situation very different from that between a bank and its client.

LAND TRANSACTIONS - INCREASE OF CRIME
As the shortage of food increases, poor marginal land holders also need cash to supplement their income. The landlords, always ready to increase their holdings, start pressuring them to sell. Since the small land holders depend on the landlords for employment, they resist such pressures with difficulty. The end result of a famine situation is an acceleration in the transfer of land to the rich. This demise should be seen in conjunction with the fact that the proportion of the functionally landless population is rising rapidly. It has risen from 20% to 65% over the past generation and will probably continue to rise. The terms for the transfer of land are set by the rich, usually at values less than half of the normal land value. In this way, an inequitable social structure is reinforced. Unfortunately for the poor, the moneylender provides a service that few credit institutions can match: he immediately makes the money available without paperwork.

A famine situation doesn't only affect the stomach: it starts tearing up the cohesive elements among the poor themselves. People start exhibiting behaviour that is not socially acceptable or tolerable in normal situations. Joint families or groups that normally eat together, split apart. There is unwillingness to share with siblings, inlaws or relatives. Deference, cordiality and mutual respect deteriorates. Quarrels over ownership of property become acute. Petty theft and serious crime increase. Whatever links the poor share

21

because of their common destiny, splinter.

SOCIAL DISCONTINUITY

The BRAC report brings to our attention a social characteristic they describe as discontinuity.   In rural Bangladesh, the individual household is the production unit. Although it usually consists of a nuclear family, extended family units are not uncommon. At this level, most decisions are taken regarding the cultivation system, the deployment of labour, the cropping technique and similar issues. This does not exclude, however, that several households will tend to associate in clusters or groups. In Bangla, such groupings are referred to as *dal*. These are informal social formations based on proximity and/or political allegiances that often play an important role in regulating inter-household cooperation. For our understanding, the term faction might be more descriptive. The degree of cooperation and interaction is high among households aligned with the same faction. The interactions have political as well as important economic, social or ideological implications. Members of a faction provide each other with mutual support when there is conflict; they engage in casual loan transactions, mutual labour exchanges and information exchange. The faction is structured vertically. It usually has an internal hierarchy in which the positions of dominance and authority are determined by the degree of an individual's wealth. Thus, those who have the moneylending capacities sit on top. They control the largest portion of the village resources: land, credit, trading, relief operations and employment opportunities. Of course they bring their influence to bear on the local administration. The poorer households constitute the large bulk of the faction members, the base of the pyramid. They associate with a certain faction only to the extent they gain some security and protection from it. It is a loose tie and a poor household may easily switch allegiance to another faction which better meets its needs. To some extent, the top must deliver its promises, lest support for them or their candidates during elections for local office diminishes. A household's association with a faction is determined largely by the nature of the personal relationship it maintains with the members. Kinship ties and the proximity of houses are the two most important factors at work. Clusters of homesteads often belong to the same faction.

The effect of vertically dominated factions among the poor is to minimize their horizontal linkages. The feeling of solidarity and common cause observable among the members of a faction contrasts sharply to the lack of solidarity and cooperation between factions. This discontinuity seems reflected at the national level in Bangladesh in the large number of political parties. The divisions tend to block out horizontal and large-scale attempts of cooperation among the poor

22

in economic or social affairs. The conflict generated takes the forms of interhousehold disputes and hostility, barriers to a free-flow of reliable information, and subsequent suspicion and lack of cooperation towards development efforts directed to the poor.

FROM NATURAL DISASTER TO SOCIAL PROCESSES
Rural factions are another dimension of a social relationship configured by dependence and exploitation. Factions arise and expand as a result of vested interests and rivalry between its leading members. Often the fight between these personalities is fierce. Violence, intimidation and trickery are commonly used means to gain ascendency and control of the local resource situation. Relief operations directed to the poorest are exposed to the cynicism that derives from a viciously competitive milieu. The local leaders, or leaders to be, systematically gather support and expand the power of their faction by holding out the promise of benefits or economic support to the poor who will give their allegiance. The highly unequal distribution of limited resources in the rural areas, along with their control and use by a few, is the socio-economic source of a relation of dependence. The exploitation materializes in the grossly unequal economic exchanges most clearly illustrated by the low wages paid for agricultural labour and the exorbitant interest rates charged for loans. And the exploitation is continuously at work whether or not those involved in the dependency relationship are conscious of it. To sum up: The relationship between natural disasters and social processes is essential for an understanding of the rural situation in Bangladesh. Poverty is not a fortuitous, self-inflicted condition; it is a result of processes at work within the society. These processes are clearly perceived and understood by the poor themselves.

ATTITUDES TO FAMINE RELIEF
Ubiquitous poverty and frequent famine situations demand constant attention to relief programmes. To assess and develop effective relief programmes, the victims themselves should be asked their opinions about relief assistance. What are their views on the various types of relief programmes? Quite typically these programmes are always conceived behind the desks of the agencies concerned, isolated from the views of those directly affected. As we shall see later, Grameen has made a beginning in changing this through its innovative relief operators in Rangpur district.

The BRAC studies bring forward several insights which we share from our own observations and interviews. It is a sad reflection on our own ideas and attitudes that we must "rediscover" that poor people are very honourable, that they value pride and dignity. People do not like to be given what they need,

23

and find it demeaning to accept relief without earning it. In BRAC's assessment, the Food For Work programmes (FFW) are preferred because they allow people to *claim* their food. It is a right people feel they acquire through their own work.

Poor peasants also had clear perceptions about the abuse of relief programmes. Local leaders often skim off excess relief supplies by fraudulently enlarging the lists of people declared needy in their area. It was stated that relief supplies were even used by landlords to feed and pay their own hired labourers. Flour, say the poor, is less suitable for relief than grain because it can be more easily adulterated. Overall, the poor resent that they never know what their leaders are writing and doing. They recognize the waste and feel frustrated that their own views and ideas about relief are not registered. The poor themselves suggest they should take charge of relief supplies and their distribution.

The BRAC study reveals that the poor are well aware that the only way to combat their problem would be to act together as a group. Their ideas centre around the collective production of goods and services. Relief agencies should take note that the major demand is not primarily for food or other kinds of temporary relief, but more for various types of inputs which can help the poor generate income on the basis of existing skills. Interestingly, the most preferred input is credit. Aware not only of the potential benefit of pooling funds together, the poor also recognize the potential impact of collective action on the social environment.

THE SOCIAL NEGATION OF WOMEN
This description of the culture of poverty is incomplete and inaccurate without an analysis of a predominant social reality: the socio-economic negation of women. A fruitful starting point for this discussion is the work situation in paddy production. In Bangladesh, rice accounts for about 75% of all food grains grown. Without doubt, it is one of the most labour-intensive crops to cultivate and irrigate. Post-harvest rice production comprises a sequence of equally labour-intensive operations such as field stacking, transportation, farmyard stacking, threshing, winnowing, drying, soaking, parboiling, drying, de-husking and finally polishing and storage. From winnowing onwards the work is done within the homestead and exclusively by women. In addition, it is the woman's task to tend fruit and vegetable gardens, care for animals, make all the meals and finally, care for children. Her work starts at sunrise and may finish as late as nine or ten in the evening. There are few opportunities for rest. A time-allocation study shows that the average peasant woman spends 43% of her time on activities related to farm production, about the same on

actual household work, and about 11% on child-care and other family matters. (5) This is the situation when the household owns or leases some land. Women in landless families face a different situation.

Purdah and bari. The social reality of *purdah* and *bari*, allow us to understand a little the kind of norms affecting women's role in rural Bangladesh. The interpretation of *purdah* enjoys a wide continuum of practice in Islamic cultures. In rural, poor areas of Bangladesh, it means that women should not be seen by males outside the family. The logical extension of this norm is that women are largely restricted to work that is possible within the *bari*, i.e. the family homestead. Religious decorum prefers women to wear a standard garment which covers the body completely and loosely if they travel outside of the *bari*. Not to, would threaten the public image of the family. Men especially would feel disgraced. A high social and religious prestige is associated with the observance of *purdah*, although its observance varies according to the economic situation of the family. Only the very wealthy can afford to observe *purdah* strictly. Very poor Moslem women do carry out trade and small business activities in public, forced to by economic necessity. However, they must then sustain the negative status attached to this condition, despite an attitude concession made on behalf of widows and destitute women. What's important to realize is that the main economic consequence of *purdah* for women is that, in general, they must confine themselves to income-generating activities located in and around the homestead. When business activities require travel to markets or other villages for purchase, trade or selling of goods, women rely on husbands, brothers, sons or other male relatives to carry out this aspect of the work.

The labour situation. The majority of poor women who find paid employment, work almost exclusively as domestic labourers or in rice processing in nearby wealthier homesteads. In the rice-husking process, women use a traditional mortar hollowed out in the hard clay ground in combination with a foot-operated pestle, a *dheki*. With the introduction of diesel or electrically-operated rice-husking mills, this opportunity is diminishing. Husking by mills is cheaper than by traditional technology. The result is a worsening of the situation of poor families dependent on the supplementary income from this source. Again, wealth is transferred to households which are already wealthier and to the rice mill owners. Ownership of rice mills becomes, for women, a primary development issue.

The study referred to above (5) reports that in the busy harvest season, women in households with one or two acres of land were on average 3.5%

25

overemployed. In comparison, the landless and poorest women were up to 36% underemployed. The most common complaint of the poorest which applies most acutely to women, is the lack of employment or income-generating opportunities. Other studies undertaken at BARD (6, 7, 8) confirm that women's labour in the final analysis is underutilized. Women work but their level of productivity can be further improved. Lack of access to extension services is a major feature. The methods through which women more fully could utilize their potentials are not available to them. Their worsening situation is accelerated by the overall economic decline which has reduced severely the real wage for male agricultural labour. In the larger perspective, a major force in this process of pauperization is increased landlessness. As we discussed earlier, the social discontinuity, dependence relationship and seasonal occurrence of deep economic distress, including famine, collutes in a continuous process of land transfer from the poorest part of the population to the more wealthy. At the same time, the general population increase leads to increased fragmentation of the land.

Marginalization. Together, these social, economic and technological forces are leading to a marginalization of women in the labour process. Even more disturbing is the pervasive social devaluation of women which accompanies intensified marginalization. The social negation of women is the end result of a culture of poverty. However, to ascribe this situation to patriarchal attitudes alone is too simplistic an explanation. As we have tried to indicate, such attitudes must be seen in the context of the existing adverse socio-economic conditions. It is well documented in development programmes and research that a woman's status in the household and the community rises with an increase in her personal income and control of assets.

The social negation of women is reflected in other sectors and practices not directly considered economic. For example, the health and nutritional care of female children is often neglected among the poor. (9) Strictly speaking, this is not due entirely to the factor of poverty. What food there is, is not distributed equitably within the family. This appears due to at least three interwoven factors which, in the long term, make sons economically less dispensable than daughters. Marriage, inheritance laws and the role of the male as provider place sons in a position in which they are perceived by parents as the future source of social security in their old age. Daughters marry and leave; they are viewed as a cost from which others benefit in the long term. Attitudes and practices therefore are inclined to favour sons to the detriment of daughters. We point out the relativity of this analysis and the exacerbating role of poverty. As everywhere parents incline to love and care for all their children. Considerable variation will be found in the degree to which parents treat sons and daughters unequally. However, there is enough documentation to show that gender favouritism is practiced. At meal times, the best food or the bigger portions will often be given to the sons.

Overall, the female child is less well fed, less looked after, is less likely than her brother to attend school and receives less medical attention. The inadequate food intake for women, which begins approximately from the age of six, aggravates an existing low nutritional status. This has been brought about by generations of malnutrition as well as food practices that affect women during pregnancy and the post-partum period. Women are the smallest of the little people. As a result, female infants tend to have a higher mortality rate in Bangladesh. It is probable that in former periods of history, a set of protections accompanied the tradition of child marriage. Now, however, a cost-benefit consideration has become the central factor influencing the practice in a setting of economic desperation. For women, the implications of child marriage are premature deliveries which cause widespread mortality among young mothers. Taking the population of Bangladesh as a whole, women have a higher mortality rate than men.

Violence against women. In any culture, the crime rate rises in periods of acute unemployment and economic distress. In Bangladesh, this occurs in the rainy season when communities are fragmented and isolated from each other by water. From these myriads of waterlogged islands, crimes cannot be easily reported for investigation, and crimes against women hold a lower priority. Recent studies document that rape, physical torture and murder are not uncommon during this period. (10) Although, for a variety of reasons, there are still gaps in the research data base, several disturbing, initial observations can be made. The police records and newspapers document murder as a major crime against women. Husbands uniformly stand as the single most reported assailant in the murder of women, which usually takes place within the homestead. The cause of death, often preceded by long periods of torture, is by beating and kicking or using sharp weapons. Rape, the second major kind of crime against women, appears to be on the increase. Young girls and female children from 5 to 15 years are usually the victims. Also, a hidden type of violence exists which results in suicide by women. It appears that women in the prime years of their youth, 15 to 25, revert to suicide in sheer desperation. The studies reveal that women in lower socio-economic levels are vulnerable to emotional disorders such as anxiety, neurosis and depression.

Dowry. The final and very dominant issue in the negation of women is dowry.

The predominant reason for violence in the home is dowry-related quarrels, or quarrels related to the family's and particularly the wife's belongings. Traditionally, dowry is a Hindu custom which, only in recent history, has been adopted by Moslems. Earlier in Islamic tradition, the practice was quite the opposite. The groom or his family paid in cash or in kind a sum to the bride which symbolized her worth to the bridegroom. This was called *mahr*. From an economic interpretation, the practice of giving *mahr* is a consequence of and expression of an appreciation for the need for female labour in the groom's household. The practice of dowry, which is more and more widespread, correlates with the decreasing size of land-holdings and the resultant decline in the importance of female labour in post-harvest processing activities. The decreasing demand for wives is accompanied by an increasing demand from potential grooms for higher payments. Dowries of 10 000 taka are not uncommon. Such a sum is a crushing burden propelling a vicious downward spiral which tosses the family deep into debt and dependency. It is a small step from social negation to physical obliteration. Women who commit suicide frequently resort to the few technologies modernity has offered them: burning themselves in kerosene or swallowing insecticide.

THROUGH THE WOMEN TO THE POOR

Donor agencies, development planners and programme implementors are constantly lamenting that projects do not get through to the poorest of the poor. And in that dilemma, women are the hardest to reach. A mounting number of evaluation reports confirm this. At the same time, there is an emerging rhetoric about women as the socially most legitimate venue to development. However, operationalizing this in a practical programme has not been achieved on a large scale. It is well acknowledged that there is a clear connection between the social and economic status of women and the nutritional and welfare status of their families. However, even in projects which try to circumvent social or gender barriers, experience indicates that social negation and exploitation continue. Cooperatives are a good example: Men not only assume most management positions but also enjoy a disproportionately larger share of the resources and opportunities generated. As we have pointed out, within the culture of poverty itself there is a stratification which promotes conflict. It is characterized by factions, rivalries, intrigues and gossip. There is a significant material difference between the absolute landless and those owning a small plot of land. Particularly because of women's role and situation within this constellation of problems, it is felt that development initiatives should address them directly as a priority. But the "how" of it and the scale of the need have presented seemingly insurmountable hurdles.

THE CONTEXT OF THE NATURE

The situation of the poor should be seen in the larger context of natural disasters in Bangladesh. For decades the discussion has been flowing back and forth--like the floods and tidal waves themselves--on what it would be right to do or whether it would be right to do anything at all. Should the floods be managed through comprehensive flood action plans? Or, are the floods natural recurrent phenomena people have to learn to live with and survive in? If the Ganges is controlled by dams what are the ecological consequences? And the economics - who would benefit, the rich or the poor? If flood barriers were built to contain the water in Rangpur, how many million people would be displaced? There are so many rivers in Bangladesh that one may call it the land of rivers. Eighty percent of the land area is flood plain zones. More than 90% is swampy low land, the alluvial gift of the great rivers Brahmaputra, Ganges and Meghna and 240 smaller rivers (11). The problematic results of human manipulation are also manifested here. The shifting of the Brahmaputra course through the Jamuna channel between 1889 and 1930 is responsible for recurring floods in Rangpur, Bogra and Pabna districts. Mymensingh was ravaged in 1938. Memorable floods of recent times took place in 1954, 1955, 1974, 1987 and 1988. Similarly, cyclonic surges ravaged the Bangladesh coast in 1960, 61, 63, 65, 69, 70, 85, 86 and 91. Flood control activities have shown limited results. There is also the question of the effect on soil fertility when diverting the flood water. The situation that created the land in the first place, will be discontinued. Of the 82 000 square kilometres land vulnerable to floods, only 18 000 has so far been protected. An effective strategy depends on effective collaboration with the SAARC countries: India, Nepal and Bhutan; India, as a big neighbour and upper riparian country, carries a heavy moral responsibility to respond to the appeal of Bangladesh. Paradoxically, in a situation of so much water, drought is another of nature's ravages.

THE CONTEXT OF THE NATION

One cannot discuss poverty in Bangladesh without thinking about the polity, the State as a political entity. The factionalism, bickering and violence on the local level is but a micro-reflection of the larger context. While in India, in spite of fragmentation in castes, religious and local identities, the poor masses seem to have retained a common faith in the State, at least until now; one is more uncertain about the situation in Bangladesh. The psychology of the poor appears to be one of mute disinterest. Confronted with the colossal ravages of nature and the nothingness of whimsical state intervention, the poor are sceptical to the capabilities of the forces above. The Bengali have a great sense of the need for softness in civil society, but merge this paradoxically with

29

fiercely anti-establishment feelings. Ever since the British advanced to conquer India through Bengal, the Bengali have rebelled against oppression. But the poorest among them are sometimes too emaciated for it. Is statehood eluding the Bengali in spite of or perhaps because of its democratic election? Greed and graft, violence and killings among financial powers and political parties are now at a peak. Political authority seems unable to hold the diverse social elements together in a common democratic framework. This is the stage the ever more self-confident extremists storm onto these days. Honoured Akhter Hameed Khan said it long ago: "Unity, discipline and improved methods - if we can follow these three principles in Comilla, we can develop within thirty years as did Japan, Germany and Denmark". The much less revered, Lee Khan Yew of Singapore said recently almost the same: "The exuberance of democracy leads to undisciplined and disorderly conditions which are inimical to development". (12) The profound issue is whether political reform should follow economic progress or vice-versa. The answer is not simple. Undoubtedly Singapore, Taiwan and South Korea all achieved their remarkable economic development through discipline enforced by political strongmen and are now easing their way into a more democratic style of governance. If standard of living is the measure, unrestrained democracy appears to be faltering. Looming over the situation in Bangladesh just now is the sorry result of the graft and decay of social responsibility in the ruling classes, just as reproduced so recently by the democratic experiment in the Philippines. One should not question the fundamental democratic values, human rights and social accountability, but one should study ways in which these can be wrought out of a situation of social discord and discontinuity. It is the simplest of truths: A house cannot be built from the ridge of the roof. Work must start with the foundation in the millions of homesteads and thousands of small local communities. It is in this respect we hope the book shall enable the reader to discover Grameen does much more with poor people than just being their Bank.

THE SONGS FROM POVERTY
Why should we assume always that poverty is poor in everything? The culture of poverty has other assets aside from its practical skills. True it is hard to laugh on an empty stomach and harder still to sing when one is out of breath. Life *is* hard in Bangladesh. But the head and the heart together are part of everything. There is an old literary tradition in an equally old alphabet. The rich oral tradition with its songs and eloquent tales is palpable in the daily lives of people in rural Bangladesh. And people's singing is there for the ear that cares to listen. The boatman's *bhatiali* song still floats hauntingly over the waters. There is desperation and agony, but also great tenderness in the Bengali people.

PEOPLE'S BANK
PEOPLE'S MOVEMENT

*The cessation of action brings death
to the organization through
factionalism and inaction
- a basic personal sense of identity
can come only through the drama
of moving experiences - of action.*
SAUL ALINSKY

After seventeen years of remarkable practical achievements, it is time
Muhammad Yunus is set on the world stage among two of the other greater
actors in the field of community organizing and community participation for
development, Saul Alinsky and Paulo Freire. What is happening within the
Bank and among its members can best be understood on a backdrop of the
international experience in the issue of participation over the last thirty to forty
years.

CONFLICT OR PROCESS
All three share profound insight into people's participation, but Yunus reaches
a very different conclusion on practical action. While both Alinsky and Freire,
to some extent, advocate conflict and confrontation as a means of synthesizing
action for liberation and development, the Yunus approach is analytical,
process-oriented and non-confrontational. Its strength is competence in
organizational development. To counteract and supercede oppressive
structures, it builds alternative, more effective and enabling socio-economic
frameworks through which people can participate in action towards their
liberation. And it attempts to do so on a large scale.

ORGANIZING THROUGH ACTION
Saul Alinksy is the practitioner who probably best understood the nature of
conflict as an asset in community participation, in social change and in problem
solving. To him, community participation is organizing for power. His

organizing work began in Chicago's notorious Back-of-the-Yard slums in the late 1930's. Later, he helped organize communities throughout North America, from the black ghetto of Rochester, New York, to the Mexican-American barrios of California. He also worked with North American Indians and his organizing approach was tried and modified in India and the Philippines in the 1960's.

The Alinksy approach in community organizing is based on the idea that community organizing and social change is generated through a tactic of confrontation between the community and the targeted part of the establishment. Conflict is used by the organizer as a force in the organizing process itself. Change comes from power and power comes from organization. The job of the organizer is to give the community the feeling that it can do something. While people may accept the idea that organization means power, the crucial turning point is when people experience this in action. Action is as critical to the organizing process as oxygen is to breathing. The organizer simultaneously encourages conflict and builds power for participation in the game. No one can negotiate without the power to compel negotiation. Anything else is wishful thinking. To attempt to operate on a basis of goodwill rather than on the basis of power is foolish and impossible. The following are some of the Alinsky tactics for community organizers.

- Power is not only what you have but what your antagonists think you have.
- Never go outside the experience of your community. If you do, the result may be confusion, fear and retreat.
- Whenever possible, go outside the experience of your antagonists. It causes confusion.

Human beings are quite aware that everything in life is functionally interrelated. However, they are able to segment and isolate values, issues and other factors and this fact has implications for building and galvanizing action. When organizers begin to analyze issues in terms of this duality, they start to identify the clues on which direction to take. Alinsky points out that these contradictions and their accompanying interacting tensions are the creative departure points for the organizer. This grasp of the duality of all phenomena is vital for the organizer's understanding of politics. It frees her or him from the myth and the oversimplification that one approach to problem solving is positive while another is negative.

A reason seldom exists to oppose or to try and alter traditions. People's traditions and customs are interwoven in the fabric of their experiences and must be respected and understood. But understanding is not the same as just being aware of people's prejudices, beliefs and values. It is understanding people in terms of their relationships and attitudes toward one another. Equally important is the analysis of their relationship toward the outside. Overall, it is understanding the community in terms of its knowledge of people in the world: the recognition that this is people's identity. Community organizing and participation is about actualizing community identity. Alinsky is convinced that a common cause of failure in campaign work, for example is the lack of real respect for the dignity of people. An organizer will succeed only if she or he is truly fond of people and unflinchingly trusts people's ability to create their own future.

Underlying Alinsky's organizing approach is a fundamental respect for the autonomy of a community of interests as the social entity of primary importance. The organizer must aim to create a social and political situation which enables the community to negotiate for its rights from a position of power. Despite its emphasis on conflict with the larger society, it seems as if the approach in essence rests on the notion of endogenous development. The source of power is within the community itself. It is in the people's capacity for social sense-making and selfhood, people's capacity to generate knowledge about their reality. Although Alinksy's method grew out of the specific conditions of the North, which foster an ideology of competitive and aggressive values, its assumptions about selfhood and the right to participate with equity in the larger society are shared with many process initiatives in the Third World today. Yet, his ideas are more for organizing instantaneous action in situations of political confrontation. He pays less attention to the long-term nitty-gritty of organization development, of institution building with a self-sustaining economic base without which a community cannot plan any future action.

ORGANIZING THROUGH CONSCIENTIZATION
Paulo Freire followed in the footsteps of Alinsky, but took a slightly different tack in his *Pedagogy of the Oppressed* published in 1970. Freire presented mass-illiteracy as the major structural problem caused by oppression of the poor majority by the powerful classes in society. According to him, the problem could be solved only by changing the oppressive structure. The means of doing that was through popular education. Freire provided both a philosophy of education and of development, seeing the latter as emerging from a critical awareness of the causes of problems. He emphasized the direct link between emotion and motivation as the basis for action, and the need for liberation and development to rise from the grassroots up through a process of reflection and actions. Freire is perhaps more process-oriented than Alinsky with the animator

playing a central role in facilitating a process of community dialogue aiming at critical awareness. Freire delineates the role clearly: At all stages of their liberation, the oppressed must see themselves as people engaged in the vocation of becoming more fully human. Reflection and action become essential. True reflection leads to action but that action will only be a genuine praxis if there is critical reflection on its consequences. To achieve this praxis it is necessary to trust in the oppressed and their ability to reason... While no-one liberates themselves by their own efforts alone, neither are they liberated by others!! The key concept in Freire's thinking is conscientization. It is a process focused on the intellectual development of the individual, although in a group context. Yet, the Freirean approach gives little indication as to how people should organize themselves for action. Freire's thought has influenced adult literacy work all over the world, particularly in Latin America a movement has emerged that combines popular education with social activism both through media and grassroots organizations. Attempts in Africa have been less successful.

ORGANIZING THROUGH PROCESS

Alinsky and Freire are paramount contributors to the articulation of the practical problematique of challenging oppressive forces in society. Their precepts can be traced in the strategies of many social-change movements in the Third World. From their practice over the last decades, the limitations of these strategies are beginning to emerge. To be in opposition generates power to overthrow power, but is this enough to generate energy for a development from within, once the State is taken over? History documents that revolutionary movements once in control easily become governments as oppressive as any. A more equal distribution of resources among people is not enough to justify that the same governmental institutions and the same structure of State are perpetuated. This is the point where both left and right, East and West, have so far failed. There has been little understanding of the imperative need for building alternative, enabling institutions and even less understanding of how to do it. The radical cry has always been for structural tranformation within the State, but the attempts at innovation around the premises for organizational and institutional forms facilitating a participatory process that empowers all its citizens have been feeble. Also, the need for making such institutions economically sustainable has not been seriously addressed.

This is the point where Yunus takes a major step forward, well ahead of his contemporaries. The Yunus approach to participation is a learning-process approach, but it should be noted, not only from the point of view of individual or group learning. It is, above all, organizational learning and development.

34

The issue is to develop an organization which is responsive to the needs of the participants and capable of sustaining this responsiveness.

CRITICAL FIT

Central to such an approach is the concept of "critical fit". David Korten has elaborated this concept (13). Firstly, there is a critical fit to be achieved between the development programme of the organization and the needs of the participants: the particular resources and services the programme makes available to the community must fit the particular needs of the community as these are conditioned by the larger social, political and economic context. Next, arises the question of the fit between the participants and the organization itself. How does the community define and communicate its needs? And, how does the organization adjust its decision-making and implementation processes to effectively respond to these expressed needs? Whether the organization's actions build or diminish the problem-solving capacity of the community is ultimately determined by the way the fit is achieved. This is the point at which empowerment of the participants should take place and development of the community should ensue.

Between the programme itself and the organization, another critical fit must be worked out. This involves the mutual adjustment between the specific tasks required by the programme and the distinctive competence of the organization. Considerations on one side concern the members of the organization and what they must do to produce the inputs required for and by the community. On the other side are the factors of organizational structure, routines or technical capabilities that influence the provision of these inputs. It is on the background of this fundamental paradigm of the individual, collective and organizational learning process we shall analyze and describe the structure, programmes and operation of Grameen Bank.

The doel birds in Rangpur. To describe the Bank is a little like attempting to photograph a flock of doel birds sitting on the telephone lines in Rangpur District. The blue doel birds have such long beautifully curved tails. The flock is an intriguing configuration of notes spread on the lines, a sheet of music in the sky, but the moment you have the flock in focus and snap the shutter, it flies off and settles in another configuration on another set of telephone lines. Many will want to copy Grameen Bank and wish to lay their hands on the organizational blueprint for its success. However, if they do not have a feeling for the doel birds in Rangpur and their music, they are likely to fail.

35

In our interviews with staff members we tried to nail down the structure of Grameen Bank, but the responses always took unexpected turns. Elucidations of economics and the business of banking were punctuated by value statements with many different implications as indicated in the following:

- "The credit we give is a means for poor people to restore their dignity."
- "We do well, but we are not a perfect organization; we are a human organization."
- "Eighty-two percent of the members in Patuakhali are women. The men are there for mental balance. Women are much more particular."
- "The poor cannot fight on an empty stomach. Our credit gives them the stomach."
- "If there is a result among the poor, they cannot be ignored anymore."
- "I was so afraid when I started as a bank worker, but I did it, even though I had not taken rice for many days."
- "These were the disbursement figures last month, but now they are very outdated."
- "Today we are sure it works like this. It may not work like this tomorrow, because we always evaluate."
- "Yes, I am the Zonal Manager in Dhaka but next week I will be heading Research and Development at Head Office."
- "We don't think it was an error. It was a new idea, but it did not work."
- "Our credit is a catalyst. It comes and goes and leaves behind some change."
- "A bank worker should count his money, not his steps. He must be good at walking."
- "This is a section today. It will be made into a department after the rains."
- "We can always afford to make new mistakes, but we must not repeat old ones."
- "The most correct development indicator is the nutrition and health status of the poorest 40% of our population."
- "This country is a warehouse of malpractice; we must demonstrate we can do better."
- "The question of resource constraint is blown out of proportion by the economic planners. In our work with the poor, we have to start out with what we have."
- "At Grameen Bank we talk much, but at the same time we work much."
- "The Koran says that drops of honey in a baby's mouth makes it grow to speak good things. A beehive can contribute 80 taka a week to pay off a house loan."

- "Once they have credit, the loanees solve 80% of their problems themselves. Perhaps 20% are solved with the help of government or other agencies."
- "As long as our system can detect the problems, there is nothing to worry about."

When visiting Grameen Bank offices, even in the new building, one is struck by an environment of modesty and equity. From the head office to the branch office, the desk of the Managing Director is of the same simple, sturdy design as that of a branch manager. The senior staff have their own offices, which is a necessity for their level of responsibility. But these offices are sometimes adorned with incubators being tested or plant pots along the wall being observed for the first sign of seed sprouts. Obviously, some staff have more authority than others, but only by virtue of experience and merit. The differences in status and salary are just enough to enhance the pleasure of promotion and make it a motivating reward. There is a willing ear for those who want to communicate, but the few telephones are guarded closely against abuse. Staff members are at ease and move around as much as they sit at their desks, but freedom is not absence of supervision. There is abundant trust in the willing spirit, but there is also a pragmatic awareness of human weakness.

Management and staff members work creatively together, comporting themselves with openness, perceptiveness and self-confidence. They gladly listen to the advice of an expert, but prefer to test out the propositions in their own way rather than taking them on face value. The leadership is talented and inspiring indeed, but so is the performance of the general staff. Competitiveness is fostered for the benefit of the commonality. There is a strong belief in discipline and supervision while there is encouragement and support. At the first sign, corruption is treated immediately with dismissal. All doors are wide open for the new idea, but judgement is exercised.

Some organizational modes of thought. Although not stated explicitly, the Bank appears to process information and promote decision-making according to the following generative modes of thought:

- Information is not kept secret. The organization is transparent, both to insiders and outsiders. All staff are involved and informed. Information is diligently pursued. Certainty is preferred, but ambiguity is tolerated.
- Errors are absorbed as experience and converted into opportunities for learning.
- Decisions are advance adaptations to changing circumstances. Plans are tentative outlooks, but with a strong sense of direction.

- Creativity is actively promoted. Conformity is discouraged. Attitudes and talents are not considered to be by inheritance alone: staff become good performers by virtue of what their organizational environment allows them to learn and realize.
- Social accountability and participation emerges from discipline and supervision.
- The more equal people are, the better they communicate and collaborate.

Deep thinking with creative twist. From such modes of thought Yunus has inspired, over the years, the development of an organizational culture quite unique in its approach to practical problem-solving. His staff members frequently appeal to the need for "deep thinking" when they discuss professional matters with outsiders. Taking their cue from Yunus, they mean looking at and describing problems in new, innovative ways. From the point of view of the more complacent observer, the results are surprising sometimes almost eccentric, but always intellectually refreshing in their newness. The approach springs out of this series of Yunus maxims:

- Every problem has a simple solution. A problem and its solution are two sides of the same coin, they are always together.
- A problem is only half the truth. A problem and its solution makes up the whole truth. Discover the whole truth.
- If you don't find the solution to a problem it is because you don't understand the problem.
- If you can comprehend the problem properly you are half-way to the solution.
- The solution is born in the womb of the problem. Artificial solutions do not last long.
- A solution cannot be found away from the problem itself.
- you must immerse yourself totally into the problem before you can start touching the surface of the solution.
- As you go deep into the problem you come close to the solution. This is the sure route to the solution.
- Neither can I solve *your* problem, nor can *you* solve *mine.* If it appears that I have solved your problem, it was possible only because I made your problem mine.
- Look for the solution where the problem is. It is intermeshed with the problem itself.
- Each problem may have many solutions, but there is one which is the best. Keep trying to get the best.
- A problem is a state of a particular configuration of events.

38

"Grameen trainees," writes Yunus "will hear these statements many times during their training period. Grameen tries to make them believe that they can find solutions to all the problems they'll face and also to feel that facing a problem is fun--you get a chance to test your wits."

Grameen Bank was not a preconceived plan, it was an idea that evolved and continues to evolve as a response to a situation articulated among the poorest in rural Bangladesh. It signifies a break with conventional development economics and cannot be described in the usual frame of management and organization terminology. It is a structured learning process more than it is an organizational structure.

A SOCIO-ECONOMIC FORMATION
Perhaps it is easier to understand Grameen Bank if we consider simpler organizational forms. Let us say it is a cluster or formation of interacting social and economic functions, in short, a socio-economic formation. When people are part of, i.e. participate in, such a formation, it means something simple to them. Quite literally, it means to stand together and to move together, to have an intention together and to act together in pursuit of that intention. This is literally what a people's movement is all about. Such a formation is expressed both in a physical or spatial arrangement and in the thinking, the feeling, the attitudes and the behaviour of the participants, right down to their body language. Most significantly, it is a social design in which people participate by making themselves socially and economically accountable to each other. It is a people's movement.

A conventional organization, such as a commercial bank or an agricultural extension agency, operates as an entity, as something cognitively different from its social environment. It interacts with the individuals surrounding it and develops friendly, hostile or indifferent but mostly depersonalized relationships to them. The interaction is a very limited one and people exist apart from the organization. In contrast, a socio-economic formation goes a long step further. It absorbs more and more of the social environment in itself and recreates it in a process of continuous transformation. It is formative in the sense that people create through it a new social and economic environment for themselves. It is the personalization of a participatory process. Grameen Bank does not have clients but members.

From individualism to self-control. The assumption that social development will occur when people change their attitude and behaviour has, until recently, dominated development literature. Changing people's attitudes and behaviour

39

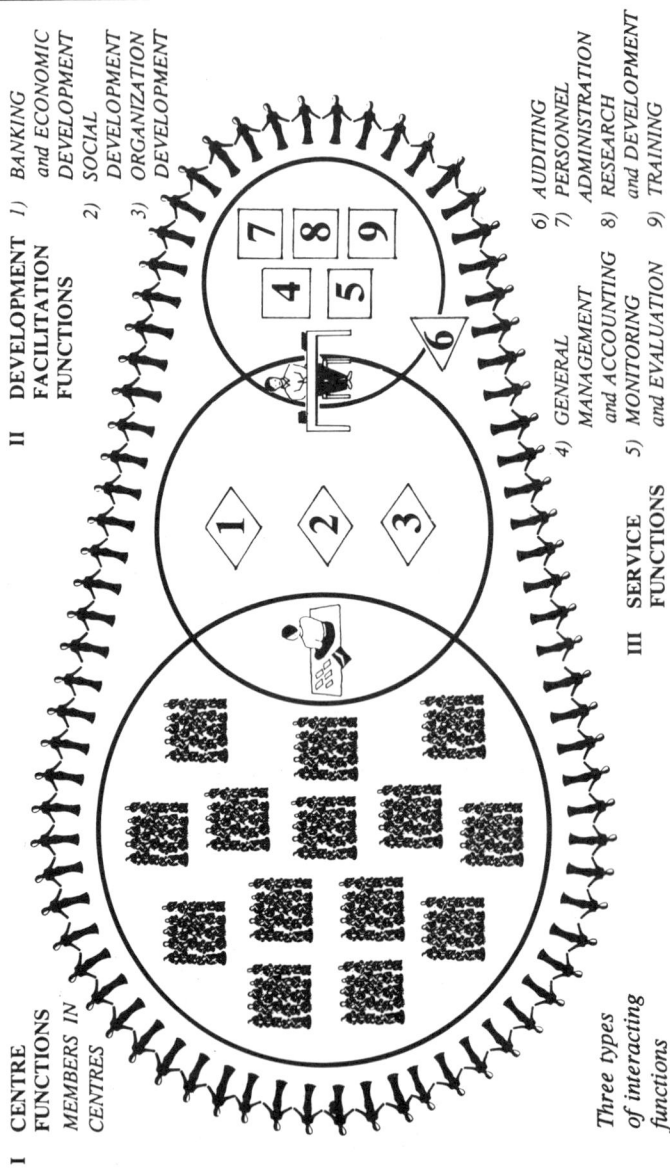

Figure 1

A SOCIO-ECONOMIC FORMATION
THE GRAMEEN OPERATIONAL FUNCTIONS

I CENTRE FUNCTIONS
MEMBERS IN CENTRES

II DEVELOPMENT FACILITATION FUNCTIONS

1) BANKING and ECONOMIC DEVELOPMENT
2) SOCIAL DEVELOPMENT
3) ORGANIZATION DEVELOPMENT

4) GENERAL MANAGEMENT and ACCOUNTING
5) MONITORING and EVALUATION

III SERVICE FUNCTIONS

6) AUDITING
7) PERSONNEL ADMINISTRATION
8) RESEARCH and DEVELOPMENT
9) TRAINING

Three types of interacting functions

is the declared or implied objective in scores of intervention programmes from family planning to horticulture. It is an educationist way of thinking about social reality and change which has not been fruitful, based as it is on the social assumptions of Northern societies. The North largely takes its starting point in the individual. The importance of individual rights for persons who make themselves accountable to society is not in question. However, when we take for granted that the individual is the only starting point for social analysis or polemics, we run straight into problems. One consequence is that we attribute to individuals, qualities, attitudes and habits which actually are features of the environment. It may be more fruitful then, to assume that behaviour will change if the social environment is changed. Behavioural psychology is founded on this basic tenet. In our view, the philosophy of Grameen Bank places a paramount emphasis on the social environment. Its essence is supervision and a discipline of strong social and economic accountability.

MANY INTERACTING FUNCTIONS
To describe the Bank only in terms of its sections and departments would not adequately explain the basic programmes and communication processes it sets in motion. We prefer to look first at the many functions of the Bank as a socio-economic formation. Then we will describe the various management units where interaction takes place and the particular designations and responsibilities of the actors themselves, staff and members. With this as a basis, we hope the reader should be able to place the later descriptions in a wider perspective.

Figure 1 shows the three types of functions Grameen Bank is engaged in and where they overlap and interact. Please keep in mind this is a "Functional Chart". In Grameen Bank, there is no discrete unit or section called "Organization Development" or "Social Development" but these functions take place as aspects, components or processes of many sections, departments and management levels of the Bank. Below we offer brief, general introductions to the three types of functions which are explained in more detail in successive stages throughout this chapter and the next.

I   **Centre functions.** Centres are comprised of the landless poor who carry out responsibilities and activities as part of their work to further their own development individually and collectively.

II   **Development facilitation functions.** If the situation of the poor is to be met effectively, three interrelated processes have to be set in motion. We categorize these processes as three functions which serve to facilitate the development the landless poor endeavour to achieve through their work. They include: (1) The banking and economic development function which makes credit available; (2) The social development function which makes information and supplies available; and (3) The organization development function which is engaged in the continuous development and management of the socio-economic formation as a whole to ensure it is optimally appropriate for its purpose.

III   **Service functions.** Specialized operations are required which carry out a variety of services directly or indirectly related to the social and economic development of Grameen Bank members.   These operational functions correspond to the names of the sections and departments in the Head Office of Grameen Bank.   Some of these operations also exist at the zonal office level.

Let's examine these functions more closely:

I   **Centre functions**

All the work of Grameen Bank springs from, and focuses on, the activities of the landless groups and their centres. People organize themselves in groups of five.   Then six groups of five members each join together to form a *centre*. Therefore, a centre usually comprises thirty members.   The name, centre, derives from the obligation of the six groups to construct a meeting-centre, a place where they can discuss their concerns and conduct their bank business. At the time of writing there are over 50 000 centres in operation, of which about 46 000 are female.

Landless groups. The poor who want to become members of the Bank are encouraged to form *groups* by finding five like-minded people who are in a similar economic condition and enjoy mutual trust and confidence.   Whereas group members must be inhabitants of the same village, only one member of a household may be in a group.   If several people from a household want to join the Bank, they must take membership in different groups in the centre or in another centre entirely.   Similarly, relatives must not be in the same group. Membership in groups and centres is according to gender.   Women comprise

THE CENTRE OF ATTENTION

To the members, the centre house is the first tangible result of their collective effort. Once built, it becomes a symbol of their solidarity and the meeting place for making decisions. After the meetings their children gather for school in the same shelter.

43

their own groups and centres and so do men. This decision is given in the social milieu of Bangladesh which is predominantly Islamic.

Each group elects a *chairperson* and a *secretary* who hold office for one year only. They cannot be re-elected until all other members have had the same learning experience that accompanies the responsibilities of these positions. The group chairperson is responsible for the discipline in the group. Members conduct their business with the Bank through her or him at weekly meetings. All members are obliged to attend these meetings and to be fully aware of the rules governing the activities and procedures of the group.

When a new group is formed, it is kept under close observation for a month or two by bank workers and other staff to see if the members are conforming to the discipline of Grameen Bank. If satisfactory, two members will receive their loans and be observed for a month or two to ascertain if they pay their instalments regularly. Only then will the next two members be eligible for loans. The fifth member of a group will receive her or his loan when the second set of loanees have established their reliability. Usually, the group chairperson and secretary are the last to receive their loans.

Social collateral. The second set of loans are not approved until the individual accounts of each group member are settled. Thus, the group members interact in a micro-network of mutual accountabilities. The individual is kept in line by a considerable amount of peer pressure. Equally, an individual is sustained by a considerable amount of peer support. This is the whole basis for the singular fact that Grameen Bank can give loans without demanding a collateral surety. Social collateral replaces material collateral. The credibility of the group as a whole--and its future benefits in terms of new loans--is in jeopardy if one member defaults on loan repayments. In practice, what often happens in the case of financial difficulties is that the group arrives at a private arrangement to pay a member's instalment. This is one of the reasons the Bank has a repayment rate better than 97%.

The group makes decisions on all bank matters on a consensus basis. The chairperson is expected to be the spokesperson who voices the group consensus at the centre meetings. Therefore, the homogeneity of the group is essential. Through trial and error, the Bank has settled on a group size of five. Initially, loans were given to individuals, but this procedure quickly proved itself uncontrollable for Bank staff. Then the idea of peer control was introduced and groups of ten or more were organized. However, these were found too large to be effective. The necessary self-discipline did not emerge and the meetings became clumsy to conduct. Agreement was slow to take place and the chairperson's overview of the group's situation was complicated by its size. In the end, five members turned out to be the most practicable size. Corresponding to the five digits of a hand, it is also an easy figure to communicate.

In the early stages of the Bank's development, group formation on the basis of a similar activity was also monitored for its effectiveness as a cohesive element. It was found that groups based exclusively on specialized activities, such as cow fattening or rickshaw pulling, did not function too well because the members came from different places and could not meet easily. The spatial and social closeness of being from the same village emerged as a major premise for a well-functioning, cohesive group. In conventional credit systems, the company is ultimately responsible for ensuring loan repayment. In Grameen Bank, this responsibility is placed with the group and may extend to the centre. If a group member behaves in an undisciplined manner, for example, by not attending meetings or by not repaying loans regularly, the remaining members may, by unanimous decision, impose a fine. In the same way, they may decide to expel a member for chronic breach of discipline. In such cases, the member to be expelled must repay the total loan before leaving.

A member may leave the group at any time as long as any loan is fully repaid. If a member leaves without repaying the entire loan, the responsibility for paying the balance falls to the remaining group members. Any person may join a group if its members unanimously agree and the person meets the qualifying criteria set by the Bank.

Centre meetings. The regular centre meeting coincides with the weekly repayment of instalments. Early in the morning the six groups meet in the centre house and are assembled before the bank worker arrives. During the meeting, current issues of interest to the members are discussed, various problems are raised, repayment of loans and other bank business is conducted, and decisions of concern to the centre are taken on a consensus basis.

Over time centre members have arrived at a seating arrangement which makes it possible to conduct their meetings more effectively and efficiently. The six groups assemble in rows of five. Each row is one group. Each chairperson sits on the far right of her or his group followed by the secretary and then the remaining members. Normally, the centre chief's group will occupy the first row. (See Figure 2). Although the number of people in a centre may vary, more and more the optimal size of thirty members is the practice. Larger

Figure 2

THE MAINSPRING IN THE MOVEMENT

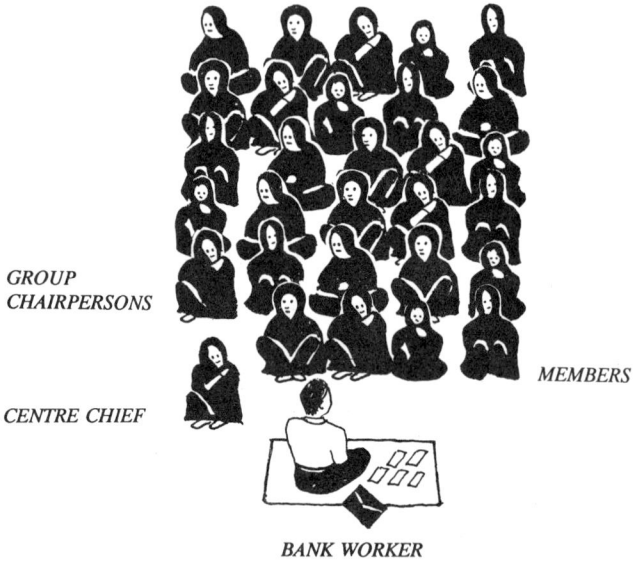

GROUP CHAIRPERSONS

MEMBERS

CENTRE CHIEF

BANK WORKER

THE CENTRE

*6 groups
in each centre.
5 members
in each group.*

Weekly meetings of women in the shelter of their centre is the clockwork, the very mainspring in this people's movement made of hard work, money, accountability and dignity.

46

centres do not allow for the same degree of participation by individual members and eventually divide to form two centres as necessary. During the meeting, the group chairpersons conduct the bank business on behalf of their respective members. From among themselves, the group chairpersons elect a centre chief and a deputy centre chief who hold office for one year only. It is a rule that new centre officers must be elected after a year has expired, and bank workers are increasingly supervising to see the rule is followed. Even a particular month of the year is specified for the elections so the whole process can become a standard matter of practice.

Centre chiefs ensure attendance at the weekly meetings, payments of loan instalments, overall discipline and generally conduct the programme of the meetings. If a centre chief regularly breaches discipline, she or he can be removed according to certain rules and a new person will be elected. Both the group chairperson and the centre chief are involved in the essential task of supervising if members are utilizing their loans appropriately. Any misbehaviour in this regard is reported to the centre meeting. Office holders in groups and centres are not paid for their work.

One of the most significant features of the centre meetings is that *all bank business is conducted openly* in front of the members. There are no private transactions, much less any shady deals. Every member knows what is happening and can assess her or his own position in relation to others. Carrying out all transactions in public and dealing with problems together, combined with the rotation of office holders by obligatory yearly elections, severely mitigates the entrenchment of vested interests and constellations of power. At the same time, the openness of the procedures prohibits individuals from misbehaving. The fear of public exposure is a heavy disincentive for inappropriate actions. Thus, the centre meeting reinforces a relationship of social and economic accountability that is established in the groups. The individual members are very aware that they enjoy the benefits of membership only if they play by the rules of the game. This is a premise for community participation that is rarely articulated much less treated with any seriousness in the literature on the subject. It entails subjecting oneself voluntarily to a combination of self-discipline and communal discipline.

The issue of discipline for the common good is reiterated during the meetings. Within the rules and regulations that members have accepted, the centres are quite autonomous in their decision making. It is up to them to decide what to do with the opportunities the Bank offers.

The complete set of rules and regulations applying to groups and centres are specified in *Bidhimala,* the Grameen Bank's bylaws. (See Annex 1). Also in the bylaws, provision is made for the advent of larger landless associations. To date, the members have pursued this opportunity informally and usually in response to an injustice. It seems they feel their interests are adequately taken care of within the centres. It is difficult to say if landless associations comprising several centres would actually formalize in the long term.

II Development facilitation functions

To facilitate the development activities the landless poor carry out through their centres and groups, to respond to the needs they voice, and to develop theorganizational tools for an effective facilitation of the whole participatory development process, is a complex challenge. It requires a high degree of organizational talent, creativity and hard work by the Bank staff. These facilitation functions are not necessarily located in or carried out exclusively by one department or section. It is characteristic of Grameen Bank's way of working that some functions are spread over a network of many actors within the Bank. However, in order to maintain an overall perspective of Grameen Bank's operations, it is more useful to define these activities as independent functions. They are discussed according to the following headings in the order given: (1) Banking and economic development, (2) Social development and (3) Organization development.

(1) Banking and economic development. Development has always bypassed the landless. In rural credit schemes "rural" has been synonymous with "agricultural" and therefore, by definition, excluded all those engaged in a multitude of other subsistence activities. And women constitute the group most removed from the possibility of credit. To some degree, the small farmer has been reached but at the cost of the poorest of the poor. One main reason is the landless poor are not able to provide a collateral surety for loans. Consequently, in conventional banking practice, they do not qualify as potential clients. It is the stated purpose of the Grameen Bank, on the basis of a democratic principle of equal opportunity, to provide banking services to the poorest. Credit is simply considered a human right. This purpose is detailed in the Grameen Bank Ordinance. (See Annex 2). In a situation of severe resource constraints and within the framework of the national economy, it is the Bank's view that credit can be offered only at the official, current rate of interest. At the time of writing it is 20% per annum. In principle, the banking function should be profitable or at least generate enough income to cover the operational costs of the Bank as a whole. These costs are bound to be high. The possibility of defaulting and the lack of collateral surety can only be countered by intensive supervision within the centres and by a monitoring and evaluation system that gives early warning. This extent of supervision requires investment in a large number of staff as well as procedures for accounting and control. Many small loans with weekly instalments add heavily to the amount of work to be done. Loans from external sources have been necessary to finance the Bank's expansion. Nevertheless, the banking and economic development function manage to forge a path marked by an exceptionally high degree of economic self-reliance. It is the Bank's intention to continually maximize its self-reliance and autonomy. It has already largely succeeded in doing so.

(2) **Social development.** The social development function in the Bank's work can be traced to the days when it was an action research project. From the beginning, the social development emphasis was on women. They were seen as the people facing the greatest need. As importantly, women were considered the most effective point of entry for an improved standard and quality of living in their families and communities. As well as carrying out the fledgling provision of rural credit in Jobra village in 1976, the first female bank employees were informally discussing matters of health, nutrition, family planning and education with women loanees. Under a tree, in a courtyard, in a villager's house--wherever the meetings for loan collection were held--it was as much an occasion for the exchange of socially-needed information, for encouragement and motivation, for confidence building as it was an economic exchange. The essence of Grameen Bank, ultimately, is social development and empowerment. The catalyst in the process is credit. Without the catalyst, the social development is thwarted.

Although Grameen Bank always recognized the need for credit and social development to go on hand-in-hand, other banking institutions in Bangladesh found this unorthodox and unacceptable. In the early stages of its development, Grameen Bank could not support an intensive social development programme because it does not have immediate economic returns. However, aware of the long-term investment value of education programmes for women particularly, the Bank was determined to integrate such a dimension into its overall services. As the Bank expanded, its social development programme for women loanees required more organization, facilities and financing. For these reasons, Grameen Bank sought outside funding and, by 1980, in consultation with UNICEF, had planned the first phase of a two-year training programme for women. New phases have been added over the years and the arrangement is still funded by UNICEF and some support from GTZ. As the Bank becomes increasingly more self-reliant, it foresees carrying this programme with its own funds. The women members themselves, it is felt, will demand it.

Grameen Bank sees social development inextricably linked to economic development and its own interest as a Bank. In the short and long term, improved nutritional and health status, for example, is a sound banking investment. It correlates with increased productivity and creativity which, in turn, must influence loan turnover and stability. Most social development takes place through an intensive and extensive workshop programme primarily addressed to women. The content and processes of these workshops are described in considerable detail later. However, other social issues are raised by the Bank in the course of its work. One is that Grameen Bank will not authorize credit to a man who has two wives. Quite simply, he is not a good credit risk. Credit is to increase productivity and investment and generate savings. The Bank considers dowry an economic burden the poor can ill afford and is working hard to motivate people to marry without it. Dowry is seen to break the backs of the poor. If the practice doesn't cease, credit will only serve to inflate dowry prices.

Children's education is promoted by the Bank and staff provide advice, textbooks at cost and arrange for special children's savings funds. Specialized training or information needs are handled by bank staff who primarily serve as a liaison for their members' requests. For example, staff would identify a trainer to teach machine maintenance, but the members would make their own arrangements with the trainer. Although this is still practised, the training needs are so pervasive that now specialized workshops providing knowledge and skills directly related to loanees'income-generating activities are a regular feature of the programme. Overall, the social development function comprises a wide variety of activities integrated into almost all levels and units of the Bank.

(3) Organization development. Instrumental to the operational competence and capacity of all other activities in Grameen Bank is the organization development function. Central to its efficacy is the decentralized way information is processed and communicated by staff throughout Grameen Bank. Organization development encompasses the daily management of the operations as well as the continuous development and expansion of the Bank as a socio-economic formation. The pace of expansion in Grameen Bank has been so rapid that many daily management decisions are intertwined with the continuous reassessment and projections of future needs.

Management and supervision units. To understand how organizational development takes place in practice, we describe the management and supervisory units through which the Bank operates and the staff positions assigned to each. The field-level unit having the most sustained contact over time with the loanees is the branch office. (See Figure 3). Currently, about 1 000 branch offices are in operation, numerically constituting the most predominant field management unit. A *branch office* supervises and services a maximum of 60 centres located in villages within walking distance of the branch. Walking is the least expensive and mostly the only means of communication available. Due to this physical limitation, a branch office cannot cover an area much greater than 30 square miles. Five miles is considered to be the maximum feasible walking distance for a bank worker. To some extent, bicycles are now used by bank workers but this is not always possible because of road conditions or no roads at all. In more conservative rural areas, female bank workers face strong social disapproval sometimes bordering on aggression if they attempt to ride bicycles from the branch offices to the centres. The branch manager always has a bicycle, and it is becoming more and more common for each bank worker to have one as well.

Almost 80% of the Bank's total staff work at the branch level. The branch office is the basic operating unit and is considered a profit responsibility unit. It is imperative for the branch manager to show profit. Branch workers can receive 10% of these profits as an incentive. Historically, the branch offices have reached profitable levels within the fourth year of operation, a period required to form a sufficient number of viable groups and prepare them as viable borrowers. Now, profitability is frequently achieved earlier.

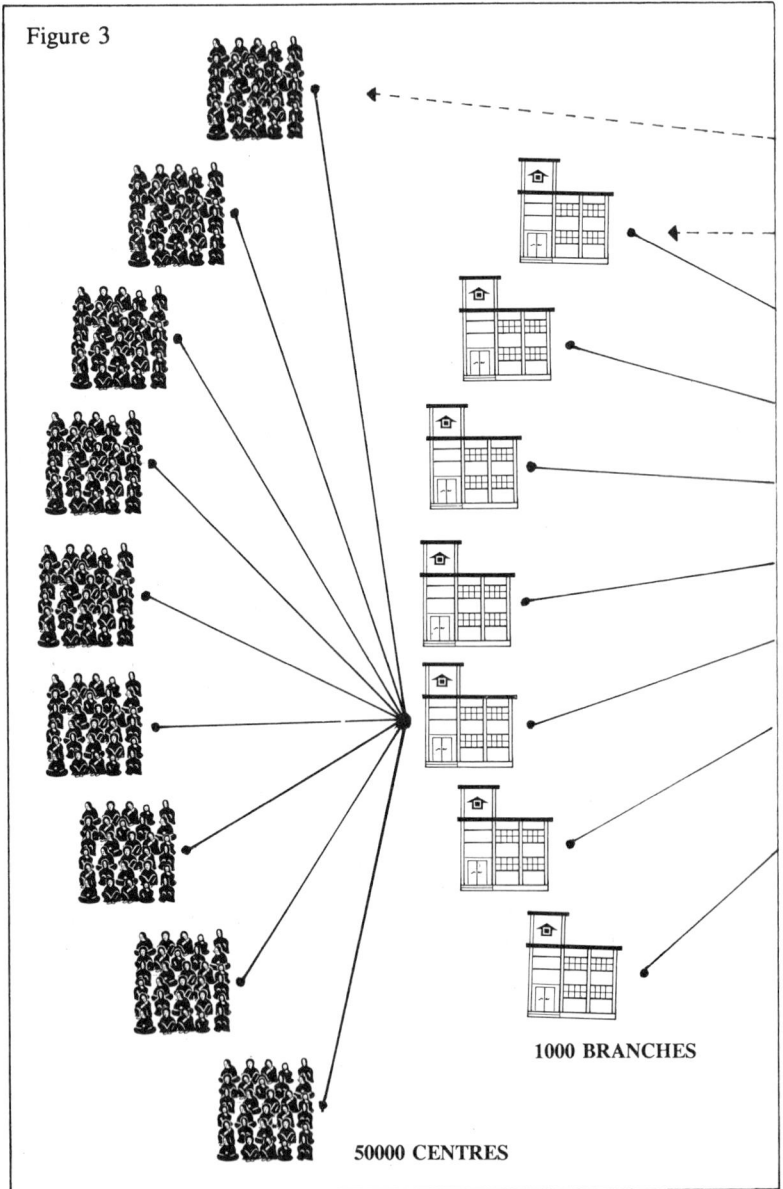

Figure 3

1000 BRANCHES

50000 CENTRES

54

THE GRAMEEN ORGANIZATIONAL DESIGN

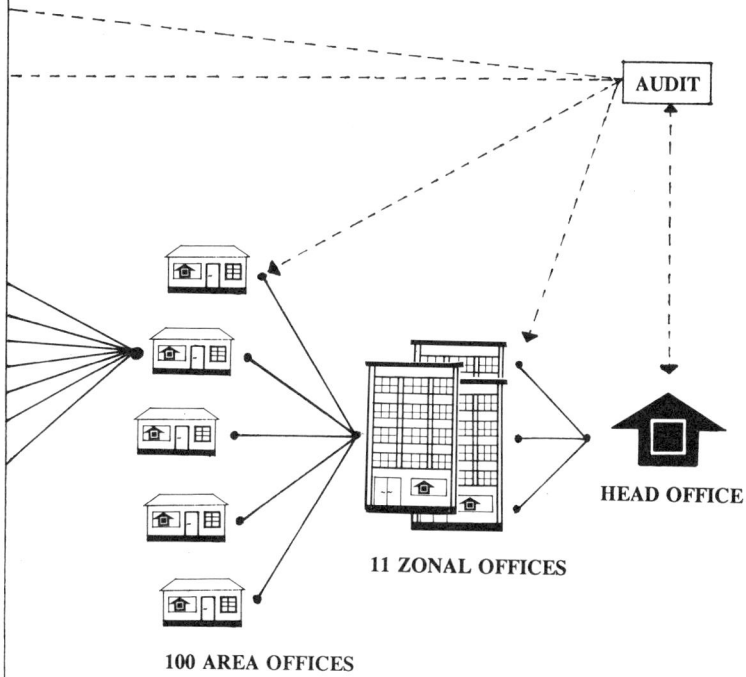

AUDIT

HEAD OFFICE

11 ZONAL OFFICES

100 AREA OFFICES

Numbers are approximate

About 10 branch offices are, in turn, supervised by an *area office*. Usually located in a small town, the area office services an approximate area of 400 square miles. For transport, motorcycles are in use both by area managers and their programme officers. However, these are purchased by the officers through loans from Grameen Bank. Characteristic of Grameen Bank is the high level of autonomy granted to the field units. The area office manages itself. Its accountability occurs in its reporting procedures to the *zonal office*.

The zonal office is the head office for a zone which, by and large, corresponds to a government district in Bangladesh. With five area offices under its supervision, a zonal office is located in the district capital and has one vehicle for transport. Eleven zonal offices are now in operation located in Bogra, Chittagong, Comilla, Dhaka, Dinajpur, Faridpur, Rajshahi, Rangpur, Patuakhali, Sylhet and Tangail. These offices service 44 out of the 64 districts in Bangladesh. Although they operate in a very coordinated fashion, the zonal offices are highly independent, almost autonomous units. Finally, the *head office* for the whole of Grameen Bank is located in the capital city of Dhaka.

Categories of staff members The *branch manager* is responsible for a branch office. He is assisted by one accountant/senior assistant and six *bank assistants*. Each bank assistant supervises and services on average two centres a day or a maximum of ten centres a week. In addition, branch offices used to have three bank worker trainees who received practical training by participating in the office work and accompanying the bank assistants in their daily routine. Since there are several categories of bank assistants, to avoid confusion we shall refer to all of them as bank workers. During the period of rapid expansion there may also have been one to three officer trainees assigned to a branch office for a period of time. Figure 3 illustrates in a simplified manner the organizational structure at field level.

The *area manager* is a senior officer in charge of an area office. His main collaborator is a *programme officer*. An area office may have one programme officer. Together with the area manager, they are very intensively engaged in supervision of the work in branch offices and their centres. A programme officer has the capacity to supervise well, around eight branch offices. Also stationed at the area office are officers who consolidate or control accounts, statistics and other data before forwarding to the zonal office. Trainee officers are often posted to area offices and participate in the work. All area managers and programme officers have formerly been branch managers and know the ins and outs of the operations in the villages. Area managers are authorized to

STAFFING IN FIELD OFFICES

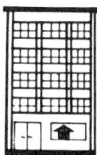

ZONAL OFFICE	--------	Zonal Manager	-1
		Principal Officer	-1
		Senior Officer (SG)	-4
		Senior Officer	-5
		Officer	-3
		Senior Assistant (SG)	-3
		Senior Assistant	-4
		Bank Worker	-7
		Typist	-2
		Driver	-2
		Peon-Cum-Guard	-3

			35

AREA OFFICE	--------	Area Manager	-1
		Programme Officer	-1
		Senior Assistant	-1
		Typist	-1
		Driver	-1
		Peon-Cum-Guard	-1

			6

BRANCH OFFICE	--------	Branch Manager	-1
		Senior Assistant	-1
		Bank Assistant/ Bank Worker	-6
		Peon-Cum-Guard	-1

			9

handle all decisions for their areas, but if they feel the need for advice, are free to consult the zonal manager.

The *zonal manager* has a staff numbering around thirty-five. His main collaborators are senior principal or principal officers in charge of accounts and fund management. The function of monitoring and evaluation is a priority in the activities of the zonal office. Most zonal offices have several senior officers who are responsible for a major part of the social development programme in Grameen Bank. For the reader's easy identification of their role in Grameen Bank, we prefer to call them social development officers. Although the zonal office holds the major responsibility for carrying out the social development programme of Grameen Bank, a few area offices have social development officers assigned to them. A zonal manager works in close contact with the area managers who all attend management meetings once or twice every month in his office.

Management functions at head office. A link to the formal government system in Bangladesh is provided through the *Board*. As stipulated in the Grameen Bank Ordinance of 1983 (See Annex 2), it is constituted by the Chairman, the Managing Director, six Directors appointed by the government and four Directors from among the borrower/shareholders. In the spirit of empowerment this proportion of representation has been changed. Now, only three representatives are named by government while nine directors represent the landless--all of whom are women. Thus, the landless have a majority vote in the Board. Revised in 1986 and 1990, the Grameen Bank Ordinance provides for fifty percent of shareholders to be women. In reality, female members hold 92% of the shares while male members hold 8%. Moreover, women may not transfer their shares to men, but the opposite is allowed. The Board is in charge of the general direction and superintendence of the affairs and business of the Bank. It may, "for the purpose of ensuring efficient functioning of the Bank and facilitating transaction of its daily business, delegate to the Chairman, Managing Director or any other Director or any officer of the Bank any of its functions subject to such conditions as it may think to impose." The Board provides a formal link to national institutions while it ensures that the rural poor have themselves an institutionalized opportunity to decide over Bank policy. Increasingly, the members hold shares in the Bank and it might be envisaged that a general assembly of shareholders would be the ultimate governing body in the future. Eighty-seven percent of the shares are now owned by the landless.

58

Sorbocha meetings. The overall daily management of Grameen Bank is the responsibility of the *Managing Director* supported by a small personal staff. His work should be seen, however, in close connection with that of the Sorbocha Committee, the "Highest Committee". The sorbocha meetings, which are comprised of the Managing Director and the Deputy Managing Director, the General Manager and the Deputy General Managers, are held up to twice a month. Very often the Managing Director will refer matters for decision to this meeting rather than taking decisions himself. The meetings work out decisions on policy or implementation issues until a satisfactory consensus is reached. The meeting is not adjourned before agreement is reached and the decisions have the backing of each participant.

Consensual approach. The same consensual approach is applied in the zonal managers' conference. Twice a year, the eleven managers meet in a marathon three-day session during which they exchange experiences and hammer out issues and decisions for further development of the Bank in their respective zones. If one of them is not convinced of the utility of a certain proposal, the rest must convince him or else modify the proposal. Just as the branch and area managers enjoy considerable management autonomy, the zonal managers have a great deal of freedom in running their zones. However, to ensure that the Bank progresses along the same lines in each zone, it is necessary to have agreement on major policy and implementation issues. Once a consensus decision is achieved, the rule is that it is binding. At the most, a zonal manager can delay implementing a decision, if there are practical reasons to justify it. But, he cannot fail to implement it. During these meetings, the head office management assume a role as resource persons and observers. The principle is that decisions concerning the practical development of Grameen Bank should be left to those who do the job, but everyone needs to be well informed. The decisions of the meeting are compiled and circulated immediately to all offices. Progress and performance are evaluated in each zone and the reports distributed to all.

In general, as the Managing Director points out, "Head Office still avoids taking unilateral decisions. If it has to frame new policies or rules or regulations, it will make a draft and circulate the draft among departmental heads and zonal managers for comments and modifications. If the subject covered by the draft is of greater importance, copies of the draft will go to the area manager. Depending on the seriousness of the matter, those who receive the draft may send their comments in writing, or each recipient may hold his internal meetings to debate the issues and come up with reactions. After all the opinions and reactions are received by the head office they are sent to a standing committee, the "drafting committee", which reviews all opinions and suggestions and prepares the second draft. "

Special purpose committees. The sorbocha committee is surrounded by a network of special purpose committees organized around issues of recruitment, promotion, training, hostel management, construction tenders, construction implementation, and procurement among others. A committee is constituted by staff members from various units considered relevant to its purpose. Committees develop plans for their particular area of responsibility and supervise implementation. The decision-making process is consensual. They decide on a course of action themselves or feed recommendations for action to the sorbocha meeting in a continuous process of communication and interaction. The decision-making process is a crosswise function rather than a top-to-bottom one. The organizational principles of matrix organization and of ad hoc task forces is extensively utilized by the Bank, but the practice could also be further expanded on. Committees or staff members are encouraged to take decisions on their own rather than referring them upstairs. An initiative or a new idea is hardly ever met with a "No!" but with "Maybe". "Let us try it out and see." Grameen Bank is practising the kind of open and consensus-oriented management approach expounded in textbooks on advanced management, but which few organizations or corporations realize in practice. It is an unwritten rule that any query or proposal from loanees or staff members is responded to quickly. If it isn't, the staff concerned consider themselves free to act on any necessary decisions. Although there is a strong and charismatic Managing Director, he practices collective leadership and delegation of authority to an extent rarely seen. The Organizational Chart and procedures of Grameen Bank are quite standard in their formal presentation. What is remarkable is the practice of these in reality. (Annex 3)

Corporate pride. The result of the above approach is an organization development and management function which anticipates events, planning for them in advance. Also, a continuous flow of ideas is generated for improving the Bank's services to the landless poor which are tested and rapidly implemented if found successful. It could be argued that bureaucracies deserve the staff performance they get. At worst, hierarchical management systems produce apathetic, disillusioned and inefficient employees. At best, they release the talents of a few only. The genuine practice of open management in Grameen Bank elicits an unmistakeable self-confidence and commitment in its staff which greets the visitor like a breath of fresh air. Combined with a high degree of economic self-reliance, it lays the basis for the development of a healthy corporate pride.

III   Service functions

In the following we describe the five service functions of Grameen Bank and refer the reader again to Figure 3 for the overview glance.

(4) General management and accounting. This service function concentrates on fund management and an extensive accounting system. It deals with pension benefits for the staff, service regulations and disciplinary matters. The effectiveness of Grameen Bank as a whole is obviously dependent on the accurate and effective processing of financial information and the rapid response to the financial needs of other functions at head office or the zonal offices.

Overview of statements. Monthly financial statements and overviews including a balance sheet and a profit and loss account are ready for the Managing Director by the seventh of each month. Taking into consideration the difficulties of rural transport and communication, this is a remarkable feat which is accomplished in the following way. The branch manager brings his monthly statement personally to the area office by walking or bicycling. Often the timing corresponds to his attendance at a monthly evaluation meeting for all branch managers. The area manager brings the statements of all his branches to the zonal office at the time of a monthly meeting for all the area managers. The zonal office collects and consolidates the information and sends it on to head office by messenger. Head office does the accounting, compiles the information and prepares the cumulative financial statements for the month. The financial needs of the zonal office for the coming month are assessed and dealt with concomitantly. For their general information about the Bank's overall position, a *consolidated monthly statement* is sent in return to the zones, areas and branches. The record keeping required by a branch manager is considerable. In addition to the monthly statement, he is obliged to work out weekly, fortnightly and quarterly statements. As we shall see later, even a daily statement is required for monitoring and evaluation purposes.

61

Fund management. Particularly important for an overview of the financial situation of a branch is the weekly statement. Available on Sunday, it reflects at a glance any discrepancy between instalments due and repayments made. Although a branch manager can request supplementary funds from the general manager in head office, he is encouraged to manage efficiently the branch's own funds through various regulations. It should be stressed here that money is handled physically in the Grameen Bank only at the branch office level and in the centres by the bank workers and the loanees. At an earlier stage, supplementary funds required by a branch office were transferred directly from head office to the branch offices. Now, this function is shedded to the zonal offices as head office transfers funds to these only. All the transfers are done through existing commercial bank channels.

Every day branch managers personally deposit the cash received from loan payments in the nearest commercial bank. It should be made clear to the reader that the branch office is the basic profit-making unit in Grameen Bank. The fund management is decentralized. The Branch charges 20% interest to its loanees and borrows money at 12% interest from the zonal office. Therefore, its profit margin is 8%. After depreciation of assets, a branch may have 250 000 taka or more in yearly net profit. As penalty interests are charged on untransferred amounts, the branch manager is motivated to keep funds revolving rapidly.

One of the key and largely unrecognised factors in the effective fund management of Grameen Bank is the weekly instalment. It allows for a very rapid revolving of money which increases the Bank's potential to generate its own funding. By and large, a zone as a whole will not need supplementary funds from head office for its routine transactions. It will tend to be self-sufficient in funds. Exceptions are the funding needs for purposes of further expansion of the Bank's services or for particular purposes such as joint enterprises or transfers to its sister organizations such as the Krishi Foundation. As a rule, a zone as a whole will need extra funds only if disbursement exceeds the recovery of money. During the dull period brought about by the monsoons in Bangladesh, disbursement will tend to decline while weekly recovery is maintained at the same pace. This is due to the fact that loans are given on a yearly duration. On the other hand, if disbursement is slightly higher than recovery, it demonstrates that a demand for money and a potential for further expansion exists. At the branch level, it has been the experience that individual loans tend to stabilize in terms of loan amount. This trend has been changed lately by the introduction of new types of loans. Grameen Bank is consistently searching for ways to ensure its autonomy and efficiency. A fund management approach is to accept savings deposits on a large scale from its individual loanees, from the various funds accumulated by the centres and from the richer part of the rural population. The latter is seen as a potential way of transferring access to resources from the local rich to the local poor. Grameen Bank will pay a normal deposit interest. In rural Bangladesh, the commercial banking system is well developed and Grameen Bank's operation so far has been interwoven with this and dependent on it. To expand in the area of deposit banking might mean severing some of these ties, so the Bank has not implemented this line of action fully. Only about 500 branches in remote areas are engaged in deposit banking. But rural saving is seen as worthwhile exploring from the perspective of fund management and socio-economic development. In rural areas, savings are normally bigger than investments with the investments kept in urban areas by the commercial banks. Depositing savings in Grameen Bank would ensure that these financial resources remained accessible for the rural areas themselves. It is clear that rural savings would take the form of many small deposits. The benefit lies in the characteristic that these deposits are usually long-term. Since the branch managers are encouraged to manage their branches in a profitable manner, the Bank is aware that adding deposit banking to their duties might possibly divert their attention to the richer part of the rural population. The matter is, however, continuously under consideration.

$$\boxed{5}$$

(5) **Monitoring and evaluation** is one of the clues to the smooth functioning and rapid expansion of Grameen Bank. At any time it is the source for its preparedness to respond swiftly and effectively to the needs of the poor. Intense attention is paid to the performance of individual staff members; inefficiencies are nipped in the bud and merit is quickly rewarded. Extensive records are being continuously updated. Monitoring and evaluation is valued for its present and potential contribution to future management and organization development beyond the function of keeping an eye on the operations. Factual data are important but equally important are the qualitative aspects of what is happening among staff and clients. An effort is made to encourage staff to write *narrative reports*, integrating them into the formal, quantified reporting procedures. Staff are urged to be creative and bring forward their own personal views, ideas and criticisms. Perspectives of the members and their situation are documented through data collection in training assignments and the social development programme.

Figure 4

BOTTOM UP MONITORING SYSTEM

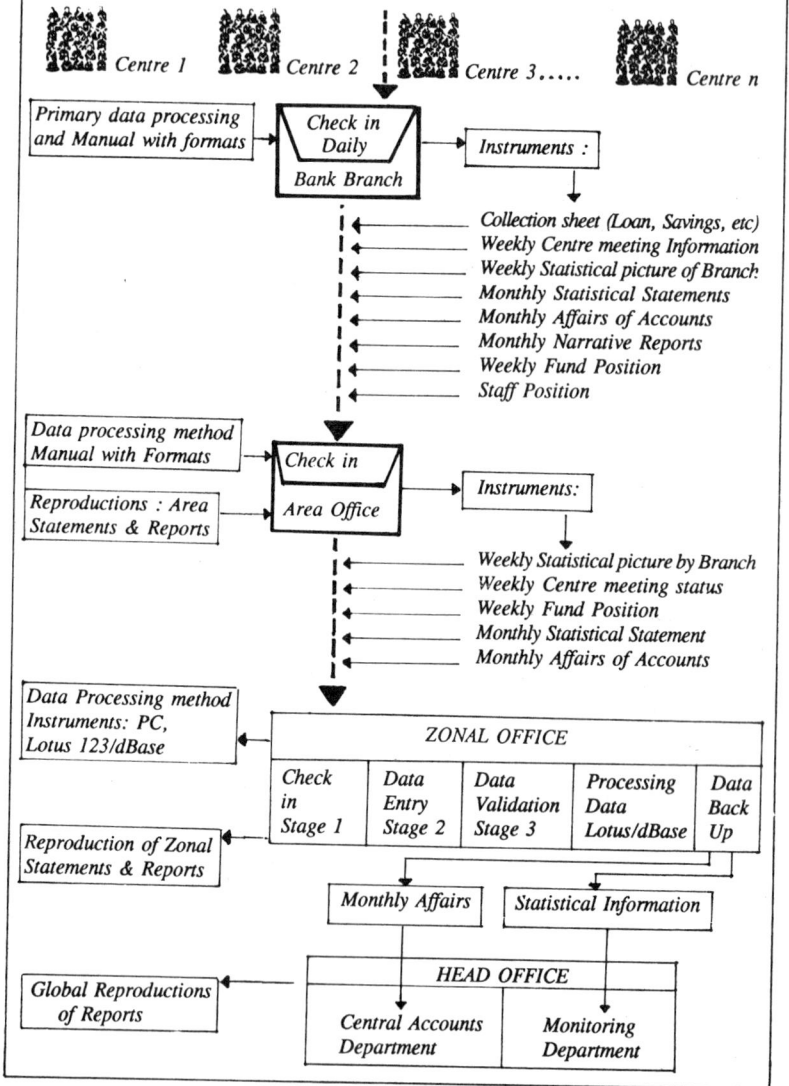

Centre 1   Centre 2   Centre 3 .....   Centre n

| Primary data processing and Manual with formats | Check in Daily Bank Branch | Instruments : |

Collection sheet (Loan, Savings, etc)
Weekly Centre meeting Information
Weekly Statistical picture of Branch
Monthly Statistical Statements
Monthly Affairs of Accounts
Monthly Narrative Reports
Weekly Fund Position
Staff Position

| Data processing method Manual with Formats | Check in Area Office | Instruments: |
| Reproductions : Area Statements & Reports | | |

Weekly Statistical picture by Branch
Weekly Centre meeting status
Weekly Fund Position
Monthly Statistical Statement
Monthly Affairs of Accounts

Data Processing method Instruments: PC, Lotus 123/dBase	ZONAL OFFICE				
	Check in Stage 1	Data Entry Stage 2	Data Validation Stage 3	Processing Data Lotus/dBase	Data Back Up

| Reproduction of Zonal Statements & Reports |

| Monthly Affairs | Statistical Information |

Global Reproductions of Reports	HEAD OFFICE	
	Central Accounts Department	Monitoring Department

Grameen Bank is unique in its gathering of socio-economic data to monitor and evaluate the viability and impact of credit to the landless. As we discuss later, trainees carry out thorough case studies of the poor which become part of the monitoring and evaluation data base. The scale of this can be appreciated by realizing that the Bank during its intensive expansion used to train 400 to 500 people a year. Socio-economic data are also collected by social development officers in the course of their work with women members. These data are analyzed and the results variously incorporated into staff meetings, training and management decision making. Through all management units and among their personnel, there is a continuous flow of information. Without exception, staff members we interviewed demonstrated a remarkably detailed knowledge of the Bank's operations and plans for the future.

The Monitoring and Evaluation function was upgraded to a fully-fledged department in 1986 and has since then developed a very professional and precise Management Information System (MIS) which includes an Early Warning System (EWS). The whole system is computerized, demonstrating an international standard, possibly ahead of what is practised by many large national and multinational corporations. The information gathered is applied to a remarkable degree in daily management of the operation and for future scenarios. Beyond that, the size and quality of information offers a special opportunity for understanding change and development in the rural areas of Bangladesh. Figure 4 gives a simplified outline of this bottom-up monitoring system.

The basic concepts are transparency of the Bank's operation and insurance of loan quality, management quality and earning quality. So far, the indicators being concentrated on are those for normal and abnormal rate of expansion. Computer modelling is applied extensively in financial and operational planning. For example through its MIS, the Bank can study whether it is likely to operate profitably under a special set of projections. The focus is particularly on the performance of the branch offices as they are the basic income-generating units. The system can project a five-year scenario for branches or zones, assisting the managers to look ahead, improve their focus, telling them where they should look and why, and what they are doing right or wrong. The budgets are monitored quarterly with percentage assessments of deviations. It is considered particularly important that branches are not overlooking the cost aspects of their work decisions. Since 1990 the general budget deviation has been brought down to below 5%. Deviations up to 10% are handled at the zonal level. In excess of that, head office takes action.

The Monitoring and Evaluation function aims at giving management the global overview of the Bank's operation at the same time as the information is broken down to give full updating on details. However, management now face a situation of information overload. One remedy adopted is printing of graphs and histograms; another is consolidation of information in summaries distributed to a circle of senior officers who review the material and feed action points to the departments concerned. This procedure has proven to be effective, although it is clearly a stopgap measure. A process for rationalizing and reducing the amount of information is now ongoing. For readers who wish to pursue more detail, a complete list of the periodical statements of the Bank are reproduced in Annex 4. This function is responsible also for publication of the Annual Report, usually available in June the following year.

It is characteristic of Grameen Bank's unorthodox approach that it does not have a separate information division or unit. This activity largely pertains to monitoring and evaluation with its comprehensive data accumulation and report preparation. Aside from the obvious value of this information for decision-making, it also reflects the Bank's attempt to set in motion a learning process. To reach Grameen Bank staff members and facilitate dialogue among them, monitoring and evaluation has the additional responsibility of compiling an internal staff newsletter called, *Uddog* (Initiative). Bank workers and other field staff are the main contributors, sharing the experiences arising from their work. *Uddog* contains a lively variety of touching personal reflections, critical evaluations, workshop experiences and insights.

<6|

(6) **The Auditing function.** In the usual conventions of banking, the audit function is independent and external. This applies to Grameen Bank which has a standard external audit of accounts as stipulated in its Ordinance. In response to its many particular requirements and to meet the needs of a rapid expansion, the Bank is developing its own *internal audit function* as well. This function has undergone decentralization with an audit office now located in each zone which remains independent of the zonal office. Coordination of the internal audit function is the responsibility of the audit section in head office. On an average, a branch office would be audited every second year. The selection is, however, randomly made. Several criteria are applied: the monthly statements are scrutinized for discrepancies; branch, area or zonal office may have requested an audit or there may be mishappenings that require attention. The general opinion is that since the zonal audit offices were established, mistakes

have been reduced by more than eighty percent. The audit offices operate with a small staff of three to four experienced officers recruited from the field.

A branch audit may require up to ten days and includes a fairly high degree of verification through field inspection in the centres and in the homesteads of individual loanees. The auditors work according to an *audit manual* which prescribes a variety of audit procedures and techniques for detecting operational irregularities and guiding the branch staff. The head office audit section has designed a format in line with the above strategy to assess the progress of an audited branch at a glance. This brief assessment with qualitative remarks is submitted to the Managing Director for his perusal and advice. One of the following five qualitative remarks sums up the direction of performance of a branch office between two points of audit: A-Impressive progress; B-Satisfactory progress; C-No progress; D-Situation has deteriorated; E-Alarming deterioration. The most recent practice is that reports are submitted to Zonal Manager while the Managing Director receives a consolidated summary. Branch offices which show impressive progress are sent congratulatory letters and the ones with disappointing performance are alerted to the state of affairs. These letters inspire the branches which are doing well, and put the weak branches on the spot.

We are not bloodhounds. It is indicative of the spirit in Grameen Bank that staff do not talk about mistakes, theft, bribery, corruption, fraud or embezzlement. They all use the term mishappening. It is a considerate way of naming human frailty. Yet, it does not exclude mishappenings being dealt with resolutely whenever they occur. The auditors prefer to look at themselves as social workers among the Bank staff. In their view, auditors have an unfortunate, negative reputation. News of their arrival precipitates an audit panic. This is not helpful to the staff and their work who, in turn, treat auditors as undesired. The Grameen Bank auditors are attempting to change this image and attitude. "We are not bloodhounds," they emphasize, "but watchdogs for the benefit of all." They are not competitors, spies or rivals, but associates who prefer to work in harmony with staff towards their common objectives. Their starting point is trust rather than mistrust. While they consistently apply their auditing skills, they work very deliberately to dismantle some of the lingering staff psychology surrounding the usual narrow definitions of an audit. Along with providing a corrective check on banking functions, the auditors provide consultative advice to the field staff.

Both mishappenings and successes. Grameen Bank auditors have evolved an approach which they call the positive and negative auditing principle. It works on the basis that good procedures and successes are given as much emphasis as mishappenings. The auditing reports demonstrate that a remarkable amount of learning often takes place among the staff as a consequence of an audit. To date very few incidences of fraudulent behaviour have been found, although they do occur. So far the observation of the auditing staff is that innocent mistakes take place which they perceive as a necessary part of the learning experience for a branch office.

Before departure, the audit team holds an open discussion about its findings with the branch manager and his staff. The purpose is to arrive at a mutual understanding of what works well and what does not. The senior audit officer makes written comments on this discussion to qualify whether or not he finds the explanations about shortcomings satisfactory. Complete openness is binding on the auditors. There are no secret findings. In a concluding paragraph of the report, the senior audit officer lists which steps should be taken to improve the performance of the branch. The narrative report is handwritten and may be up to 25 pages. The zonal auditor is at liberty to express his personal perceptions and ideas about the appearance and performance of the branch, its manager and staff members.

$$\boxed{7}$$

(7) **Personnel Administration.** With a number of staff members in the range of 12 000, the personnel administration function faces a particularly demanding task. Expansion in the Bank's services has provided many opportunities for staff promotions and has depended heavily on the motivation of staff members. As expansion tapers off and the emphasis changes from horizontal to vertical expansion, promotion opportunities become fewer while the demand for quality delivery in the Bank's services increases. To keep effective track of the performance of such a huge number of people, the personnel administration is maintaining a partly computerized record keeping system. Detailed records are kept on each staff member's education, personal history and performance during training and subsequently in her or his posting. Updating is based on regular reports from supervisors. Credit is given for new ideas, narrative reports from the field, contributions to *Uddog* and similar initiatives. The personnel administration unit recommends candidates for promotion, but the final decision is taken by a promotion committee.

Grameen Bank represents a clear career opportunity for youth in Bangladesh, particularly young men with endurance and incentive. Opportunities for employment are limited in Bangladesh and the Bank offers even the longer-term prospects of promotion. To encourage motivation and to ensure that employees, if they wish, can qualify for positions in other credit institutions, Grameen Bank has adjusted its post designations to correspond with those of commercial banks. Also salaries are the same as or slightly higher than those of colleagues occupying parallel positions in nationalized commercial banks. Recruitment of trainees is an ongoing process in a bank whose services cannot possibly meet the needs of 50 million people for decades to come. Upon receiving a request from the training function in head office, the branch managers place job notifications in their respective areas. From one branch as many as 50 to 60 applications may be received. The various branches forward the applications to the zonal manager who reviews them, makes a short list of candidates, and sets dates for interviews. A staff member from head office travels to the zonal office and selects which candidates are to appear for a final interview in Dhaka.

Note: Recruitment, staff development and training have been one of the most essential elements in Grameen Bank's enormous and successful expansion. Since understanding this feature is of special importance to people who wish to replicate the Grameen model, we retain our earlier description of these functions as practised and validated during the years of horizontal expansion. Recent changes are commented on as required.

Trainee branch managers must have a Master's degree in any subject. It is a myth to think that only students trained in business and commerce are suitable candidates. We met branch managers who were graduates in Bengali, Management, Literature, Statistics, Music, Rural Development, Sociology, Economics or Astrophysics. Since experience in Grameen Bank is weighted equivalently with academic qualifications, as long as a bank worker displays the capability, there is no barrier to her/his promotion to branch manager. Male bank workers are required to have twelve years of school (i.e. a Senior High School Certificate). However, women with a minimum of ten years of school are eligible to become bank workers. To really open up the possibility of having women as bank workers in Grameen Bank, it was necessary to lower the academic requirements for their entry. In Bangladesh there are fewer women than men with the same educational level and this inequality is compounded by social limitations to physical mobility. Since government law requires a minimum of twelve years of education before a person can qualify to work in a bank, the Board of Grameen Bank sanctioned the exception of lower entry requirements for women due to the needs of its field services. This decision took into consideration the cultural reality of a predominantly Muslim country where it is more acceptable and appropriate for women to meet and serve women.

The Bank has not been as successful in recruiting and promoting women as the leadership hoped for. Currently about 9% of all staff members are female and only 30 women are branch managers. The main reason is that female candidates are less available for the type of work Grameen offers. To really appreciate the significance of this, think of purdah and the stigma, especially in rural areas, attached to women walking independently to and through strange villages, realize that in Bangladesh, banking has always been a male-dominated profession. Often seen accompanying newly-recruited female trainees from the districts to the Grameen Bank training courses in Dhaka, are two or three male guardians. Relatives fear for the safety of their daughters and wives from a social and physical point of view. Explanatory as these reasons are, they do not account for the predominance of male staff in the Bank. Among the rural poor, Grameen soon establishes enough credibility so that numbers of female staff would be well tolerated in many districts. More likely it is due to the exigencies of very rapid expansion and the lack of a targeted policy decision.

8

(8) **Research and development.** Many of the ideas generated by staff members for further study, evaluation, development and testing are taken up by this function. As the Bank intensifies its vertical expansion and works on continually improving the quality of its services to members, so does the role of research and development. Skill-development, management, new or modified technologies, health and nutrition, horticulture, agriculture and aquaculture are some of the areas pursued. As mentioned, no idea is accepted or rejected at face value; it's met with an open attitude. An idea may be a seed to a useful plant, but first let's see if it germinates. The work of research and development has been, and still is, very practically oriented. Prototypes of new technology are acquired and tested if there is a potential demand for it among the loanees. Whether for use by individuals or in joint enterprises, the prototypes are tried out on a small scale in real life situations and the performance carefully assessed before the technology is introduced on a larger scale. For example, a Chinese power tiller was tested by a centre in Rangpur. Found sturdy, reliable and economical, it was adopted subsequently by centre members as a joint enterprise. The sales representative for the power tiller was mobilized to provide training in the skills of using and maintaining it. The centre has been renting out the service of the power tiller, the loan has been repaid, and the enterprise has proven very profitable for its members. An

70

incubator for chicken and duck eggs, however, did not fare so well. Since it operated on kerosene, the incubator offered the promise of being appropriate because electricity is unreliable or non existent in rural areas. The producer claimed it would hatch about 80% of the eggs successfully. However, testing revealed that only 20% of the eggs hatched. Now research and development staff are testing an electric incubator capable of retaining heat over periods when there are cuts in the electricity supply. The Bank is trying to minimize the incidence of bad investments for its loanees which works to minimise credit risk as well. Incubators have proven to be suitable for joint enterprises in areas where electricity is available.

Other technologies such as hand pumps, tubewells, oil separators, carts for transport, beehives, winnowing machines or rice mills are being or have been tested. Adoption of a new labour-saving technology and acquiring the new skills it may require are sometimes more complex than anticipated. On trying out an improved potter's wheel, it was found that the new foot-pedalled turntable had a flywheel too small and light to provide the steady speed potters were accustomed to. The frequent pedalling it necessitated interfered with the rhythm and steadiness of the potter's hands as they worked the clay. In spite of its labour-saving potential, the potters rejected the new turntable. Another new prototype with a much larger flywheel was subsequently undergoing testing.

The services of Research and Development are very concrete. In the economy of the poor no resources must be wasted, but straw from the rice fields is sometimes burnt and cattle urine is used for nothing. In Chellam, Sylhet, a specialist is now assisting the branch manager in researching the possibility of using straw as cattle fodder. It is mixed with urea in airtight bags. The process makes the straw more nutritious and smaller quantities of fodder give larger quantities of milk or meat.

The SIDE programme. As time went by, research and testing became more systematized and extensive in the SIDE programme which stands for Studies-Innovation-Development-Experimentation. Supported by foreign funding, the programme is implemented by two action research departments within the Bank, Research and Development and Technology Projects. An explanation of its function is central to understanding the origin and development of the Grameen sister organizations described in a later chapter. This programme was designed to undertake studies, identifying and supporting innovative actions, taking up developmental and experimental projects aimed at introducing and testing new technologies, new management strategies and new scales and areas of operation.

One of its main purposes is to support the borrowers in the leap from individual to collective enterprises. Initially, Grameen followed the procedure already tested in its operation: the facilitation of borrower consensus for entering into a collective enterprise. SIDE's only contribution at this stage was the introduction of a new idea or new technology. This led to the setting up of enterprises with power-tillers, wheat-threshers, winnowing machines in the agricultural service sector or collective production units such as edible oil crushing mills, small handloom factories, and mechanically-driven potters wheels. Later, SIDE introduced other types of enterprises: bee-keeping, high-yielding khaki campbell ducks, poultry incubators, production of fuel-saving cooking ovens. These initial small steps with local technologies were encouraging and valuable experience was gained in the many management problems occurring in collective enterprises.

This overall early experience set the stage for a bigger leap in both technology and management. Opportunities were offered by the Government of Bangladesh, whose Ministry of Fisheries invited Grameen to take over a huge pond aquaculture project in Serajganj, a project which had collapsed because of poor management. Grameen decided to take it over as a SIDE enterprise and constituted an innovative management of SIDE staff. The management approach proved very effective for entering into larger production or business enterprises. At the same time, Grameen could ensure that the poor benefitted justly through their collective labour-contribution to the projects. Systems were also introduced for their involvement in the decision-making processes. Some of these enterprises are now on their way to becoming path-breakers not only for the Bank's members but also for the economy of Bangladesh as a whole. These are the Joysagar Fish Farm, Chokoria and Satkhira Shrimp Farms and the Deep Tubewell Project.

Approach to economic empowerment. SIDE has been experimenting at several ownership-management levels : from one-centre collective activities to multi-centre collective activities managed by Grameen members themselves. A new style of management was introduced when Grameen got involved in ownership and management directly. The rationale behind Grameen's direct ownership was that the borrowers were risk-averse and did not have the management and technical knowledge to run these larger ventures. They also lacked the political clout to overcome social barriers. Grameen decided to take up the challenge and overcome the management, technical, financial and political obstacles before asking the poor to bear any risk. Because the bank itself is owned by the borrowers, anything owned by the bank is, in effect, owned by the borrowers.

This situation of indirect ownership by the Grameen borrowers is viewed by the designers of Grameen Action Research as an interim phase. They see a three-phased scenario. In Phase A, Grameen directly owns and operates this type of "start-up" and "taken-over" enterprise. In the meantime, an independent Trust is established which has the prime objective of changing the socio-economic status of the landless poor. In Phase B, the enterprises owned and operated by Grameen will be handed over to the Trust for ownership and/or management. In Phase C, the Trust will develop the methodology and the legal framework to gradually transfer the ownership and management to the Grameen borrowers. This process is now far progressed. Although, in Phase A, these enterprises are referred to as Grameen-owned, each enterprise is a separate entity for which an independent book of accounts is kept. Income or expenditure of the enterprises do not enter the accounts of Grameen Bank itself. The enterprises appear there as clients borrowing money. Grameen is neither benefitting from their profits nor responsible for their losses. In effect, Grameen is keeping these enterprises in an informal trust, while the process of formalizing them proceeds.

When initiating an enterprise of this type, SIDE is playing the role of an entrepreneur or promoter and takes upon itself the responsibility for being a path-breaker. This is based on the hard-won recognition that it is not yet within the capacity of Grameen borrowers to embark on a big collectively-run enterprise and cope with all the odds against them. Economic empowerment is a complicated longer-term process that is likely to succeed only stage-wise. SIDE does the developer's work and brings the enterprise to a cruising level while creating employment for Grameen borrowers and their relatives and opening up new business opportunities for them in related activities. Through its long experience Grameen has come to the conviction that this approach offers the best prospects for the poor. Too many failed joint enterprises substantiate this conclusion. The chances for the survival of technologically-upgraded projects with complex management structures is greater than the conventional way of facilitating group-formation and waiting for people to come forward and take the entire risk on their own.

Breaking the barriers. The Bank is convinced that the technology and management barriers for the poor can be broken down through this pragmatic, experience-based, organizational approach. Again Yunus demonstrates that the critical factor in economic empowerment of the poor is not concientization alone but institution building and an enabling organizational framework for participation. He envisages that small, medium and even very large enterprises can be owned and managed by the poor, and not the least, by women. These independent enterprises can network and influence government policies. In

Yunus' view, the SIDE strategy is particularly effective in taking over all the un-utilized, underutilized and even negatively-utilized resources of privately or publicly-owned enterprises of which Bangladesh is replete. Already being effectively realized in a variety of projects, the vision of Yunus is to carry through this organizational enablement on a large scale with three types of enterprises characterizing this vertical expansion. (14)

(a)   Activities involving adoption of new technologies such as new seeds or new high-breed varieties of poultry, but not necessarily in the form of collective enterprises.

(b)   Collective enterprises organized and operated by Grameen Bank group members.

(c)   Enterprises owned and operated by SIDE. Fisheries appear to be one very attractive area of action; deep tubewells and irrigation generally are others.

$$\boxed{9}$$

(9) Training. The training function has been the lifeblood of Grameen Bank. On the premise that experience is the best teacher, over 80% of the training time is spent in the rural areas where the branches are located. Training as experience serves many purposes. It quickly weeds out those who do not have the stamina or inclination for the physically demanding nature of Grameen Bank field services. It immediately demands that the trainee must rely to a considerable extent on her/his own resources. It plunges a person into direct contact with the poor of Bangladesh which largely curtails any inclination to interpret poverty as a charitable abstraction. Of most importance to Grameen Bank is the significance of this training for the long-term policies and practices of the Bank. Very few staff positions in head office are recruited directly (approximately 5%). Most head office personnel have been trained in the rural areas and then worked there for a very long period before taking a position in the head office in Dhaka. This means that the field experience is central, one which guides and informs the focus and direction of policies. It is the yardstick by which subsequent judgements and decisions are made. It inhibits the possibility of far-fetched theories and unviable suggestions wasting too much staff time. Essentially, the Bank has been evolving through the interaction of four dimensions: self-reliance, cooperation, innovation and empathy into the daily meaning of poverty. The training programme takes its starting point here, and this practice is reflected throughout all levels of the Bank's operations. Because of its emphasis on training, Grameen Bank established its own Training Institute with dormitory facilities which was in operation by 1987.

Six months in real-life situations. As we have discussed, the branch office is the most critical unit of Grameen Bank because its staff directly serve and interact with the loanees on a regular basis. For this reason, great emphasis is placed on the training of branch staff who are the bank workers and branch managers. Lasting for six months, the training, with some minor variations in emphasis, is the same for each. Alternating between the training courses in Dhaka and the branches in the rural areas, the training programme allocates the time periods as follows:

At the Training Institute: (Fixed days)	At the Branch Office: (Approximate days)
2	56
7	56
7	56
7	

For many it will come as a surprise that the training is introduced with only two days at the Institute. But this is deliberate. To a maximum extent the trainee must learn through coping with real-life situations. This includes not only the work itself, but problems and discomforts associated with the living conditions in rural Bangladesh. From the beginning trainees are given the worst idea of what they can expect. For example, branch manager trainees are asked, "What can you cook?" Especially for male university graduates this amounts to culture shock and quickly rids them of any conventional ideas they might entertain about banking as a 9 to 5 office job. At the branches, bicycles are the only transport available for the managers and increasingly for the bank workers, and these are on the basis of a personal loan. Trainee branch managers, however, are instructed not to use bicycles for their work in visiting groups and centres or in generally carrying out their tasks. In this way, they share the daily experience of the bank workers they will ultimately supervise. Also, the hardship faced by the landless who are chronically without transport becomes physically understood and not easily forgotten.

Mastering the forms. In the course of the training, all the banking forms and ledgers used at the branch level must be mastered. Normally this takes about 16 weeks. As part of the two-day overview, the trainer briefly introduces these forms and supplies a complete set to the trainees for the duration of their field work. However, the main objective of these two days is to give the trainees assignments which they will carry out in their first eight weeks at the branch. To assist them, they are issued a guideline which is discussed in class first. The guideline does not provide detailed information to be followed in a prescriptionary manner, but presents instead an open-ended format to avoid stereotyped responses to tasks or problems that the trainees encounter. For the most part, it is a list of questions around a topic. As Yunus says, "To arouse curiosity in the mind of the trainee and to stimulate interest in the learning itself is the primary goal of training." From the outset, emphasis is placed on facing situations self-reliantly and flexibly within the rules and regulations of Grameen Bank. For each assignment, the trainee is able to refer to the accompanying guideline. After this minimal introduction, the trainees report to their respective branches finding their way by train, bus, boat, rickshaw, foot or, more usually, by some combination.

Action research/Case studies. During the first eight weeks, each trainee must write in detail case studies of two borrowers, one female and one male. The case studies emphasize a life history approach, collecting information on the borrower's parents, childhood, marriage, experiences and conditions of living. Economic data such as the wage rate or income generated, seasonal differences in labour demand and the local price of essential commodities are also gathered. Through these case studies the situation of the loanees before and after their participation in Grameen Bank becomes evident to the trainee. Two very firm instructions guide this action research and the recording of the case studies. Firstly, trainees must record the information exactly as the loanee tells it. They are not allowed to embellish the responses or offer interpretations. In other words, the trainees are discouraged from concocting their own ideas or affirming their own prejudices about how the poor live and think. Secondly, the trainee is instructed to carry out the case study in the borrower's house at a time she/he finds convenient. The Bank places a high priority on the case studies being done thoroughly and according to the method stipulated. Effectively, the method forces the trainees to listen. This act of listening confronts them with a personal account of poverty and its lifetime implications. Through this exercise, trainees witness for themselves what are the worst manifestation of society--which is the rationale for the task and explains the importance attached to it.

Transport means walking. Although bicycles are now frequently in use, transport still means a lot of walking. Communication becomes a particularly difficult problem in Bangladesh during the rainy season. Even in the dry seasons, walking is often the only way by which many villages are accessible, and that means walking barefoot, since shoes will be destroyed by the mud. In the first eight-week period, trainees are required to identify the communications system, that is the roads and transport available in the area covered by the branch. For example, they would find out which roads are open in which seasons and the kinds of transport being used. Another task is to draw a *map of the area* that shows the location of public buildings, banks, offices of private organizations, among others. The knowledge of the infrastructure and services available in an area allows the bank worker to offer this information as it is needed and requested by the members of Grameen Bank. For the branch manager trainee, it is an essential task to perform in order to have an indepth knowledge of the area when taking over the administration of an existing branch or when establishing a new one. While the trainee is taken through a valuable learning process, she/he is gathering important baseline socio-economic data for the Bank. Upon completing the first eight weeks, the trainees return to the Training Institute for seven days. The class usually comprises thirty trainees from thirty branches drawn from all five zones. The week proves lively and fruitful as the main emphasis is on the *sharing of experiences* by the trainees. Thrust into a learning situation by performing the same tasks in various parts of Bangladesh, the trainees are able to compare and contrast their insights and experiences and to begin identifying commonalities and differences.

Peer to Peer. In the last two sessions of these seven days, students are encouraged to ask each other questions not only on their experiences, but also on their specific knowledge of all aspects of the work. Grameen Bank finds that peer to peer questions and responses are an effective method of facilitating discussion, healthy competition and learning. Since all the trainers have spent considerable time in the field, they can draw on their own experiences to facilitate and graphically enliven the discussion. Also, during this first seven-day period at the Institute, the *Bidhimala* or Constitution is discussed. (See Annex 1). It is mandatory the trainees know the Bank's rules and regulations perfectly. Their assignments are reviewed and, if not satisfactory enough, must be repeated or completed in the second eight-week phase. The trainers issue a new set of tasks to be carried out by the trainees upon return to the same branch.

The training proceeds in this way for the subsequent phases of the programme. Just as the case study assignment provides an understanding of the social and economic milieu in which Grameen Bank operates, other tasks are developed and assigned based on the responsibilities and demands of the work situation. Tasks are specified for identifying the target clientele groups in the villages (i.e. the landless as defined in the Bidhimala and the Grameen Bank Ordinance), for gaining an understanding of group dynamics, for determining market prices, for disbursing loans, for intensive supervision and management of loan recovery, for training new groups of prospective members, for rendering required advisory services on the basis of established and felt needs, and for administering the branch. Trainees must demonstrate they know in every detail how a branch operates. They must have visited at least 15 centres and have followed up on the loan utilization of two to three borrowers in each of these centres. In addition, they must report on special projects or joint enterprises in the area. In the end, the trainees know in great detail how to start work in an area and what to do.

Not a machine. Throughout Grameen Bank, staff are motivating the people directly under their supervision to perform better: bank workers to members; branch managers to bank workers; programme officers to branch managers; area managers to programme officers. Before departing for their new posts, branch managers are instructed by trainers to build a branch better than the one where they were trained. The trainees are reminded, "It is not to replicate mechanically what you have learned. You are an artist, not a machine." The last session of the training programme usually ends with a play written and performed by the trainees on the basis of their experiences. The Managing Director and other staff attend the closing ceremony giving a final address before the trainees leave to take up their positions.

Assigned to a branch. The trainees are assigned to a particular branch and remain there for the entire training period. When they first report to the branch, they take with them a letter of introduction in which the time of reporting to the branch and the time to return to the Training Institute are registered. If this form with the branch manager's signature is not received by Head Office a week later, action is taken to find out why. By remaining in one branch, trainees quickly realize they are part of a team whose support is essential. Although self-reliance is emphasized, it does not conflict with team work but complements and strengthens it. The only time a trainee might be transferred to a different branch in the course of the training is if reports on his or her performance from the branch manager do not tally with those of the trainer. This is a rare occurrence--99% of the time the field reports and trainer's assessment correspond. Reports on the trainee's performance are also made by the area and zonal offices. When new officers are assigned postings, they are never placed in the branch where they were trained, but encouraged to contribute to better performance in another branch office.

Attitude change is really what is taking place in Grameen Bank among members, trainees and staff. The important point is that this change is taking place among *all* the actors. Attitude change is not limited or relegated to the members. Trainers remarked to us on the personality growth they observed in the trainees. With each phase of the training, the students exhibited more confidence and deeper perceptions about rural reality in Bangladesh and their own relationship to it. As the staff reminded us, "Commitment isn't a prerequisite for starting work in Grameen Bank, it evolves in the process." Grameen Bank's management and organization development approach might be characterized as profoundly pragmatic. Always a stimulating dynamic is created between self-interest and cooperation. Branch managers are considered responsible for good trainees. They are obliged to see that assignments have been completed. If the trainees perform poorly, the branch manager is rated accordingly. One important line of promotion for branch managers is to become trainers, so it is in their direct interest to assist and motivate the trainees. Essentially the best managers are picked as trainers, which shows the priority Grameen Bank places on the education of its personnel. Recently, a grading system was introduced which requires that bank workers and branch managers take oral and written exams after one year of work.

For many years the Bank practised the rule that staff members could not be posted in their home areas. The reason being that such posting would expose them to undue pressure from relatives, neighbours or acquaintances. This has been resented by staff, who often had to stay away from their families for months at end. Now the Bank has recognised this element of staff welfare and allows posting in home areas, but minimum 20 km away from homestead.

Although strenuous and sometimes monotonous, the human appeal in the bank assistants work is strong and they often express pride in it. In the village they are somebody and evolve a close relationship with the people. A female bank worker would be addressed *Apa* which means sister, and often with special fondness as *Khala*, which is more intimate, meaning mother's sister. Male bank workers are addressed as *Bhai*, brother, or *Chaca*, uncle, by the children.

Exponential increase in trainees. Ideally, three to four trainees are attached to a branch, but the upper limit is six. After a certain time, the trainees added labour becomes an asset to the branch, which does not provide their salaries. Trainees receive a subsistence salary from head office. A branch must have been in operation for one year before it has the experience and capacity to take on responsibility for trainees. At any one time, 30% of the staff members, the experienced core, train the other 70%. As mentioned in the introduction, a process is set in motion in which a steadily increasing number of branches means an exponential increase in trainees which, in turn, means an increase in the number of branches. To illustrate, in 1978 the first Grameen Bank branch in Jobra was one year old and could train a maximum of six people--some bank workers, some branch managers. In 1979 there were two branches more than one year old, hence the possibility of training 12 people. However, in 1983, there were 21 branches eligible to train, and in December 1985, 152 branches had the capacity to accept trainees. By December 1986, 226 branches were ready to train and a total of 500 branches at the end of 1989. By December 1988, the Bank had achieved its objectives in the number of branches and the 4000 trainees needed to offer credit services to one million clients. The training function is an escalating horizontal development which never needs to be shortened in time or content for the sake of keeping pace with expansion as in most development initiatives, or sacrificed due to financial constraints. In Grameen Bank, training is inherent to its expansion like a stem to a plant. This is the main secret of the bank's acquired growth potential and the main reason for its spectacular horizontal expansion. Now the Bank's training function has come to another stage.

GROWTH AND SHEDDING OF FUNCTIONS

To understand the effective and startling expansion of Grameen Bank, we must examine its growth as a historical process. The Bank has not grown vertically as a centralized decision-making pyramid which fosters a burgeoning bureaucracy to deal with a complexity it finds increasingly difficult to manage. The dilemma awaiting the actors in governmental organizations based on this well-known model of growth is their belated realization that decentralization was needed instead. The bureaucratic mentality finds itself trapped in a Catch 22 situation. Complexity becomes inoperable and intolerable yet it seems impossible to set in motion the reverse process of decentralization in order to ease the complexity.

Once hierarchies of functions have been established, once vested interests, positions of power and privilege have fossilized the actors in bureaucratic attitudes and routines of behaviour, the organization inertia seems irrevocable. Decentralization becomes the topic of consultant reports rather than the subject of implementation. To describe Grameen Bank in terms of decentralization would be a disservice because it was never centralized in the first place. On the contrary, a process of horizontal growth has taken place where decision-making powers and operational functions are continuously shedded outwardly from head office to new units of action. It can be described as a spatial participatory growth phenomenon which is facilitated by organizational talent and managerial skill, but powered forcefully by a deep commitment to outreach, to be of service to the widespread rural poor. What emerges is a socio-economic formation in continuous growth and transformation, an organizational framework for a truly self-sustained people's movement.

Shedding of functions. When the Bank expands into new districts, general management functions and decision-making powers are shedded to zonal offices. Other functions are similarly shedded. Social development, for example, undertaken by programme assistants originally stationed at head office is very soon transferred to the zonal offices. As the number of branch offices grow, area offices become necessary. In practice 10 branch offices require an area office if the optimum level of supervision is to be maintained. The zonal office sheds some of its general management functions and decision-making powers such as supervision of the accounting procedures at the branch office or approval of proposals for individual loans to the area office. Currently, aspects of the monitoring and evaluation function are being carried out by the zonal office and the audit function is, as already mentioned, decentralized to the zonal level. Zonal offices take over such functions as maintaining bank accounts and fund management, budgetary control, programme supervision and personnel administration.

Earlier we discussed some of the constraints to the growth of individual branch offices. Despite these constraints, it is probably an optimal unit as it is presently constituted and the profit making centre of the Bank. From the point of view of information processing and interaction, more staff would lead to the old, intertwined problem of complexity and control. Rather than expand the area under their responsibility, branches multiply. In the older, more established branches, this opens up the possibility of directing more attention to improving the quality of the banking services. By adding more and more branch offices, the zone grows horizontally and, upon reaching a critical size, a new zone is created. Growing towards its critical size, the zone becomes a complete banking function, a Grameen Bank in its own right. In essence, the zonal office becomes a Grameen Bank Head Office. The development of the whole initiative is likely to gravitate towards a federation of Grameen Banks. In this process of horizontal growth, the original head office may become a secretariat or information clearing house for the federation. Certain aspects of a few functions such as monitoring and evaluation, research and development, supervision of training and similar activities which benefit from access to overall information would likely be retained.

81

Figure 5

TIME SPENT IN CENTRES

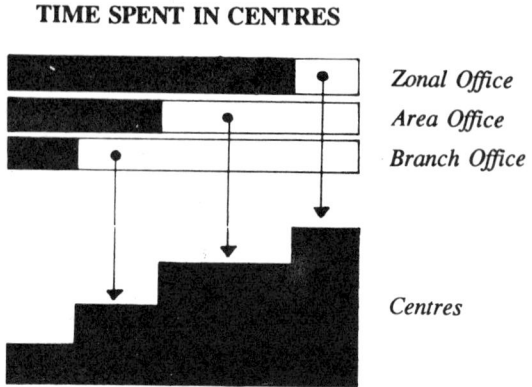

Zonal Office
Area Office
Branch Office

Centres

Approximate worktime spent supervising branches and centres. Zonal managers travel at least 5 to 8 days every month on inspection. Area and programme officers spend up to 25 days engaged in centre activities. Branch staff spend most of their time in contact with centre members.

ROTATION OF BANK WORKERS

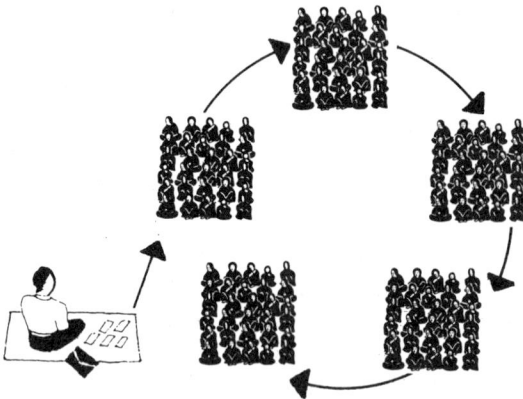

Bank workers, branch managers and other staff are frequently rotated. It broadens everyone's experience and hampers entrenchment of vested interests.

As we have pointed out, the exponential growth in training capacity has been one of the basic premises for the horizontal growth of Grameen Bank. The Bank has been able to channel new collaborators continuously into its expansion process in the staff categories of bank worker, senior assistant and branch manager. At the same time, the need for staff for other functional and management levels has been satisfied through continuous promotion of staff members largely on the irreplaceable basis of experience and performance. This is an insurance against discontinuous or stagnated growth. If any signs of deterioration in the quality of some personnel are detected, new cadres of experienced people are ready to meet the challenge. At this point in time recruitment of staff members to branches has been stopped.

Rotation of staff. An important mechanism for continuity and smooth operation in the Bank is the vigilant rotation of staff members and centre officers. It is mandatory that new centre chiefs are elected every year. Within their respective branches, bank workers are rotated so that every year they service a new set of 10 centres. Although female bank workers are, for social legitimation, assigned to the areas where they are from, male bank workers are never posted to their home area. (See Figure 5). After a two to three year period at one particular branch office, branch managers are transferred or promoted. To function responsively and effectively, the head office in Dhaka needs to draw continuously on experienced staff members from the zones. To ensure this, trainees and staff members are posted to the zones to gain the field . experience instrumental in developing their perspective and work potential.

Two main advantages are gained from this pattern of staff rotation. First, staff members have access to a wide range of experience and develop a detailed knowledge of the ins and outs of the organization. Later, this will benefit both themselves and the organization as they move through promotional channels. The second advantage is more preventive in nature. The frequent transfer of staff members, particularly bank workers and branch managers severely curtails the establishment of vested interests, favouritism or malpractice. The possibility that the occasional staff member may go astray is never dismissed.

THE DISCIPLINE OF ACCOUNTABILITY
The simple fact that Grameen Bank deals with money has a double significance for its successful operation. Credit is a resource the Bank places at the disposal of the landless poor. At the same time, the money is a tool the Bank uses to supervise the performance and progress of its staff members. The flow of money has always been a precarious issue in development programmes, but in this case it is the money that makes the programme eminently superviseable.

For example, the quality of the loans given by a branch office is a clear indicator of the performance of the branch staff and the centre members. It can be established accurately by an analysis of the repayment records because they document whether the loans are, in fact, *bona fide* collectible assets that the Bank can expect to convert into cash in an orderly manner. The presence of money serves to establish financial accountability between people and this extends into a wider social accountability. The performance of each and every bank worker can be followed day by day. The figures she or he records are the very measures of progress or lack of it. The same is the case for each branch manager and his office, for each area and for each zone. If the loan disbursement or repayment figures drop a particular week in a particular location, there is reason for concern and remedial action. If these figures go up, there is reason to believe the bank worker is doing well. The ongoing monitoring and evaluation of statistics and narrative reports, and the regular contacts between centre chiefs and bank workers, and bank workers and branch managers, create a situation of strong mutual accountability. Lagging performance is quickly discovered and corrected and good performance is quickly rewarded.

Intensiveness of supervision. In government extension services how painfully familiar is the situation where the extension worker has not seen a supervisor for several weeks and the salary so desperately needed is months in arrears. There are few, if any, services to offer the clients and very little educational material in support of an extension talk. The disheartened extension worker is simply not motivated to walk long distances to repeat a lesson that farmers have heard many times before. Accountability and work motivation diminish in correlation to the supervisor's lack of responsibility towards their extension staff, not to mention the clients. To add insult to injury, most extension workers live with the daily frustration of coping with decisions taken by superiors who do not understand the real situation that must be addressed in the rural areas.

The intensive supervision in Grameen Bank contrasts sharply with the above description. In Figure 5, we have approximated the amount of time the different managers spend in contact with bank workers and the loanees in the centres. Let's take the example of a zonal manager who may spend more than 8 days a month visiting area and branch offices, centre meetings with bank workers and taking up issues at member workshops. His frequent presence has a strong supervisory and motivational effect on his colleagues, but equally important is the flow and exchange of information this stimulates. As a result of these interchanges, he has access to first-hand and high-quality information for decision making. Supervision is, indeed, central in Grameen Bank daily operations, but it should not be interpreted as an oppressive or fault-finding mechanism. It is a highly supportive and trusting activity.

The bank workers' performance is pivotal to the Bank's progress. They have a hard job and it is very important their commitment is sustained. There are two different sources from which they find support and take encouragement. The first source is knowing they are backed up in their endeavour by an organization that follows their work and appreciates good performance. The second source of the bank workers' commitment is the landless poor themselves. The attitudes held by bank workers go through a preliminary stage of change while they are trainees. In the course of their work, as they see their own efforts making a tangible difference to people's lives, their commitment grows. They can observe firsthand how people gradually improve their situation through disciplined and energetic activities in the centres. The work itself motivates and has its deeply human rewards. Not far away is the realization that their own situation could easily be the same as the loanee's. How the Bank manages to sustain a good relationship to its 12 000 bank workers is obviously of critical importance for its future.

Bank workers often become involved in the personal lives of the members, helping a destitute widow settling a family dispute or giving legitimacy to a dowryless marriage by attending the wedding ceremony. Human bonds are disrupted and tears are sometimes shed when bank workers leave for a new posting. From a deep sense of protocol the poor feel an obligation to gift-giving. However, throughout Grameen Bank the unwritten rule that no gifts from loanees may be accepted by employees under any circumstances, is unanimously practiced. Whether it is a bowl of rice, a basket of fruit, a clay pot or a woven mat, a gift--no matter how humble--cannot be taken. Flowers in bouquets are accepted for guests but even the traditional bestowal of garlands is discouraged. The step from gift-giving to petty corruption is too small to risk. There is an equally important consideration: laying the basis for a sense of decency, equity and dignity in the relationship between members and employees. It serves the same purpose as the straight back and the forthright response discussed below.

Pragmatic discipline. A large-scale participatory initiative cannot start out as a casual and free-for-all workshop seminar. The most immediate task to face is establishing an organizational context of financial and social accountability in the communities. In Grameen Bank this is done through the creation of centres in which discipline finds various expressions. As already pointed out, discipline and self-control are demanded from staff members as well as from centre members. Again and again people are reminded that if they break the discipline in their own activities, Grameen Bank collapses. One zonal manager said to the women in a workshop, "Think of your loan repayment like your own heartbeat". The discipline in the centres is the backbone of the whole enterprise. The peer pressure in the groups combined with the openness of all financial transactions in the centres literally forces the individual to exert a considerable measure of self control. On their part, the Bank staff recognize the effort and treat people with a great respect.

The discipline Grameen Bank imposes on its staff and members is unique among development projects. The fact that people accept the discipline and recognize its benefits should not be considered so extraordinary. It demonstrates a human potential we tend to undervalue. Grameen Bank provides people both with an economic resource, credit, and with a social environment that re-establishes accountability, the fundamental premise for participation in any society.

The culture of poverty is in the stance of the landless. It is expressed in the bent back, the fallen glance, and the low inaudible voice. It is an emotional vote of no-confidence in the self. In a sense, it is a bodily collapse that influences the mind and vice-versa. Self-image and body posture are two sides of the same coin. Grameen Bank recognizes that people's dignity grows out of a straight back. The Bank workers attach great importance to people in centre meetings, look at them directly as they talk, standing straight, and speaking out loudly and clearly. Over time this approach also has evolved special procedures for opening and closing centre meetings, workshops and other Bank gatherings. Members observe a special salute and reporting procedure. They shout slogans, reiterating in unison their development decisions, and carry out a programme of exercises together. These performances are all expressions of discipline and self control, individually and for the common good. They are the embodiment of standing together and moving forward together in a people's movement.

Participating in these meetings in the centre houses or community halls of Bangladesh, we experienced reminiscent feelings of the meetings of the Norwegian Labour Party's youth phalanx, the "Framfylkingen" in the Thirties. There were the same inspiring speeches, the same reiteration of the issues in the slogans, the concern for solidarity and the sense of awakening together. And, as then, people were not all that particular about the details of the "drill". They enjoyed it, but were quite pragmatic also. We find centre meetings to be an ingenuous blend of informality and structure, of frankness and unity.

86

PROGRAMMES
AND PROCESSES

The weight is not difficult
the problem is how to hold it.
Numbers do not matter,
what matters is the metaphysics ...
It is in the heart
that the real truth lives.
ANONYMOUS FOLK POET OF
BANGLADESH

When Grameen Bank establishes itself in a new district of Bangladesh, it does not arrive empty handed. It brings with it an economic and social development programme which has evolved over the last seventeen years in a process of continuous interaction with the landless poor. But the programme is not imposed on people. It is merely a well-tried starting point for a new participatory process which is open to further modification according to local conditions, priorities and needs. As we have underlined earlier, the Bank's approach to the local community and its development is process-oriented and has a long-term perspective. It is activist, indeed, but not short-term activist and confrontational. It is pragmatic and tactical, but does not yield on its principles or objectives. It may well take a step backwards for a while, if it sees an opportunity to take three steps forward in the longer term.

The prevailing view that guides practice is that the economic and social obstacles to progress are more likely to be overcome through competence, strength and dignity growing from within the landless poor themselves and, above all, to be overcome through an enabling organizational development. Grameen Bank sets out to prove that the weight is not difficult, but how to hold it requires a steadfast heart and a single-minded purpose.

The programme involves people in a long-term learning process. Through participatory efforts and joint experiences, people gradually build by themselves knowledge, in particular organizational and managerial skills enabling them to cope together with increasing levels of complexity. In this way, the programme realizes the ideas of an endogenous and self-reliant development. Structural transformation is more likely to occur as a manifestation of strength and competence in management and decision making. As intimated earlier, this approach to social and economic change has much in common with the social democratic approach that has guided progress in the Scandinavian countries.

When Grameen Bank opens a new branch office, the procedure it follows illustrates its process orientation. Prior to locating a building, the very first task of a branch manager is to prepare a socio-economic report on the locality and community under consideration. This is an extensive fact-finding study which takes the incumbent two to three months to complete. During this period, he generally seeks lodging with an educated man such as a school teacher, whose role is neutral in relation to the community. The study comprises an overview of the geography, economy, demography, and the transport and communication infrastructure of the area. Social and cultural factors are taken into account and an analysis of the local power structure is made.

Upon approval of the report by head office, arrangements are made for a big, *general public information meeting* to be held. At that meeting, the branch manager introduces himself and explains Grameen Bank's purpose, rules and programme. In particular he outlines the procedures for forming groups and centres, encouraging the landless to return to their villages and form groups of like-minded people in similar economic conditions. He explains that once they have formed groups, the landless are welcome to report to the Bank's staff.

Since the meeting is an open invitation to the public, the local elite can see for themselves that the initiative is for the benefit of the poor only. The premise of the meeting is that it is an information forum, and not one for the purpose of eliciting discussion. Therefore, only Grameen Bank representatives are allowed the floor. The constraint on discussion serves to confine the elite to the role of observers equitably and amicably in the company of everyone. In this way, alienation is largely avoided while the important group formation process is getting started among the poor.

Staff and members of Grameen Bank are urged to concentrate on building their own economic and social strength. By performing well and having a professional and dignified public image, it is felt the Bank can only gain in stability and continuity. In its relationship to local elites, therefore, protocol is the guiding stance, not confrontation. By any measure, the Bank is a young initiative. An amusing indication of its success in the rural areas is that all the political parties of Bangladesh claimed some connection to it in their platforms as early as the election of 1985.

Among senior staff members there is the opinion that the role of the local power structure has been overplayed in the social science literature. Most analyses inadequately describe and understand the reality of poverty, placing an exaggerated emphasis on local elites. Certainly the constellation and abuse of power are factors not to be underestimated. However, in the course of its experience with local elites, the Bank has met with both collaboration and resistance. More often than not resistance is minimal or non-obstructional. The factors of time, patience and perseverance are proving effective in situations of antipathy.

In its efforts in the rural areas, the Bank works side by side with governmental and non-governmental agencies. There are over fifty million landless poor in Bangladesh and the services offered by these agencies do not even begin to meet the need. Grameen Bank sees itself working in complementarity to voluntary or private organizations and government extension services, adopting towards them a neutral and independent stance. Upon the opening of a new branch in one area where a private organization was also working, its representative approached the Bank's zonal manager expressing his dissatisfaction. "Well," said the zonal manager, "you give me a list of all the people you serve and we will only disburse loans to the rest."

For purposes of administration, Bangladesh is organized into Divisions, Regions, Districts and Upazilas. Currently numbering 487, the upazilas constitute one of the smallest administrative units. They are intended to be the basic unit of local level planning and implementation in coordination with national development policy. Although the customary protocol is observed in relation to the Upazila development councils, field staff are requested not to negotiate or socialise with the officials. This is a precaution to ensure that Grameen Bank's image as a bank for the poor remains clearly that. Care is taken to locate branch offices away from the upazila offices and the upazila chairman's village is often the last to be covered by the Bank's services. In reality any conflict of interest is minimal and temporary since the upazilas are most concerned with local judicial matters and the development of infrastructure. Another concern is to avoid placing a branch office in view of a mosque to offset possible initial disfavour from the local religious leaders.

89

When a branch opens its own building in the locality it serves, it is quite an event. The local interested elite may attend, but what they witness is the foundation stone being laid by a representative of the landless themselves. In Sylhet Zone, Nurjahan Bibi was the chief guest of honour on June 16, 1991, the official opening of Lamakaji Bishonat branch office. Her name is commemorated in the foundation stone.

THE PROCESS OF GROUP FORMATION

Following the branch manager's public information meeting, the idea of a bank which gives credit without collateral sparks a lot of discussion in the nearby villages. Reactions of disbelief, scepticism and hope circulate among the landless along with reservations of mistrust and fear. There is a predictable initial resistance voiced by some of the local elite. Most of these reactions are expressed succinctly in a passage from *Jorimon*, (12) a collection of case studies in which "The story of Bachaton", is a woman's testimony of human survival in the face of heart-rendering conditions and events. In the course of her adult life, Bachaton experienced ostracization and physical abuse from her husband's family, abandonment by her own family, a husband who became paralytic, the death of two of her children, war, famine and flood. Most of her married life was spent in a makeshift hut enduring the ever-present hunger of her children as well as the daily humiliations and degradations that accompany the desperate, chronic search to alleviate want.

When she became a member of Grameen Bank, Bachaton recalls facing all kinds of criticism, "The very parent-in-law who never showed any sympathy in all her years of trouble suddenly became highly anxious to warn her of the impending danger. Her father-in-law said, "You can never repay the money you take from the bank. In the end, you will put handcuffs on me too." But Bachaton turned a deaf ear and went about her way. Since he could not do anything to her, he abused her openly. He raised questions of honour and prestige. Meanwhile, within the neighbourhood, Bachaton's joining the group created mixed feelings. Some people were extremely critical while others felt she had done the right thing. In this latter group belonged the lower class and the poor. The strongest attack came from the village elders, the leaders and the religious *mollahs*. They could not accept the fact that women could become group members so easily. They declared, "This work is against our religion. Women going to Bhuapur to get money, women talking to me, women holding meetings! All this is against the system of *purdah!*" Many said, "The day of judgement is near. That is why we are witnessing such perversity." Besides, plenty of rumours were circulating in the village concerning the Grameen Bank: "First, the loans will be given and then the loanees will be taken away to the

Sunderbons." "The women are being given loans so that they can be used as tiger-feed." "The bank men have evil intentions." "If you cannot repay the money, you will be thrown into jail." and so on."

Later in this case study, the author points out that many of these critics reversed their opinions entirely, even becoming supporters of Grameen Bank. The others are silenced simply by the growing presence of organized units of people. In our interviews, many loanees recounted similar experiences. At first villagers would say "Grameen Bank will send you away to an island." "Grameen Bank will cheat you." One villager who threatened the first women loanees in the area of Beltoil, Tangail, is now himself a member of Grameen Bank. The enticing and pragmatic opportunity opened by Grameen Bank overrides reservations and resistance and like-minded groups of people begin to arrive at the branch office.

Disbursing loans is not a simple matter of course in Grameen Bank. First, the candidates are obliged to participate in a *group training programme* which is a minimum seven days of continuous instruction. Under the supervision of a branch manager, this is a major responsibility of the bank workers. The training includes teaching thoroughly the rules and regulations of Grameen Bank which involves, for example, understanding the purpose of the various Bank procedures, knowing in detail the responsibilities of the group chairperson and the centre chief, explaining the potential of fund-saving schemes for joint activities or children's welfare, introducing the issues in the social development programme and learning to write one's signature.

Aside from the practical purpose of this training in terms of the Bank's efficacy, it has another implication which we feel has been overlooked. It ushers in feelings of achievement, self-worth and a sense of order in people's lives. Referring again to Bachaton, the rules and regulations seemed strange to her in the beginning. "Before this, she had never attended a meeting, never signed any papers. She was doing these things for the first time in her life. She even went to Buhapur to collect money from the bank. This was a tremendous change in her life. For the first time, she came to feel that she was of some value. Payment of instalments, handing in of weekly savings, attendance at central meetings, seeking permission from the centre chief in case of visits outside the area--all these appealed to Bachaton's mind." (12)

Although the minimum group training period is seven days, there is no upper limit to its extension. More often, 15 days is required but, for some it may continue for a few months. The Bank does not give up on people. A former branch manager who now works in head office recalls how one 60 year old woman took six months to learn to write her signature. While she was cooking, she would practice it with a stick in the sand. Working with dedication, the branch manager and bank workers helped her in this persistent endeavour until she succeeded.

Early in this training, the group is asked to elect a chairperson and a secretary from among its five members. Very soon the chairperson will be expected to know and carry out a set of duties and responsibilities relating to the group and centre. (See Annex 5). Eliciting whenever possible, a social and experiential form of learning, Grameen Bank has devised a simple way to demonstrate savings as an individual and collective responsibility. It also serves to assess a person's dependability. Each group member must contribute one taka per day into a common savings fund for the duration of the training. The fund is kept in turn first by the chairperson, followed by the secretary and then the remaining members. Trust is essential in relations with the Bank and among group members, and this procedure can indicate an individual's capacity for honesty and reliability with an asset held in common. It is the beginning step in establishing the fundamental relationship of social and economic accountability in the community.

At the end of the seven days, the branch manager assesses whether or not the training is adequate. If so, he gives a *provisional recognition* to the group. If not, he will specify a further period of training. The group is again examined orally, usually by the programme officer. The examination is thorough and members may be rejected or further training may be recommended. Special attention is paid to ensure that group members share the same attitudes and economic status. It is crucial to Grameen Bank's operation that the basic groups are homogeneous social entities. Experience shows that the processes of group formation and training are critical stages for long-term stability. If the discrepancies in social or economic status are too great in the group, the potential for equity in matters of decision making is lessened. At this time the programme officer will also take the opportunity to visit the trainees' houses to see if the candidates really qualify for membership according to the rules and regulations. If all group members are found acceptable and well-versed in the procedures of Grameen Bank, the programme officer accords the group *formal recognition*. Only then is the group a formal entity which can engage in transactions with Grameen Bank.

At this stage, the recognized group can turn its attention to the steps involved in getting loans. One of the truly remarkable features of the innovative credit system of Grameen Bank is that the groups themselves are allocated certain decision-making powers. Again, the significance of this has not been appreciated. From the beginning, loanees are not passive recipients of credit. They are actively integrated into the decision-making process around it. The loanee has a part to play individually, as part of a group and as part of a centre. The Bank has its part to play. What is taking place is a set of complementary and overlapping decision-making powers, responsibilities and accountabilities around the focal point of loans by all the actors involved.

Over the years, loans have been given for 442 recorded purposes. No activity is found "unworthy" as long as the group and the Bank are convinced a person can earn an honourable income from it. Musical instrument making, umbrella repairing or fan making by hand are as viable as boat building, weaving or paddy husking. The activities are grouped into eight broad categories: (a) Processing-Manufacturing, (b) Agriculture-Forestry, (c) Livestock-Fisheries, (d) Services, (e) Trading, (f) Peddling, (g) Shopkeeping, and (h) Collective Enterprises. Most loans are given for the categories a, c and e. Specific activities accounting for the greatest loan volume are milch cows, paddy husking, rice/paddy trading, cow fattening, rickshaw pulling, bullock tillage and various kinds of shopkeeping.

There are clear differences between leading income activities undertaken by men and women. Men engage more in various kinds of trading; women invest more in milch cows and paddy husking. (16). An interesting feature is that the recipients of small loans up to 1500 taka tend to invest up to 150% of the loan amount. Among the poorest, the capacity for saving is remarkable and testifies to their skills in resource utilization.

The first set of decisions incumbent upon the group is deciding the amounts of the loans and which loanees will receive them. Two conditions apply to these decisions: 500 taka is the largest amount the group can sanction without higher approval and only two members may at first receive loans. To this second condition, it is preferred that the secretary and chairperson are the last group members to receive loans. In practice it works like this: The group selects two members for loans. After a short period of time, three to four weeks, if they have shown they can observe Bank discipline and meet their payments, the next two members become eligible for loans. The same requirements apply to the second set of loanees after which the last member may receive a loan. If the first set of loanees do not comply with the rules satisfactorily, it curtails the opportunity for the rest.

THE LOAN PROCEDURES

In Grameen Bank the experience to date is that the first loans tend to be small, with women choosing smaller loans than men. First loans range from 500 to 1500 taka but usually increase with each consecutive loan. Contrary to all the assumptions about the poor being unreliable or succumbing to opportunism, what many first-time loanees suffer is a lot of anxiety before receiving their loans. Bachaton's first loan was 600 taka to invest in paddy husking and red chillies. "She had great qualms about the amount she asked for. Her fear was, "If I cannot repay the money, if there is some loss in my business, where do I get the money from?" (12) When group members and a bank worker combine knowledge through an open discussion of the viability of a potential loan, misinformation or exaggerations regarding local values usually become apparent. It is in everyone's interest that a bad loan does not jeopardize the future prospects of other members.

After the loan amount is agreed upon by the group, the loan can be proposed for approval. This involves three successive separate approvals which receive final sanction by the area manager. It is the centre chief's responsibility to start the formal proposal process by filling in a *loan proposal form,* signing it and giving it to the bank worker. In turn, the bank worker completes her or his own loan proposal form and hands them both to the branch manager. After consulting with his colleagues about the various loan proposals, the branch manager will follow up with visits to the respective groups and centres. In these visits he will check again on the viability of some of the loan amounts and the stipulated business activity. He will also take into consideration the group's observance of bank discipline. The branch manager is responsible for assessing all the loan proposals and finally recommending them. They are then consolidated on a list and sent to the area office for appraisal. The programme officer has the power to reduce the loan amount or refuse it, but has no power to increase it. On the programme officer's recommendation, the area manager gives the final authorization necessary for releasing the loan. In effect, the area manager endorses the programme officer's opinion which itself is already based on a thorough decision-making and supervisory process. Although this may appear to be a set of time-consuming steps--and would be in most bureaucracies--once a loan has been proposed, it is approved and the amount disbursed within three to seven days.

Once a loan is approved, the branch manager issues the loan money along with a *loan pass book.* Loans over 5 000 taka need special approval by the area manager. A loan is given for one year, to be repaid in 50 equal weekly instalments. These 50 weeks cover the 100% repayment of the principal while the remaining two weeks of instalments are reserved for interest and a fee set aside in an Emergency Fund which is explained later. The calculation which is streamlined for simplicity is made as follows: The Bank charges the current official rate of 20% interest on loans. This corresponds to about 10.15% average interest considering the weekly repayment is amortized over 50 weeks. The borrower will pay 80 taka as her weekly instalment during the first 50 weeks. In the 51st week, the interest charge on a loan of 4 000 taka would be 407 taka and 25% of that or 102 taka is the premium for the Emergency Fund which falls due in the 52nd week. This procedure for the Emergency Fund was practiced up to 1991 when a change was made. The members now pay a fixed charge which amounts to 5 taka per thousand for loans in excess of one thousand taka. Thus the fee for the Emergency Fund has been reduced significantly. At the same time loanees have the option of paying the interest in two amounts: one in week 51 and the other in week 52 to reduce the stress.

Loan disbursement - an event. At the branch office, the longest moment in loan disbursement is observing the women signing their signatures with painstaking concentration. It's not long in time really, but in the touching total absorption the action demands. For hands familiar with steady hard work, holding a pen is an unsteady, unfamiliar experience that requires mustering all one's courage. Old women, young women, frail women, women who endure, come to the branch offices in the afternoons to receive their new loans: general, group fund, housing or others.

Loans are disbursed every afternoon from Saturday to Wednesday, the main workweek in Bangladesh. Thursday is reserved for closing the week's accounting and reporting. Each woman buys and brings her own stamp required for the loan form. The bank worker who is assigned to her centre is entirely responsible for processing the loan. The loanee is required to sign the Loan Application Form and the Loan Disbursement Form as well as the original loan proposal. Witnessing this with their own signatures are the loanee's centre chief and group chairperson (or another member from her group instead) who must accompany the member at the time of her loan disbursement.

In Jawabazar-Chaltak Branch, the afternoon we were there, about 30 to 40 loans were processed. One of the women had come for a group fund loan. She was borrowing 1 000 taka to pay an examination fee for her brother. She would repay it at 50 taka a week with no interest charged. These were the conditions decided by her group members.

95

At the centre meetings which take place early in the morning on a regular day each week, the bank worker records the instalment in the loan pass book of each member. Known as the heartbeat of Grameen Bank, the weekly instalment begins as soon as the loan is disbursed. It places the member in a situation of immediate accountability to other members and the Bank. At the same time, by ensuring the rapid rotation of the available funds, the weekly instalment is a major factor in the Bank's good fund management. The innovation of the weekly instalment emerged quite early in the development of Grameen Bank's delivery and recovery system. This arrangement was preferred because money is a scarce resource in poor households. It became apparent that people found it easier to manage their funds on the basis of shorter intervals between instalments rather than the more conventional practice of monthly repayments. So this accommodation was made and incorporated into practice.

Always an open forum, centre meetings for loan transactions first took place under the village tree. In these conditions, it often proved distracting to carry through the business because of passers by and spectators. Thus the idea of a *centre house,* now a requirement as centres become established, grew out of this experience with the first one built in 1979. Another practical problem faced by the Bank in its earliest stage was the question of the loanee's signature for money received. To begin with, thumbprints were used in place of signatures. But the bank workers soon discovered that for women particularly, they could not verify whether or not the print was made by proxy. Since, by custom, most women wore veils and hence their faces were not clearly visible, it became essential to obtain the loanee's real signature for banking verification. There was a situation in which one woman received three loans! When loanees can write their own name, falsification is almost impossible. Besides, when a woman signs a form, she must lift her veil just a little to see where to place her signature. This explains the importance attached to members learning to write their signatures during group training. For women and men, the ability to write their own signatures becomes a source of pride.

The need for loanees to practice writing their signatures and the need to monitor the attendance of a centre's members led to the use of an *attendance register.* Each member signs in when arriving at the centre meeting. In this way, the pen and the written language become routinely demystified and people are encouraged to learn more. It is the feeling among the first bank workers that had they pressed for signatures at the outset, the requirement would have been too inhibiting and even fewer women would have come forward for loans. As well as providing a record of a centre's continuity, the attendance register indicates if a member is living up to obligations. Keeping this register is the duty of the centre chief along with other responsibilities similar to those of the group chairperson, but more extensive. (See Annex 6). We describe below how signatures also play a central role in another loan verification process initiated at the client level.

From the Bank's perspective, regular centre attendance and the payment of weekly instalments do not, in themselves, constitute adequate supervision. Immediately following a loan disbursement, it is a regulation that *within seven days* the client must have invested the loan for the specified purpose and started utilizing the investment for income. Procedures for monitoring loan utilization start with the group chairperson who is easily able to check on how the loan is being used. If the utilization is adequate, the group chairperson appends her or his signature to a *loan utilization form* then reports to the centre chief to hand over the form. The centre chief rechecks the same member's loan utilization and, if satisfied, also signs the form. At the first opportunity, the centre chief gives the form to the bank worker who also checks on the utilization of the loan, providing as well a written description of the investment. The description is quite detailed. For example, if a milch cow is purchased, the colour will be noted, the age and the quantity of milk it provides daily and whether or not it has a calf. The bank worker turns over the loan utilization forms with their signatures and description to the branch manager who is responsible for personally checking 30% of them selected randomly. Following his field visits, the branch manager adds his signature to the respective form and then sends all the loan utilization forms to the programme officer. Similarly, the programme officer carries out field visits based on a random selection of the same loan utilization forms.

If tardy or inappropriate loan utilization is observed, remedial steps are taken to deal with it. However, issues of discipline are rarely a matter for bank staff. Mostly they are taken care of within the context of the group and the centre. The chairperson, centre chief or other members will urge an erring loanee to "Use your funds: idle funds are not productive."

How people use their loans to ensure continued productivity is obviously important to the Bank. The monitoring of loan utilization doesn't stop once a loanee has made the investment. It constitutes part of the ongoing work of bank workers, branch manager and programme officers.

When a loan is fully repaid, the branch manager issues a *repayment certificate* to the loanee which, together with the loan utilization form, is part of the deciding criteria when granting a new loan to a member. The repayment

THE GENERAL LOAN CYCLE

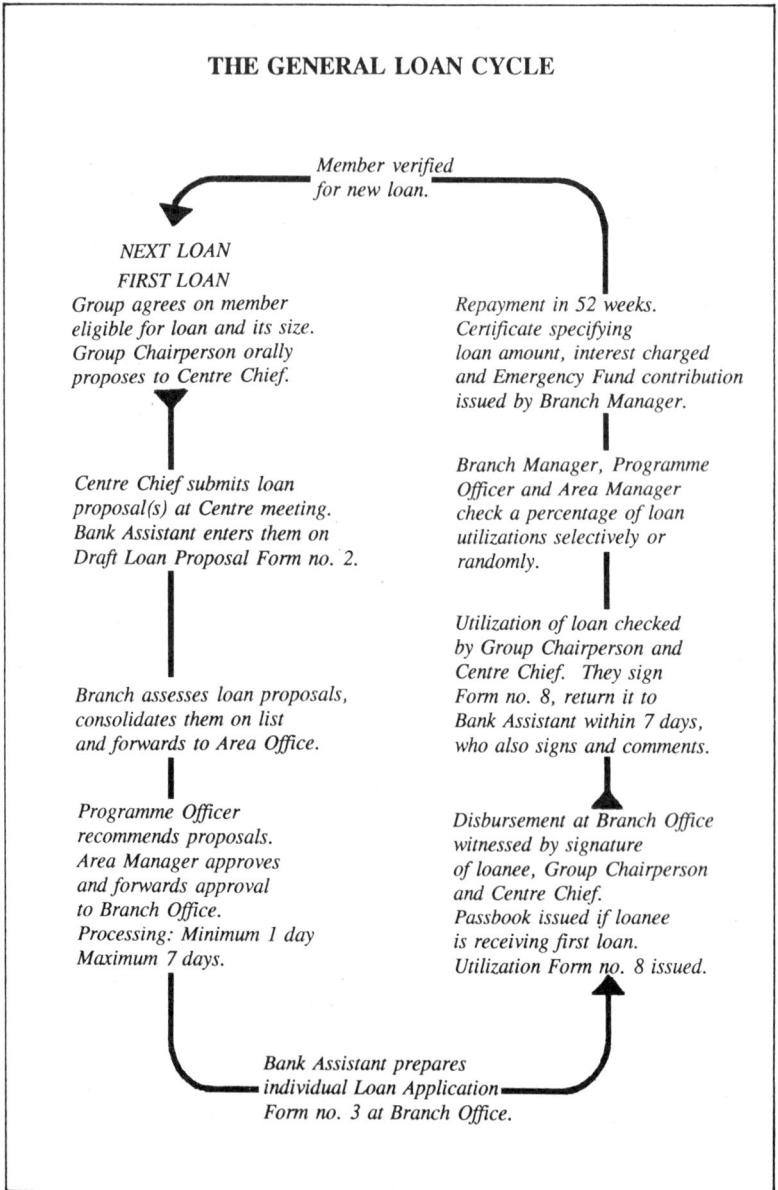

Member verified
for new loan.

NEXT LOAN

FIRST LOAN
Group agrees on member
eligible for loan and its size.
Group Chairperson orally
proposes to Centre Chief.

Repayment in 52 weeks.
Certificate specifying
loan amount, interest charged
and Emergency Fund contribution
issued by Branch Manager.

Centre Chief submits loan
proposal(s) at Centre meeting.
Bank Assistant enters them on
Draft Loan Proposal Form no. 2.

Branch Manager, Programme
Officer and Area Manager
check a percentage of loan
utilizations selectively or
randomly.

Branch assesses loan proposals,
consolidates them on list
and forwards to Area Office.

Utilization of loan checked
by Group Chairperson and
Centre Chief. They sign
Form no. 8, return it to
Bank Assistant within 7 days,
who also signs and comments.

Programme Officer
recommends proposals.
Area Manager approves
and forwards approval
to Branch Office.
Processing: Minimum 1 day
Maximum 7 days.

Disbursement at Branch Office
witnessed by signature
of loanee, Group Chairperson
and Centre Chief.
Passbook issued if loanee
is receiving first loan.
Utilization Form no. 8 issued.

Bank Assistant prepares
individual Loan Application
Form no. 3 at Branch Office.

certificate offers the poor one of the few legal protections to which they have ever had access. Within the village or within the homestead, it is undeniably clear whose assets are whose. And the institution of Grameen Bank can be called upon for legitimation. The implications of this for women particularly are discussed separately.

Grameen Bank's extraordinarily high repayment rate, from 98% to 100% in some districts, is largely due to the tight supervision and the participatory process at work in the groups of five and in the centres. In the event of default, there is no significant collateral the Bank can resort to. Moreover, it is simply not the prevailing attitude of the Bank that they would bring legal charges against the poor, the very people they are trying to serve. The only recourse is social collateral, that is, through the group solidarity and accountability relationships the members have established among themselves. It is a self-controlling participatory process. It works by nipping a potential defaulter in the bud and putting him or her back on track. Nevertheless, for a variety of reasons, it may happen that a member is unable to meet a loan instalment. In this circumstance, the group usually contributes the funds to pay their instalment while making it a private matter to collect from the member.

A group will apply its own social intelligence to a problematic situation. It may waive the outstanding amount or it may attach a penalty interest to the payment. The point is, the group or by extension the centre, will find a jointly agreed upon solution to the problem. For example, a member of one centre in Beltoil-Mirjapur Branch, died shortly after purchasing a cow. The centre decided to sell the cow and were paying off the instalments from the capital. Group members know that if they do not solve the problem, future loans for the group as a whole are jeopardized. Also, the openness with which all bank matters are treated tends to elicit a general social pressure for good performance. A member will make a great effort to avoid the public indignity of being a defaulter. In this way, the Bank does not really have to cope with such problems, it is done by the centre itself.

It is quite likely that Western observers will react uncomfortably to the functioning of social pressure which we have just described. The starting point for Western democracies is largely premised on individual rights to freedom and privacy. Yet, it is becoming increasingly clear that Western individualism is constraining to social life. People are taken up with their individuality to such a degree that they stop relating to each other as human beings. More damaging is the diminishing awareness of the human condition of interdependence. All too often freedom degenerates into meaning freedom from social accountability.

We seem to be more willing to underwrite human rights for isolated individuals than for the social and cultural context of those individuals, for example, the local community, the religious group or indigenous people as a whole.

THE POWER OF STANDING AND MOVING TOGETHER

In our many visits to Grameen Bank centres, we have had ample opportunity to observe how members take great pride in being honourable and making their payments on time. When a centre does well in its activities and in implementing its development decisions, each member has a share in the communal pride. The accomplishments of individual members, which would never have been possible without having access to credit, are also a source of pride. The spirit of solidarity has very tangible consequences for individual members.

Throughout Grameen Bank the prevailing attitude is that the group must progress as a whole. If one member is lagging economically behind and another is forging ahead, the prospering member's new loan may be delayed until the others achieve the same standard. Field staff are sensitive to the issue of differences in economic status arising in the groups or centres. They use every occasion to reinforce the message, "You must go forward together and help each other." Senior staff are very concerned with the possibility of acquired wealth by its members--modest as it is in relative terms--leading to any exploitative relations developing vis-a-vis other landless.

The existence of a well-functioning Grameen Bank centre in the community quickly takes on a much wider social significance. A participatory process which produces practical achievements also produces physical and mental strength among its members. When a centre opens its meeting with energetic exercises and shouts its slogan: *Discipline, Unity, Courage and Hard Work is Our Motto!* the effect is visible in people's eyes. As one zonal manager said at a centre meeting, "Whether you stand straight in your exercise drill or handle your money straight, it is the same thing." Grameen Bank cannot function without disciplined behaviour. In a social environment characterized by discontinuity and uncertainty, the centre provides its members with protection and power.

Below are listed some of the gratifying stories we gathered in the course of our discussions and interviews. They are expressions of the kinds of assistance and solidarity that are springing from the centres.
- Walking home one evening with his newly-purchased goat, a man was stopped by the police who falsely charged that he had stolen it. They

100

wanted a bribe and proceeded to take the man to jail. By chance, a zonal manager was passing and immediately the man gave him a Grameen Bank style salute. The zonal manager stopped to find out what was happening and realised he was a Grameen Bank member. The branch manager was promptly contacted who then quickly alerted the man's centre. Soon after the centre members turned up in large numbers at the jail to vouch for their colleague. He was released without delay.

- A member's house burnt down leaving the family with their small children destitute. The centre members came together, decided the family needed help and organized the speedy rebuilding of the house.

- A local official in Tangail District had a candidate he wanted accepted by the nearby centre. However, the members refused on the basis that the candidate was not qualified according to Grameen Bank rules. Although the official pressured them hard, the members stood their ground. In retaliation, the official arranged having two of them severely beaten and they were taken in bad condition to the hospital. Two hundred members, both men and women, from six centres turned up in front of the official's house. "Why", they demanded, "did you beat them?" and "Where is the money for the hospital expenses?". Hurriedly, the official handed over 6 000 taka in compensation for the incurred medical expenses of the two men.

- When a wife was beaten badly by her husband, the other female members of her centre gathered in front of her house. They reminded the husband that wife-beating was against the Koran. He relented and promised to improve his ways.

- Patuakhali, on the Bay of Bengal, is reputed to be one of the most conservative districts in Bangladesh. Because it is a delta where seven rivers meet, it is called the "mouth of fire" When it was announced that the Managing Director of Grameen Bank would be paying a visit to their area, the women decided to organize a procession to welcome him. The men in the community adamantly refused the idea, threatening the women if they carried out such unacceptable behaviour in public. Several hundred women marched to the riverside with beautiful garlands doing exactly what they had planned: to meet and greet the founder of Grameen Bank.

- A local politician in Patuakhali: "It is not appropriate that Muslim women

101

shout these Grameen Bank slogans in their meetings." The women: "But you weren't very bothered when we shouted slogans for you during the last election!"

- Sylhet is also a conservative district. When Grameen established itself there, the Mollahs threatened to burn branch offices and to not perform burial sites for the poor who joined the Bank. Three hundred members gathered and voiced their opinions about the Mollahs behaviour and threats. Onima Rani stated: "Nobody trusts poor people, but Grameen Bank does. We are more courageous now. To be honest is the main thing for trust. You can threaten me many times but I will not leave Grameen. If you don't want to bury me, I know that the members of my centre and the bank workers will do it."

- Centre No. 12 had a problem between husband and wife. He refused to collaborate and told her: "If you are a member of Grameen Bank, you should ask the Bank for money and not me." All the members went to solve the quarrel. They explained the advantages of the Bank to him. He changed his attitude and became very collaborative.

- One member of Centre No. 27, Hannda, a divorcee, died. Her children were in deep trouble. All the members went together to cover the costs of the funeral. After that, the bank approved 4 500 taka from the Emergency Fund to the family.

- Murul Islam wanted to "buy" himself a job as a security guard and borrowed 1 000 taka from a moneylender at high interest, but he did not get the job and he lost the money. His group helped him with 500 taka from the Group Fund, and his Centre helped with 1 000 from its Special Savings Fund. Murul repaid the moneylender and started a business with the 500. He is doing well now.

- Fatima in Centre No. 6 had managed to accumulate a capital of 8 cows. She earned money and was living well. Her husband who had left her earlier now wanted to come back to her again. She asked the centre what to do. The members advised her to take him back, but that she should not give him any money, only food. She should also demand that he herd the cows.

The strength and self-confidence of centre members does not derive only from the availability of credit or from the organizational context of the centre. Over

The strength and self-confidence of centre members does not derive only from the availability of credit or from the organizational context of the centre. Over the last ten years, a substantial *economic development programme* in conjunction with a highly diversified *social development programme* have evolved. These two programmes are tightly interwoven in the daily lives of the members and cater increasingly to their many needs. In the following we attempt to describe the programmes and the participatory processes around them.

ECONOMIC DEVELOPMENT PROGRAMME

The Bank is concerned with the poor deepening their basis of security. The consecutive disbursal of loans to the landless poor on an individual basis cannot, in itself, ensure this. The size of the loans and the return on the investment are, in relative terms, too small for much wealth to accumulate. The family still finds itself at the mercy of a number of unpredictable events from illness to floods which could plunge it once again into abject poverty. To cope with the spectrum of needs that confront the landless and to offer them security in the likelihood of emergencies, Grameen Bank has responded by creating a variety of fund saving schemes for specific functions.

Group Fund. Every group member deposits one taka each week as a personal saving. This is accumulated in an account called, The Group Fund Account. The account is managed by the group of five on a consensus basis. Over and above this, the members pay a *group tax* for enjoying the financial services coming to them through the group. When a group member receives a loan from the Bank, this obligatory deduction is made at the rate of 5% of the loan amount. The group tax is also deposited in the Group Fund account. In Bangla it is explained to the members as *mushtichaal*, that is the handful of rice a mother puts aside to save when she prepares the day's main meal. A handful of rice is not missed during the meal but, over time, it can accumulate to a sizeable reserve.

The rule is that individual members do not have any claim to the group tax. It is relinquished to the group and belongs to all members. The group fund is explained to the members as being their own "little bank". It protects them from resorting to the moneylender when they need small amounts of money quickly. Any group member can borrow from the group fund for any purpose, investment or consumption. What is required is the consent of the other group

103

members who also decide terms and conditions. It is more common than not that loans are granted for a fixed term at no interest.

The group fund is a highly successful innovation of Grameen Bank. Because of the versatility it offers, people use it to the maximum extent. The array of activities is very impressive. The 1991 Annual Report lists 350 different activities for which loans were granted from the group fund. The activities are grouped under the following nine headings: Social and Household Needs; Health and Medical Expenses; Loan Repayment; Maintenance, Repair and Addition of Capital Equipment; Raw Materials for Manufacturing and Processing; New and Supplementary Investments; Trading; Farming; and Collective Enterprise. Specifically, group fund loans were granted for a cattle shed, clothes, a niece's wedding, Nobanna festival, pond registration, medicine, cart repairing, tools for welding, bamboo groves, bamboo for ice-cream sticks, yarn purchase, goat raising, betel leaf trading, seedling purchase, and a collective enterprise in market leasing. This limited selection reveals the spectrum of needs met by the group fund and that its use for investment is quite significant.

To show how the "handful of rice" has accumulated, by end 1991, the total savings in the group fund amounted to 611 million taka, while the total amount of loans disbursed from the fund in 1991 alone was 189 million.

From a learning perspective, the group members see how quickly their "little bank" grows in size, even with such small contributions. Managing the group fund account autonomously on a consensus basis provides the members with essential ground experience in the collective management of finances. It is a concrete lesson in the benefits of collaboration and solidarity. As well, it brings into active discussion the element of planning in terms of longer-term objectives. No longer at the mercy of the moneylender, people have immediate access to their own funding source as long as they work it out with their co-members.

If a member leaves a group, she or he is entitled to withdraw only the personal weekly savings which have accumulated in the group fund. When a newly formed group is officially recognized, all members sign a declaration to that effect. If, by unanimous decision, a group imposes a fine on a member who has subverted discipline, the money received is deposited in the group fund for the benefit of all. Although the group funds in total increase to several hundred million taka, individual loans from them most often range from 200 to 1 000 taka. After three to four years of existence, a group may easily accumulate

THREE STEP SOCIO-ECONOMIC SAFETY NET

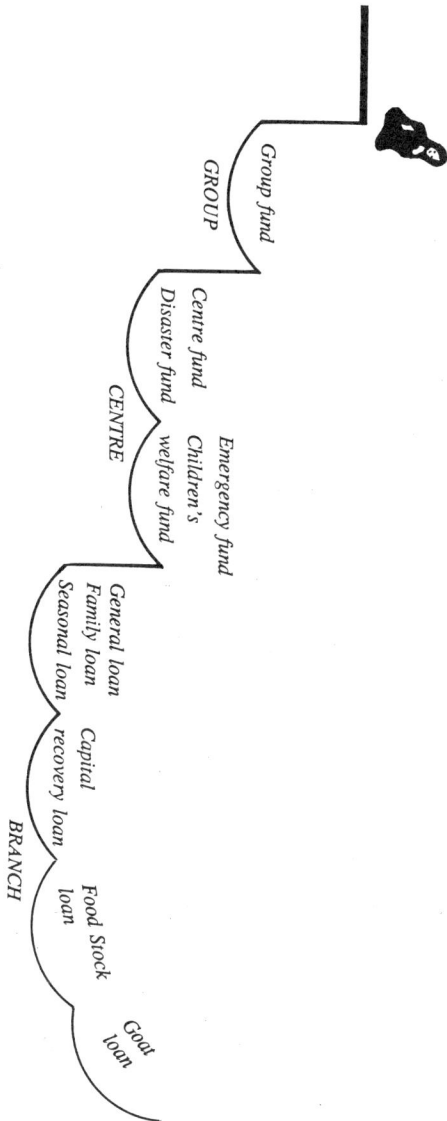

Group fund

GROUP

Centre fund
Disaster fund

Emergency fund
Children's
welfare fund

CENTRE

General loan
Family loan
Seasonal loan

Capital
recovery loan

Food Stock
loan

BRANCH

Goat
loan

In a personal or family predicament a member's first recourse is the group fund. If that is not sufficient, there are opportunities in the funds managed at centre level. In case of crisis or death, the emergency fund is activated with support to the family. The branch portfolio of loans will, in disaster situations, offer such support as capital recovery, food stock and several other loans.

7 000 taka in their group fund. At any one time, approximately 3 000 taka would be on loan to members, leaving the group with 4 000 taka in reserve and gaining interest. Only up to half the amount of paid-up savings can be borrowed by the group for loans. From a participatory perspective, the group fund is an exciting mechanism. It immediately allocates people a vital resource only they can make use of through a collective decision-making process that is entirely independent of the Bank.

Emergency Fund. Established through the contributions of all Grameen Bank members, the emergency fund is basically an insurance coverage in case of default, death, disability and other accidents. As explained earlier, it is mandatory that a borrower pay a fee of five taka per thousand for loans in excess of 1 000 taka. For example, a loan of 4 000 taka obliges the borrower to pay 15 taka to the emergency fund. The amount of the disbursement is calibrated according to the number of times a member has taken loans. The family of a first-time loanee would be entitled to 500 taka while that of a seven-time loanee would be entitled to 5 000 taka, the upper limit of the disbursement amount. Over 145 million taka are now accumulated in the Fund.

Centre members are responsible for recommending who is entitled to an emergency fund disbursement. For the fund to be operational, it requires the joint signatures of the centre chief, deputy centre chief and the branch manager. The disbursement is made in the presence of all the centre members. In one male centre we visited, a loanee had died leaving a widow with three very young children. After an introductory talk on the value of the emergency fund, the area manager gave the widow the cash disbursement and a letter of condolence from the Managing Director. The widow gave her thumbprint in lieu of signature. Always attempting to protect women, the Bank rule is that, if a husband dies who has a balance owing on his loan, his group or centre must take responsibility for repaying that balance. It is not incumbent on the wife to pay it out of the emergency fund allocation she receives.

The emergency fund also offers protection against theft and loss or damage to livestock or crops. It is also meant as a reserve for quick access in case of major crises such as cyclones, flood or drought. To date, disbursements from the fund have been relatively small, so it is accumulating capital. During the Bank's early stages, the emergency fund helped to allay its financial burden.

There can be little doubt that the group fund and the emergency fund offer the landless poor a sense of social and economic security they have never before experienced. If, as intended, the emergency fund develops into a solid insurance plan for the landless, it would be an unprecedented achievement in the annals of development. It would be an accomplishment resulting from the productivity and discipline of the poor in combination with the management services and commitment of Grameen Bank staff.

Special Savings Fund. Another part of the economic development programme is to offer the members an opportunity to move on from individual loans to joint enterprises. While group and emergency savings are mandatory, the special savings are voluntary and operate at the centre level. Depending on what a centre decides, the special savings contribution may vary from one to five taka per member per week. If members of a centre are intent on starting a joint enterprise such as fish pond cultivation or leasing a field for tobacco cultivation, they must first demonstrate that they can save money together for that purpose. The Bank will then supplement these funds with a loan. As a general rule, the Bank extends loans up to but not more than ten times the size of the members' savings. The centre collectively repays the loan. In practice, a joint enterprise loan is charged to each individual member of the group, each assuming responsibility for an equal portion of the total loan amount. In this way, it is ensured that the individual member does not perceive the large loan in the realm of the abstract. Her or his personal participation in the accountability to the collective is concretized. Although joint enterprises still are undertaken in this manner, many of these have experienced management problems and the Bank is generally now seeking other ways to facilitate the formation of larger collective undertakings.

The special savings fund, also called the Centre Fund, is used for other collective purposes as well. Often the fund will be a source for constructing a centre house. Or for meeting other expenses connected with it, such as iron sheets for roofing, furniture, mats, and a signboard. In one women's centre we visited, the members had purchased from their special savings beautiful yellow saris for everyone. One men's centre purchased shoes so they could carry out their exercises better. Buying clothes for children was a very common use of this fund.

Children's Welfare Fund. Recognizing that the future of the centres and the Bank as a whole is one, staff and members are turning their attention to the welfare of members' children. This fund becomes mandatory when a loanee takes her second loan. Members contribute one taka per week. The money is used for building or making arrangements for a modest school room, which usually functions as the centre house too, for paying a teacher or purchasing schoolbooks at cost from Grameen Bank. Similar to the group fund, the children's welfare fund is a source of small loans, but for the specific purpose of promoting small income-generating activities among children themselves which will aid in their continuing education.

We thought, at first, that members might find all these funds too demanding. But in our interviews no one complained about difficulties in meeting their instalments or contributions to various funds. To the contrary, the thought that the Bank might not be there was a source of anxiety. Again, the critical factor here is organising the instalments and the savings contributions on a weekly basis. It simply makes personal fund management easier and less stressful for the landless.

Individual Savings Deposits. In addition to the various collective savings schemes, the Bank is encouraging members to build their economic strength by keeping extra income in personal savings accounts. The absolute number of deposits and the amounts are expected to increase as members achieve a satisfactory level of consumption and see themselves served by accumulating something for the future. As discussed, the Bank considers deposit banking an important feature of its fund management in the future.

Rates of interest. As we have mentioned, Grameen Bank adopts the rates of interest set in the official money market currently charging 20% per annum for its loans and paying 8.5% to members on all the above-mentioned funds, including personal deposits.

Shareholding Scheme: To ensure that ownership of the Bank remains in the hands of the poor, and to ensure capital for future growth, it is compulsory for each group to buy shares in Grameen Bank. When the savings in a group fund have reached 600 taka, the group concerned is obliged to buy shares in the amount of 500 taka, i.e. 5 shares @ 100 taka. Each member is entitled to buy only one share. Specified on each share issued is the number of the group and its centre name. At the time of writing, the Bank has a share capital of 250 million taka of which 120 million are paid up.

Types of loans. Over the years Grameen has developed various types of bank products for the benefit of its members. Already described in detail, the mainstay has been the *general loan*. The upper limit of this loan varies in some branches, but is now usually 10 000 taka.

Seasonal Loan. This recent addition is very popular among loanees. As the name indicates, the loan is for seasonal cultivation. Conditions for its use are very flexible. A member may borrow up to a maximum of 3 000 taka which is to be repaid at the time of harvest or for a period not exceeding six months. To maintain discipline however, one or two percent of the loan capital is paid per week according to the loanee's capacity. The loan can be processed within a week. *Seasonal collective loans* are also available under similar conditions. Loan amounts up to 10 000 taka are available for a group of five and 45 000 taka for a centre of 30 people wishing to cultivate together. For collective loans, borrowers may decide if the repayment period is six months or one year. It will depend on their loan proposal. Overall, these loans tend to protect the general loan and to keep members from reverting to the moneylender. They are also proving to be a factor in accelerating a branch's time to break-even financially.

The family loan is another innovation of importance. The loan is taken by the family as a whole through the woman who is the legal recipient and pays the instalments over one year. The upper limit is 30 000 taka; generally such loans will range between 10 to 15 000 taka. To qualify, the recipient must be at least a four-time loanee of good standing recommended by the centre members who also propose the distribution of the loan within the family. For example, a loan of 14 000 taka may be distributed with 6 000 on the husband for a rickshaw and 8 000 on the wife for a milch cow. It may involve the adult children as well. The loan can be an important "bridge" to joint or collective enterprises. The family is a social entity exhibiting stronger cohesion than a group of people who have joined together on a voluntary basis. The demand for the loan indicates also that it responds to the psychology of a family where the wife has been economically successful and the husband is lagging behind. It includes the husband at the same time as it empowers the woman further. If it can follow up with support to family-oriented technology such as leasing of power looms, the Bank is into a very interesting development.

House loans. Loans for houses are a special issue. They are as much part of the Bank's social development programme as they are part of its economic one. As the Bank's credit experience and self-reliance grew, larger loans over longer periods became possible for individual loanees. Housing loans, identified early as a major need, were seen as instrumental in improving the living standard of the landless. From the viewpoint of health and stability, the situation of women and children in particular could be ameliorated. Four hundred and fifty dollars worth of housing (i.e. 18 000 taka) means people won't have to repair their houses every year, means people stay dry in the rainy season, means a place to store grain and tools which maximizes the carrying out of productive activities and the potential for earning income the year round.

Carefully thought out eligibility criteria are applied in the selection of loanees. To obtain a housing loan, a member must have received loans for at least the second time. She or he must show an excellent record in paying instalments regularly and have a perfect loan utilization record. Preference is given to the members facing the most difficult living conditions. It is required that a centre has functioned for two years before house loans are issued to any of its members. Also, the Branch should be two years old with a good record in their accounting procedures and centre discipline.

No deed - no loan. Shelter is really a women's issue. To protect women and to protect accountability to the loan itself, the Bank insists that women must have the land title deed in their name before being eligible for the loan. Either women may take a loan in order to secure homestead land or the existing deed must be transferred from the husband's into the wife's name. In our experience, there was no resistance to this on the part of husbands. Another protective stipulation is that the ownership cannot be transferred until the loan is fully repaid.

Like the general loan, housing loans do not require collateral. However, social collateral is manifested through a pledge which must be signed by all centre members who, thereby, take collective responsibility for their own member's loan in case of default. Since loans were first disbursed in 1984, more than 136 080 houses had been built by June, 1992. To be expected, well over 80% of the house loans are taken by women and the repayment is almost 100%.

The following sequence of photographs shows some of the many activities carried out by Grameen Bank members with the help of credit: poultry-keeping, paddy processing, basket-making, preparation of sweets, carpentry, rickshaw vans, sewing, herbalist medicines, petty trading of various kinds and bee-keeping. The last page illustrates the dramatic change in living standard made possible through house loans.

110

113

115

In pragmatic response to loanee needs, the Bank has arrived at two categories of housing loans: The Basic Housing Loan and the Moderate Housing Loan. The former has an upper limit of 10 000 taka while the latter has a limit of 18 000 taka. Consistent with practice, house loans are repaid in weekly instalments but at the low rate of 5% simple interest. The repayment period is calculated on the formula of 1 000 taka for each year. Thus an 18 000 taka loan may be repaid in 18 years under very favourable conditions. To our knowledge, housing loans are the only ones that loanees are encouraged to accelerate the repayment period in mutual agreement with the Bank.

In the construction of the houses, Grameen Bank has certain minimum requirements in terms of construction materials and size. Part of each house loan must be used to purchase four reinforced concrete pillars, a sanitary latrine, and corrugated iron roofing sheets. The pillars and latrine components are supplied through the Bank's House Building Materials Project and are often stocked at the branch offices ready to be delivered to loanees. Bank workers are frequently seen accompanying their loanees to the market to ensure the iron roofing sheets they purchase are of a good, standard quality. This means that the most expensive modules of construction remain undamaged after the recurring floods abate. So, the poor, pushed by poverty to opt for the cheapest and riskiest low-lying land, do not lose the most costly and essential components of their housing investment. They can literally pick up the pieces and start again. The flood does not mean that a loanee's income-generating activities have to be postponed unduly because of lack of shelter, and all the human misery that entails.

Members are also expected to plant vegetable gardens around their houses. Patuakhali and Rangpur zones are witnessing the spontaneous appearance of Grameen Bank villages: several members who receive house loans choosing to build their houses side by side in the same locality. In Patuakhali, one Grameen Bank village had Muslims and Hindus as amicable neighbours.

In some zones, it is the practice to encourage a supplementary income-generating activity along with the house loan. These activities are seen as being appropriate to enhance the economic independence of women especially and, for that reason, are increasingly reserved for them. Pigeon-raising and beekeeping are two occupations which can be established on the homestead or very nearby, so women can easily accommodate them into their daily routines. The labour involved in their maintenance is minimal and the activities yield a largely reliable and sizeable income. Five pairs of pigeons can generate a yearly income of approximately 1 500 taka. Under optimal conditions, a single

117

beehive may yield one kilogram of honey per week with a sales value of 80 taka or more. These activities can contribute substantially towards paying a house loan.

A house loan is a major event in a centre and the members often pitch in and help the loanee with digging the foundation and other preparations. Even the bank worker can be seen contributing. When a women has taken a house loan, the house eventually becomes her property and she has the deed as proof. Automatically, she is placed in a very strong position in the event of divorce or other family disputes which raise the question of property rights.

House loans after a disaster. Although in practice house loans are reserved for well-established centres, Grameen Bank is capable of responding to emergencies. In 1985, a severe tornado took place in the Ghior, Manikgong area in rural Dhaka. Members in ten of the Bank's centres were gravely affected and many lost their houses. A total of 60 members lost all their possessions. Immediately, the Bank sent out a team of three staff members to assess the situation. The team reported that 41 members required house loans to rebuild their homes. After an assessment carried out by the zonal office as well, the Bank processed a total of 547 000 taka in house loans ranging in size from 7 000 to 18 000 taka. In its own words, the team also considered the Bank's purpose was "to create brotherhood". Members organized themselves for mutual help in the reconstruction. The zonal office organized the supply of building materials to support the collective effort. Four members decided to buy land together and build a Grameen Bank village. The Bank is aware that its credibility is at stake if it cannot respond to the needs of the members, especially in emergencies.

House loans became an important issue following the floods in Rangpur in 1987. Members accounted for a total of 33 400 fully or partly damaged houses and 17 850 of these were in need of new housing loans. This time, however, the damage was of a magnitude requiring comprehensive emergency measures. On 15 October, 1989, the Aga Khan Award for Architecture was presented to Grameen Bank for the excellence of its Housing Programme.

Other loans. Some loans are reserved for a variety of appropriate technologies such as tubewells and treadle pumps. Loans for joint enterprises, also available, are explained more fully later in this chapter. A special portfolio of loans developed for emergency situations that chronically arise in Bangladesh and that drastically affected Rangpur zone is described in the next chapter.

PROCESS - FROM THE STOMACH TO THE HEAD

The economic development programme of Grameen Bank is a myriad of significant details which fit together in a complex but very functional whole. Behind every rule or practice, there is a cumulated body of experience to justify it. The Bank is firmly convinced that the first step towards real empowerment is higher caloric intake. The immediate task is to fill people's stomachs and then to offer them a series of opportunities to improve their general situation. This is done by loanees mastering ever more complex financial and managerial operations. The road from the first seven- to fifteen-day training course where the members learn to trust each other with their first group savings, to small joint enterprises where they collectively take much larger loans, is incredibly short. What loanees experience is a social and economic learning process which is thoughtfully structured while pragmatically open to modification.

The fact that Grameen Bank deals with money like any other bank is a conspicuous feature which tends to overshadow its wider and very significant social impact. By entering into group and centre processes, people restore economic and social accountability in the community. The gradual involvement in economic undertakings of increasing complexity is integrally related to people's management capacities. The weekly centre meetings with repayment discipline, discussions of person or community matters as well as successful collective initiatives of different levels over a period of two to four years, advance people's decision-making capacities and re-invigorate community self-confidence. Through this process members in centres become a viable socio-economic formation which can deal effectively with social development issues and which is capable of acting quickly in times of emergency.

SOCIAL DEVELOPMENT PROGRAMME

The most striking characteristic of Grameen Bank's social development programme is its enlightened concern with a long-term perspective. Certainly it deals with immediate needs which benefit both members and the Bank, but they are incorporated into an overall approach which is educative, qualitative and responsive. In the last ten years, different components of it have developed at different stages. And, uniquely, it is the women members of Grameen Bank who have been the impetus in formulating the Bank's priority social issues.

Earlier, we mentioned how informal discussions between bank workers and women loanees became the basis for an extensive workshop programme largely addressed to women. At the end of these workshops, it has become standard procedure that the participants formulate a set of decisions to be implemented

119

on return to their respective centres. In March 1984, a national workshop took place which was an historic occasion in the Bank's development. The 100 participating women representing the five zones existing then agreed upon *16 Decisions* which they committed themselves and the general membership of Grameen Bank to implement. These 16 Decisions have become the Social Development Constitution of Grameen Bank and are the focus for the participatory process whenever members meet. Also, the 16 Decisions can be used as a monitoring and evaluation tool to assess the impact of Grameen Bank's work. Members may rearrange priorities or give different emphases to the various decisions, but the list remains the major guideline for household or community action.

The "16 Decisions" are no abstract ideological resolution. Quite the opposite, they constitute a concrete document for action arising from and expressing the needs of the landless. Grameen Bank's role in the manifestation of the 16 Decisions has been its preceding years of facilitating development around the general values of solidarity, health, education and work. In this document, social and economic distinctions overlap. Solidarity and mutual help are as much a practical concern as building a pit latrine or drinking tubewell water. Savings and investment in collective enterprises reflect the same spirit as tree planting or growing vegetables. Abolition of dowry payments is linked with the issue of discipline, physical exercises and courage with the quest for social justice. Environmental sanitation is as important as children's education. The subject matter of the 16 Decisions has become the major focus for a comprehensive process of change.

To date the social development programme of Grameen Bank comprises three main components which distinguish the Bank as a socio-economic formation rather than a strictly economic development enterprise. Generating or supporting participation differently, these components are: a *Workshop programme*, a *Centre school programme* and the availability of *Supplies and skill training*.

WORKSHOP PROGRAMME
The major responsibility for planning and implementing most workshops is carried out by the zone, area or branch offices according to the type of workshop. However, the zonal office provides the essential coordinating function required among the different levels in order to administer the workshops effectively. At Head Office, the Special Programme Unit within the Training Department is tasked with the overall development of the Workshop Programme at the field level. Now a package of seventeen different workshops

THE SIXTEEN DECISIONS

1. The Four Principles of Grameen Bank - Discipline, Unity, Courage and Hard Work - we shall follow and advance in all walks of our lives.

2. Prosperity we shall bring to our families.

3. We shall not live in dilapidated houses. We shall repair our houses and work towards constructing new houses at the earliest.

4. We shall grow vegetables all the year round. We shall eat plenty of it and sell the surplus.

5. During the plantation seasons, we shall plant as many seedlings as possible.

6. We shall plan to keep our families small. We shall minimise our expenditures. We shall look after our health.

7. We shall educate our children and ensure that they can earn to pay for their education.

8. We shall always keep our children and the environment clean.

9. We shall build and use pit-latrines.

10. We shall drink tubewell water. If it is not available, we shall boil water or use alum.

11. We shall not take any dowry in our sons' wedding, neither shall we give any dowry in our daughters' wedding. We shall keep the centre free from the curse of dowry. We shall not practice child marriage.

12. We shall not inflict any injustice on anyone, neither shall we allow anyone to do so.

13. For higher income we shall collectively undertake bigger investments.

14. We shall always be ready to help each other. If anyone is in difficulty, we shall all help him.

15. If we come to know of any breach of discipline in any centre, we shall all go there and help restore discipline.

16. We shall introduce physical exercise in all our centres. We shall take part in all social activities collectively.

●   Formulated in a National Workshop of one hundred women centre chiefs in March 1984, the 16 Decisions might be called the social development constitution of Grameen Bank. All Grameen Bank members are expected to practice and implement these decisions.

focused on the loanees takes place in each zone. Many of the ideas for these workshops are suggested by bank staff themselves based on the kinds of social, technical and economic issues faced by the members. At least another four workshops each addressed to different levels of field staff are also arranged in the zones per year. To some degree, the workshop programme is shed to the field-level units as their capacity and need to take responsibility increases. Ninety percent of the workshops take place at the Branch level.

In the course of a year, an established zone might easily organize 250 or more workshops varying in duration from one to seven days. With eleven zones, this amounts to a total of 2 750 workshops a year. Out of the 250 workshops in a given zone, three-quarters of them are for women and the rest for men. Normally, workshops for women take place from one to seven days while those scheduled for men are from one to four days. Exchange visits might be arranged for centres in a branch, between branches or between zones and are a way of providing workshop follow-up and further motivation for women. Below is an overview of some of the major training workshops currently offered by the programme.

The 7-day workshop. The core of the social development programme is the 7-day workshop for women. Implemented at the Branch level for centre members of a particular branch, each workshop caters for thirty-five centre chiefs. The workshops are organized by social development officers from the zonal or area office. In a given zone, the minimum objective is to provide one 7-day workshop per branch every two years. If possible, the opening and closing days are attended by the zonal manager, but he is obliged to spend one full day at these workshops. The agenda of the 7-day workshops is very dense and comprehensive. Because of their centrality in Grameen Bank's programme, these workshops are described in detail later in this chapter.

Follow-up workshops - 1 day. These take place two months after a 7-day workshop. Two social development officers visit the houses and centres of the centre chiefs. Prizes are awarded to the three centre chiefs whose centres have best implemented the 16 Decisions overall. The women report on their findings, achievements or problems and renew their commitment to action. The area manager, programme officer and branch manager must attend.

1-day workshops for women. Often the purpose here is to bring together 40 centre chiefs who are new to their post. They spend the day reviewing the rules and regulations of Grameen Bank facilitated by branch or area staff.

Exchange visits. Seen as an indispensable way of internalizing and gaining knowledge, exchange visits open doors to new perspectives about what women can achieve. They combine three powerful reinforcing elements: peer learning, peer motivation and peer solidarity. When a group of women visit other centres to assess implementation of the 16 Decisions, not only do they learn from the experiences of their sisters, but their presence as guests has a considerable motivating effect. When the bank worker notifies about the intended exchange visit, the hosts--like hosts everywhere--take great pride in being well prepared. The message creates a flurry of activity and excitement. Exchange visits between centres take place in the same branch or different branches. Sometimes the visits are connected with the development of joint enterprises and may even take place between zones. The social development officers are usually involved in both planning and implementing the visits.

A centre exchange visit is for three days. The women stay as guests in the host members' houses, participate in their centre meeting and inspect their income generating and social development activities. On return, the women must report the results of their visit to their own branch and centre. A little later, the three-day visit is exchanged and the roles reversed. The branch manager reports to the zonal office on the results of the exchange.

Area workshop. Three or four centre chiefs per branch, or a total of 40 female participants, come together in this five-day workshop organized by the area office. The workshop covers general information about the Bank, practical knowledge to improve income activities and stresses the importance of the 16 Decisions. Officers from the area and branch level, and a social development officer facilitate. The zonal manager will be sure to attend for a few hours at least. "On return to my centre", one participant told us, "I will share what I have learned. For those who can read, I will give them the written materials."

Zonal workshops take place every year. It is a major event with one hundred centre chiefs, one from each branch in the zone, selected to attend the workshop on the same basis as the National workshops. In most respects the zonal workshops parallel national ones, with the emphasis on discussing issues more specifically relevant to the zone concerned. It is a very lively affair lasting five days. The social development officers and the bank workers set up a sales centre where the women display their goods, crafts and produce. There are three categories of prizes which, not surprisingly, are related to the 16 Decisions. In Rangpur zone prizes are given for best vegetable production, good discipline and centre school promotion. The workshop will finalize with a set of decisions to be implemented at the zonal level. Either the managing

123

director or other management personnel from head office participate in the event.

National workshops. These workshops for women are held every two years. One hundred women borrowers, equitably representing each of the eleven zones are selected to attend. For the lucky participants, it is a significant and exciting event. Only women who have not attended a previous national or zonal workshop are eligible for selection. Two social development officers and three bank workers from each zone are selected to participate on the basis of their work performance. Lasting five working days, the purpose is to have the Bank's operation and development programme discussed on a national level. In these workshops, the role of the senior staff and head office management is to listen while the loanees do the talking. They might initiate an issue in the form of a question such as "What have you done about education?" but the ensuing discussion is left to the participants.

The first National Women's Workshop took place in April 1982. It discussed and swore to implement ten decisions. The subsequent national workshop in July 1984 elaborated and added to these decisions which became the *16 Decisions* currently in force.

4-day male workshop. For centre chiefs, this workshop includes an exchange visit between centres. A number of practical issues around business activities are discussed with high interest. For example in some zones, participants prefer to concentrate on the problems they have with livestock. Attended by a social development officer, branch manager and other branch staff. The zonal manager is expected to be present for one full day.

1-day workshops for men. Workshops for male members are held on a much less intensive scale. An average of one or two per month are organized at the branch level usually by the area office. The agenda centres around review of Grameen Bank rules and regulations, the value of joint enterprises with advice and examples on how to proceed, and how to show more initiative in developing businesses. To determine what else should be added to the agenda or which topics should be given priority, the area manager collaborates closely with the branch manager concerned.

Family workshops are for any family members of female loanees who directly affect her daily life. This may include male guardians either husbands, uncles, brothers or mothers, mothers-in-law, sisters and sisters-in-law. Often the men don't believe what their wives say about their activities in Grameen Bank.

Female relatives often under-appreciate or deprecate the loanee's efforts. So in the day together, the area office staff and the social development officer try to clarify any misgivings or misunderstandings about the Bank. More and more it is recognized that the cooperation of the whole family is needed for socio-economic development. Staff discuss the loans, the rules, nutrition, family planning, health. They even tackle family discrimination in the preferential treatment of boys over girls. The overall intention is to increase harmony in the family and harmony with the Bank.

A one-day **Teacher's workshop** aims to motivate centre school teachers on the importance of encouraging children to continue their school in the future with special emphasis on completing primary education. About 35 to 40 teachers are brought together for the occasion.

Mother and Child Gathering. Organized at the Branch level, this is an event much looked forward to by the women, children and staff. The whole day is dedicated to games and sports. The children and their mothers participate in the fun. Why should only well-off children enjoy such activities in their schools? Stereotypes about cultural conventions are certainly challenged here as women race happily to the finish line in their saris.

Birth Attendant workshops are new in the programme and reflect the widening and deepening process of meeting the crucial needs of women. Held for ten days, they bring together women who are traditional birth attendants and female bank members interested in the profession. Safe motherhood is a life issue for women and children. Still in the experimental stage, many are planned for 1993.

Mother and Girl-child workshops. Also experimental, 150 of these workshops are to be implemented in 1993. The intention is to address a major issue in the culture: the low-status resulting from social and economic marginalization of the adolescent girl. Lasting two to four days, staff try to raise awareness and appreciation of the value of daughters. They emphasize what the girl can do and what she can contribute to the household as a productive member. One objective is to identify how the girl can carry out an activity for self-employment just like the mother. Pursued in discussion are critical attitudes and issues that impinge powerfully on being a young female person in Bangladesh: delayed marriage, spaced births, legal rights and nutrition.

A Gotcha workshop or, Grassroot workshop, is a one-day forum for listening to members of a centre which, for one reason or another, is having problems. They began in September 1992 in Rangpur due to the low morale and discipline among Grameen Bank loanees following the floods. The zonal manager makes every effort to attend but the area manager and his programme officer must be present. The morning is spent sitting and discussing any centre problem the members are facing. Spouses of centre members take part in the afternoon session when staff explain to them the various problems raised in the morning listening, in turn, to their problems. The assumption here is that the family as an interacting unit must be approached in order to restore motivation and productivity. Open-ended questions such as "What do you think?" characterize the search for people's responses. At the end of the day the objective is to arrive at first-stage decisions acceptable to everyone in order to re-establish centre discipline. In Rangpur, the Gotcha workshop is followed up by repeating the 7-day training and new group recognition for members and a 3-day training for their spouses in order to revitalise an ailing centre.

The Cluster workshop also attempts to deal with problems in centres by focusing on listening to the members for a day. Not more than two centres are brought together for this purpose. Increasingly, centre-focused day workshops such as these are a regular feature in many zones.

Skills-training workshops. The above workshops concentrate on the organizational and social dimensions of the Bank's programme. However, there are workshops addressing skill, technical and specialist knowledge needs as well. One is Skill Exchange workshops where loanees have the opportunity to share their expertise with each other, for example in mat making. Depending on the needs of the zone, staff will liaise with Ministry agencies to arrange for workshops in Forestry or Livestock care. In one series of forestry workshops, loanees learned how to establish a nursery and which kinds of trees to plant; in the latter, simple veterinary treatment was the subject and participants received a medical kit free of charge. Usually the Ministry covers the cost of their own workshops. In order to offset the cost of a treadle pump loan, one zone has a plan for branch-wise training of its members so they can learn how to sink the iron pipe themselves. Grameen members also need to be informed of 18 other schemes which are currently offered. Referred to as Project Development Follow-up workshops, the area manager is responsible for organizing these and finding the necessary resource persons. Some borrowers have great difficulty keeping track of their financial situation. An idea now being seriously considered is to have each zone suggest two centres from one branch where members would be taught basic arithmetic. If this proved feasible, then the training would be offered more widely.

Focus on Women. The United Nations Decade for Women from 1975 to 1985 highlighted women's socio-economic position in its declaration: "Women do two-thirds of the world's work, earn 10% of its income and own 1% of its property." Grameen Bank has been among the first to recognize this in practical action and outreach on a significant scale. It is also a firm belief of the Bank that access to social development is through women. Programmes for women are considered more cost-effective for the long-term consideration of benefit to families and communities. Also, there simply are not the funds available to run an equivalent programme for men at this time. The decision to direct social development programmes more intensively to women rests on their socio-economic situation, their primary concern for family welfare and their role in transferring attitudes and knowledge to their children. Poverty and hunger strike women more harshly and acutely than anyone else. Thus, when given an opportunity, women put up a more determined fight against it. In the Bank's experience, women use their earnings for the family in terms of permanent housing, clothing, nutrition, education which all add up to health, welfare and development. For men, increased earnings may well go into the family, but there is an equally strong tendency for the money to disappear into the tea houses and other forms of personally gratifying consumption. From a pure banking point of view, women have proven to be a better credit risk; they exhibit a greater social reliability and sense of accountability. In one zonal manager's opinion, "Women are much more particular and responsive to self discipline for the good of all." As women's knowledge, information, skills and income increase, so will the development of their families and villages. Grameen Bank is placing a high stake on the workshop programme for women because they will be the force that really sustains social change. There is another reason: women are the poorest of the poor and the Bank's mandate is to address that reality. Throughout our many interviews with all levels of Grameen Bank staff, we were deeply touched and impressed by the staff's awareness and genuine concern for the situation of poor women in their own country.

Economics of the workshop programme. Grameen Bank does not yet fund this programme entirely out of its own budget. UNICEF and other donors have been major contributors. A 7-day workshop would be allocated an amount to cover expenses for a meeting hall, transportation, resource persons, cooking and a daily allowance to the participants. At the end of the workshop, each participant receives a small gift such as iodized salt, seeds or seedlings which can be used on return to their homes and centres. The costs are modest, but workshops and exchange visits are major events in the community which the members attend with enthusiasm and expectation. It is a new element in people's lives: new ideas and knowledge, friendship and social bonds, pleasure and pride, dignity and new courage. Nor are they without the smaller human frailties, as participants sometimes recount. A young female member was all enthused by the exchange visit to another centre. Unfortunately she also fell in love with a host member's husband! But, the other Centre members intervened successfully.

Centre school programme. This is the best example of the Bank's appreciation of a long-term perspective. Starting very tentatively with a few experimental schools in Tangail in 1980, the programme really got off the ground in 1982 and continues to accelerate. In Rangpur, one of the more recently established zones, the density of centre schools in a branch is at least 20 and sometimes over 50. Totally, there are now 17 000 centre schools in operation. The rationale for the centre schools is quite simple: the children are the future of their parents and the future of the bank. But with 50 000 active centres there is still a long way to go. This is now a major development issue for the Bank. In the culture of poverty, the child has a role in the economy of the family. Each child contributes to survival through her or his own work. From the point of view of labour needed or absolute costs involved, few families can afford to keep children in primary school. So, other solutions must be found.

Morning classes or evening classes. The centre schools adapt to the work and social routines of the village by holding classes from 0700 to 0900 in the morning or from 1700 to 1900 in the evening, six days a week. Considered strictly as a centre responsibility, the members contribute to the school's operation with savings accumulated in their Children's Welfare Fund. The main running expense is the teacher, who is paid from 100 - 150 taka a month. This is a private arrangement between the teacher and the centre. A few teachers work voluntarily. Usually, classes take place in the centre house which is one large room or in another dwelling constructed for the purpose. The teacher may be a student with an educational level from the seventh grade upwards or a local person with some education, spare time and social commitment.

Grameen Bank's contribution is limited to supplying text books at cost price (1 taka a copy) and to the bank workers giving assistance and guidance when required. Parents are urged to send their children to centre schools as early as three years old. This gives the mother some free time and socializes the children early into the routines of school and the Bank. Centre schools fill a very real need for older children who have not had any opportunity for education. Many ten to twelve year old children of Bank members who feel awkward about starting school so late can receive at least the first two years of primary education through the centre schools. Also, centre schools are seen as one way to offset the very high dropout rate of landless children from the public school system in Bangladesh. In many districts, there simply aren't enough schools for the number of children. Often older children will use the centre schools as a place to do their homework and receive a little extra help and encouragement. The subjects taught are reading and writing in Bangla, elementary arithmetic and sometimes passages from the Koran. The children are able to recite the 16 Decisions by heart with great verve and accuracy. We discovered they even roleplay the centre's activities: one child is a bank worker, another a centre chief, another a group chairperson discussing plans and problems with great zest. Enterprising teachers introduce dances, exercise drills, plays, games, songs and even poetry recitals. Sports competitions are an annual event in the branches or zones and prizes awarded to the best students. Prizes are also given to the centre school which performs the best exercise drill. These competitions are an occasion for fun and pride and are attended by bank workers and branch managers. Visits by other field level staff are quite common. The centre house and the centre school quickly become the social centre in people's lives.

Productive children. The Bank is aware that in a society with no old-age security coming from the State, people naturally look to their children for their future survival. They have done this for generations. In explaining to members why children should be productive, one zonal manager reasoned, "You must encourage your children to be enterprising. From your profit or from the Children's Welfare Fund, give your children some money so that they can keep chickens and sell eggs. You can also give the children seeds or plants to cultivate and earn profit from it. Assist in every way to keep your children in the centre school. They should have at least first grade and know how to write their name, but I will be happy to see them having finished primary education when I come back in five years. Keep the slogans in practice so that your children become good Grameen Bank members. Don't expect your children to feed you when you are old unless you educate them. Children will destroy your savings if you don't invest in them now. They are your asset."

Supplies and skill-training. With the many initiatives in the centres and the increasing number of joint enterprises, there is a growing demand for supplies and skill acquisition of various kinds. At first, the Bank met these demands as special requests from the Centres, and this continues to be the practice. However, with certain requests reappearing on a regular basis, it was more efficient to consolidate a programme for some services. The overall coordination and continued development of these programmes is the responsibility of the Special Programmes Unit of the Training Department. The provision of seeds and seedlings is one example. Well in advance of the planting season, bank workers take orders from the centres for the planting requirements for the vegetable gardens. The need is on such a scale that the Bank can make bulk purchases which allows it to sell the item at cost to the members. The delivery of textbooks to the centre schools is another regular supply service. Also, the Bank either supplies or assists the centres in obtaining supplies of items such as cement slabs for pit latrines, tubewell equipment, water pumps, power tillers, roofing, beehives, pigeon houses, incubators, chicks and ducklings, iodized salt and alum for water purification. When a specialized service or knowledge is required in the field of horticulture or husbandry for example, the role of the bank worker is to refer the members to the nearest qualified agency for help.

Specialized skill training is arranged for members when the need for it clearly emerges or when it is directly requested by the loanees. The policy is not to push skill development, but to support it when centre members are ready for it. For example, a women's centre which had invested in rice husking machinery wasn't able to maintain the equipment themselves. Grameen Bank arranged for a mechanic to spend a few days training members at their centre. this type of training will be handled by the centre itself; the Bank's role will be to help facilitate the arrangements. It is important to note that Grameen Bank does not predecide or predetermine skill training needs. The needs that emerge are based on the skills people already have or on skills they can easily acquire and use productively.

In Chittagong, the zonal manager had organized in 1986, on a trial basis, a short course in beekeeping for women. Although a few women had expressed interest in beekeeping training, for some it involved acquiring an entirely new skill. Since this activity has a relatively high income for a relatively low investment, with the added advantage of being located near or on women's homesteads, it proved to be a particularly appropriate income-generating enterprise. Although beekeeping requires skill, it requires very little labour. Considered exploratory at the time, this training has now become one of the eighteen schemes the Special Programmes Unit offers the loanees. Implemented through the area office, these Project Development Follow-up workshops provide information and skill-training in varied areas from the treadle pumps, pedal threshers and winnowing machines to making soya milk. Having immediate relevance to people's life situation, this knowledge allows the loanee options to supplement or diversify productivity, to decrease labour, to increase efficiency, to augment nutrition at a negligible cost among others. Loans are available for many of these activities thus complementing the skill acquisition and vice-versa.

Pay for what you get. It is the Bank's unwritten policy that nothing should be given for free. An important part of the motivation for productivity and effective resource utilization is that members pay for what they get--even if it is a token amount. An equally important consideration is the Bank's necessity to recover its costs. Therefore, items such as alum and seed packets or seedlings and textbooks are sold at cost price. For many items the cost is set at one taka for convenience. In some cases, members also pay the costs incurred for specialized skill-training courses such as the fees and transportation of trainers. This is a policy the members seem to accept as fair and sound. Nevertheless, the Bank anticipates to be able to finance its basic social development programme itself by 1995.

PROCESS IN WORKSHOPS

We have just discussed the relationship between the economic and social development programmes of Grameen Bank and the participatory processes they elicit in groups and centres. We mentioned that the 7-day workshops for women play a particularly central role. In fact, they may be seen as the foundation of the social development programme in Grameen Bank. In the following we examine in more detail the organization of the 7-day workshops, its agenda and the communication methods employed.

The overall organizing of the workshops is the responsibility of social development officers who are called programme assistants in the Bank's designation of staff positions. In Grameen Bank, the position of social development officers is entrusted only to women. These officers coordinate with the branches throughout the zone to determine which require 7-day workshops. They analyze the information, decide how many workshops are possible and in which branches for their zone. They may arrange for outside experts in various fields such as agriculture or health to attend a particular workshop session. The social development officers develop a workshop plan for a year in advance which is submitted to head office for allocation of funds. Soon this function is expected to be transferred to the zonal office. Once a

131

workshop is confirmed, it is up to the branch to find an available space where the workshop can take place. Sometimes the workshop takes place in the branch office itself, if no other suitable premise is available. The staff gladly make do and adjust. In the course of their duties, the Bank workers inform the selected centres about the workshop, requesting them to choose one or two women to attend.

THE 7-DAY WORKSHOP

All these workshops are run by the Special Programme Units in the zonal offices. Due to the limitation in funding and staffing, the workshops cannot possibly include every single loanee. To take advantage of a multiplier potential, selection of participants is generally limited to women holding a leadership function in the centres. In order of preference, these are centre chiefs, deputy centre chiefs, group chairpersons or group secretaries. Normally, the 7-day workshops comprise centre chiefs from 35 centres. In some cases, two women may participate from one centre. However, the overriding rule is that if anyone in the centre has participated in a workshop once, she becomes ineligible to attend any future workshops. In this way, no one leadership function in a centre can acquire an elevated status with regard to access to knowledge or participation in the workshops. Too often in development training projects for women, the situation arises where participation in one training programme leads to a person's successive participation in others. The effect of the Bank's procedure is a horizontal deepening of information at the centre level along with continued access to the most recent information being offered in the workshops.

Workshops begin early in the morning around 7.30 am and finish by 4.00 pm in the afternoon. Women travel to and from their own homesteads every day. Breakfast, lunch and tea in the afternoon are served daily at the workshop. The branch office hires a cook for the duration and everyone eats together-- participants and staff. No exceptions are made for minor differences in the food preferences of Muslims, Hindus or Buddhists, and this has not proved problematic. To be identified as a group that "eats together" is culturally very significant. The rule is we all eat together and we all eat simply.

Seven groups of five. When the women first arrive for the workshop, they are required to form seven groups of five, each with a group chairperson and secretary just as the practice is in the centres. From the group chairpersons a "centre chief" is elected for the day, so there is a different "centre chief" for each day of the workshop. Not only does this maximize learning but also reinforces the rule in Grameen Bank about rotating the leadership function. If there is one word that expresses the core principle of the Bank, it is discipline, in this case, learning the discipline of leadership.

Each morning and afternoon session of the workshop begins and ends with simple exercises. Once the participants have taken their places in the workshop, the "centre chief" approaches the social development officer and asks permission to open the meeting. She then proceeds to conduct the exercise drill and also lead an oral drill based on the 16 Decisions. The decisions are shouted in unison as slogans, and new ones emerging from the workshop are freely added. In a society where the vast majority of people and women in particular are illiterate, the most effective, and certainly the most practical learning medium, is the slogan. As an aid, it costs nothing. Shouting slogans together is a memory drill which also reinforces the message socially. It is a reminder of one's collective responsibility for social development. It provides a simple collective feeling of confidence.

Testing the learning. As a rule, the zonal manager attends the first and last day of a 7-day workshop. On the first day, he gives an inaugural address. On the last day, he tests in an informal way what the loanees have learned in the workshop. This is not a token visit by a senior staff member. On the contrary, the zonal manager spends most of the day actively engaged in the workshop: motivating the participants, providing new information, discussing successes and problems in other centres. We have observed this in a series of workshops each taking place in a different zone with its own zonal manager.

Zonal managers, other senior field staff and the social development officers, in other words all those directly involved with the 7-day workshops, carry out four main functions: motivation, confidence-building, information transmission and promoting information exchange. Zonal managers will urge the participants to be more productive, to increase their assets, to be sure to save a little. They will offer advice on a variety of topics related to Grameen Bank rules and regulations, income-generating activities and the 16 Decisions. They are never negative about members' accomplishments; first they congratulate the women and only then do they proceed to encourage even further achievements. However, further achievements can't take place without some information inputs. The zonal manager does this by providing examples, by giving analogies, by reviewing the experiences of other loanees, by taking up issues of great concern to the women such as dowryless marriage, by offering practical advice on how to proceed, by answering questions, but above all, by encouraging the generation of ideas and initiative by the centre members themselves.

Some of the messages. Here are some rapidly translated extracts of five different zonal managers in the process of addressing and interacting with the women in the workshops.

"Before joining Grameen Bank, your only problem was that you didn't have money to start some business activity of your own. Now you can utilize your credit. It is a great source of pride for us if you prosper and develop well."

"Remember, you have to increase your assets and profits, don't let them decrease. Plant three papaya trees so you and your family will have fruit for the whole year. Invest in pigeons. It is a good business, they reproduce quickly and provide eggs as well. Out of the profit you can repair your houses with permanent materials or establish small store outlets in front of your houses."

"If you don't learn well in this workshop, all our work will be in vain. Try to utilize your loan in the proper way. When we visit your centres we want to see even better things than before."

"Love and care for your children or else you can't be a member of our Grameen Bank. Your children are very beautiful, no one would know they were the children of landless women. You children have abilities not less than city children. Now you have enough money to feed and educate your children. But also children must earn. You should have savings in the Children's Welfare Fund. A mother in another branch centre took a loan of 240 taka from the Children's Welfare Fund and gave it to her children. With that money they have earned 1400 taka."

"We don't give preference to rich people, but to the poor. If you alone prosper with your loans, it is not good. You must prosper together (i.e. the group and centre) If a mother dies, you should take care of her children. As Grameen Bank members, you are the mothers of those children."

"Remember, a man with two wives can't be a member of Grameen Bank."

"Don't keep savings in your house, keep your money in the bank. If you keep it at home, it tends to be misused."

"Now in this workshop you have made friends. Continue to exchange views and visit each other's centres."

"Educate your children. Raise them well. Make them good workers. They too must know the rules and regulations of Grameen Bank."

"In Grameen Bank, we musn't give or receive dowry. It affects family life economically and socially. It can bring financial ruin and it can lead ultimately to divorce."

"Don't be impatient to marry your daughters. If you daughter works well, enough young men will want to marry her. There are many young men who are members of Grameen Bank, so don't worry about finding a husband for your daughter. We will help you to find one."

"What is most important is to build friendship, equality and cooperation in your own centre and with other centres of Grameen Bank."

"If you have any problem, consult your friends in other centres. Together you will find solutions."

What should be noted is that people are given information they can use. They are not asked the impossible. If the Bank urges the end of dowry, it also offers real alternatives to the dilemma that presents to its members.

Replies from the women. On the last day of the workshops, zonal managers ask the participants what they have learned during the week. These are some of the subjects the women from one workshop elaborated in thorough responses: the functions of group chairperson; the functions of centre chief; the functions of group secretary; how a group decides on the amount of a loan; how to utilize loans effectively; the system of payment; the eligibility criteria for house loans; which vegetables are most important for pregnant mothers and children; how to prepare saline solution; and knowledge about medicine for hookworm.

Although this list of replies is not exhaustive, it should adequately dispel any lingering assumptions we might hold about rural people's ability to understand credit or other issues on many levels of complexity. Around the topic of credit, loanees are engaged with matters of profit and loss, investment, repayment, decision-making, management, and the implications for the long-term.

Some women expressed their feelings of both anxiety and happiness at attending the workshop. There is both exhilaration and pride in their faces, a foresightedness rare for the poor in a Muslim society.

135

Ducks eat much. Emphasized in one of the workshops was the importance of iodized salt in the prevention of goitre which was a main problem in the area. Along with her per diem, each woman received a kilo package of iodized salt to take home at the end of the workshop. It was quite a common practice at the conclusion of workshops to distribute either iodized salt, seed packages or tree seedlings to each of the participants. In this workshop, the zonal manager took the occasion to check on the progress of Thai ducks which had been purchased by a few of the women. Although the ducks and their eggs were bigger, the women said that they ate everything in sight. This was proving problematic. We couldn't help being impressed by the zonal manager's awareness of that level of detail and his obvious interest in having reliable feedback. It's not an uncommon experience that the highest level of extension workers and bureaucrats are inclined to make speeches in the abstract and disappear in a hurry. The opposite is practised in Grameen Bank. As the highest management position in the field operations, the zonal manager maintains a very direct contact with the loanees to an extensive degree.

In another workshop the women felt they had understood in more depth the 16 Decisions. As a priority they decided to implement in their centres the 8th Decision: "We Shall Always Keep Our Children and the Environment Clean."

A bundle of sticks. In early 1986, one zonal manager dwelt in detail on the potential of joint enterprises which had not yet been initiated by any women's centres in that particular branch.

"Now the time comes when we have to think a little about how we can increase our production, our assets. Do you know any road to doing this? We must begin with a larger investment. We have many loanees like you in other branches. At first, 20 to 30 members come together to start a much bigger enterprise. They discuss ideas and suggestions such as joint ownership of a paddy-husking machine or leasing land together. Although you haven't tried joint activities here, they are very popular in other branches. Others think it is odd that you haven't started.

It takes strength and a little hard work before you can qualify for this loan. As a centre, you must sit together and be very clear what you are going to do. Think about it. One stick has no strength. It can be broken easily. But a bundle of sticks has great strength. As individual loanees your capacity is like a single stick, but not if you are in joint work. (At this juncture, the zonal manager provided many concrete examples of joint activities in other centres).

Through joint enterprises, you can do bigger things and you get bigger loans. When there are profits, you share these equitably, if there are losses, these are also shared among you. Joint enterprises mean a sharing and distribution of the work. However, a joint project is no problem. It does not interfere or replace your own business activity. In fact, some of the profits from your own business may be used for the maintenance of the joint activity in the beginning stages. Also, the work is not terribly demanding because there are many of you. It's a question of organizing it properly. For example, in a jointly-owned and managed mat factory, the women each contribute only two hours work in the afternoons. As one possibility, think about fish ponds as a joint project because it is not too labour intensive, requires minimum maintenance and the profit is good.

No work is difficult. You just need to see and observe the joint enterprises of other centres. After your centre has discussed and decided upon a joint enterprise, Grameen Bank will review your applications and give you the loans."

Following this information from the zonal manager, one woman asked, "If we take a loan of 15 000 taka, what is our instalment?" Obviously, she was concerned about how such a large sum could be repaid. "Yes," the zonal manager explained, "the instalment is higher, but it is shared among you. At first you repay it by everyone making contributions from their individual work because the asset is in the fish pond, rice-husking mill or leased land for a limited period of time. "For this kind of venture particularly, you need unity, discipline and work." He concluded with, "Try to learn new activities from your neighbours. Ask your social development officers for advice. Try to start something. Develop your own initiatives. Be courageous."

See what others do! After this address by the zonal manager, some form of direct follow-up would be arranged. Either at the request of a centre or the field office concerned would organize an inter-branch exchange visit so the women could directly observe a joint enterprise. They could ask questions of their peers with whom they feel comfortable. This precipitates the most personalized and motivating form of learning. Peer identification elicits the attitude: if they can do it, so can we.

As we have said before, women are not asked to take initiatives in a vacuum. Grameen Bank is a storehouse of practical advice in both the finance and management of joint enterprises. Once a firm decision is taken by a centre and

137

the loan received and utilized, the progress of the enterprise will be carefully and regularly monitored by the bank worker and branch manager.

The Bank has changed its emphasis on large enterprises because of its experience in the management problems encountered, especially when new skills are involved. In a recent 7-day workshop in Sylhet, the zonal manager focused more on the advantages of the family loan and the seasonal loan. He recommended small joint enterprises familiar to members, such as leasing land for paddy managed by one or two groups from a centre.

WORKSHOP AGENDA

For the 7-day workshops, a standard agenda exists which has evolved over the past six years of the programme. Although the agenda is uniform for all the workshops taking place throughout the five zones, the social development officers are free to include specific areas of concern to the participants or to take up additional issues not necessarily on the agenda.

The 7-day workshop agenda is divided into three main areas: 1) Rules and regulations of Grameen Bank, 2) Area visits and 3) Health, nutrition, family planning and concrete problems of the participants. As well as scheduled times set aside in the agenda for open discussion, the social development officers facilitate questions and responses throughout the workshop sessions. They have undergone a special training programme in Grameen Bank similar to that for bank workers and branch managers. See Annex 7 for the guideline used by these officers in the 7-day workshops. Since we have largely covered the first topic area of the workshop agenda, we will discuss in more detail the remaining two.

Area inspection visits. The mornings of the third and fourth day of the workshop are spent in Area Inspection Visits. Already formed into seven groups, the participants in their respective groups each visit a different centre in the area to see how it is working and functioning. They observe how the centre is run, the starting and finishing of meetings and the state of the centre house. In general the homesteads and villages will be assessed for their implementation of the 16 Decisions such as the number of pit latrines built, vegetable gardens and fruit trees around the homesteads, the existence of centre schools. In the afternoon, these visits are followed by reports of what was seen and learned which is recorded by the social development officers. In the course of the discussion, an informal question-throwing session takes place where the women confront each other about what they have or have not observed.

"I didn't see any pit latrines."
"You missed it, there is one just behind my house."
"Where were the vegetables?"
"Oh, I have just planted the seeds."

Group discussions. The fifth day of the workshop, largely reserved for group discussion, focuses on problems raised throughout the workshop as well as reports from individual centre chiefs and other participants. These problems are taken up in discussion and various solutions are derived and suggested in the resulting process of comparison and group interaction. When programme officers and area managers visit workshops to discuss issues and suggest ways of solving problems they will say to the loanees, "There are many possible solutions. It is up to you what you do or do not accept."

Specific and practical information. In the last two days of the workshop, the social development officers are responsible for delivering a great deal of information in the widest definition of health: sanitation, nutrition, family planning and disease identification and treatment. What characterizes the information they present is that it is possible to utilize it within the range of available options in the area. What is offered is practical knowledge relevant to the women's daily lives. Very few of the suggestions require an economic investment. The women react positively to this information which is new for most.

The health information is very specific and addressed to the immediate hygienic and nutritional needs of women and their families which, with some minor adjustments, are the same throughout Bangladesh. Largely using hand-held flip charts as an aid, the social development officer will concentrate on a single issue, for example, night blindness, as a result of Vitamin A deficiency.

"Feed your children vegetables, particularly carrots and green-leafed vegetables. This is where they will get enough Vitamin A. Don't buy them from the shop; grow them in your own compound. Add fruit, fish and papaya to the daily diet. Eat at least one kind of green-leafed vegetable or fruit every day. These are not foreign to us. They grow in Bangladesh. Fish is very cheap and available in our markets."

139

Open discussion. To reinforce the message, "3" x 5" photographs of fruit, vegetable and fish may be circulated among the participants. The social development officer discusses the related issue of eye infections, cleansing procedures and when treatment is required by a doctor. Then she asks questions to check if the information was understood and invites questions from the women.

The discussion proceeds in this way covering the following topics: Vitamin A deficiency; treatment for eye infections; diet, rest and exercise for pregnant mothers; family planning; hygiene during delivery; correct procedures of midwives assisting delivery; diet and hygiene for newborn children; treatment for diarrhoea, i.e. how to make saline solution and the importance of continued feeding; vaccination and injections and their correct sequence; identification and prevention of parasite infestations; pre-school education; the importance of play, stimulus and regular exercise for children; proper diet, fresh air and adequate sleep for children; sanitation and relationship to disease, especially parasites; how to build a latrine; how to treat skin infections; how to treat mumps and measles; where treatment for TB is available.

This primary health care information can be immediately used at no or very little cost. Along with a wealth of practical advice which we have already indicated, not less than five different indigenous practices and treatments for hygiene or diseases were specified. Similarly, common treatments that were harmful were also mentioned and discussed. In the course of the explanation, the social development officer drew upon examples of problems faced by women in other centres and in other branches. In closing she urged, "Please try and practice this advice and tell it to the other members when you return. I will check on your progress during my field visits to your centres."

Family planning. For many of the women, family planning is an area fraught with a certain anxiety. Rumours, lack of adequate and accurate information, and a fear that family planning might be against their religion create responses of hesitation and uncertainty. Especially feared are permanent family planning measures. In the workshops, the value of family planning is approached from the standpoints of health, family economy, education of children and the crisis of scarce land resources. It is felt that either through a limited understanding of the Koran or its misinterpretation, Muslim women especially are reluctant to consider or adopt family planning. In this situation, the social development officers will recite passages from the Koran which show that family planning is not against the Islamic code but is, in fact, in the interest of family life and welfare with which the Koran is clearly concerned. Officers do not push family planning on women but make it clear that it is an option available to them. On request, they direct women to the appropriate agency for further information.

Supplies or assistance ensured. We wish to draw attention again to the impressive extent of follow-up in Grameen Bank field services. When women are urged to grow their own vegetables, this is made possible through the Bank's distribution of small seed packets. The social development officers not only make regular random checks on the participants and their centres to see if they are practising what they have learned, but also receive continuous feedback from both the bank workers and branch managers. Because of the social development they promote among the female clients of Grameen Bank, the officers work directly and mostly with the branch offices of a particular zone. This facilitates monitoring the impact of the workshops in terms of both the quality and extent of the practices adopted.

Social/economic - equal emphasis. From a communication viewpoint, the equal emphasis ascribed to both credit and social development by Grameen Bank is underscored by the fact that the branch manager and the social development officer hold exactly the same rank. Therefore, they interact on a basis of equal status while each has a very direct and overlapping contact with the members.

A sense of expectation. Because of the generous time available in the workshops, women have the opportunity to listen and discuss topics in some depth. In particular, it is the issue of the role of women that excites them. As one social development officer observed, "When the discussion is about women's contribution to society and family, the women are very, very happy." From his experience in many workshops, one zonal manager felt that the most noticeable change in women was their great interest in and expectation for the future. "They have", he said, "experienced a great economic improvement and are interested in further change and development." In other words, for the first time in the lives of many women, the future held hope, a tentative sense of certainty. For us as foreign observers, the self-confidence expressed by the women in workshops or in centres was striking. They spoke freely and at length. Upon invitation, they were quick to ask us all kinds of questions. This contrasted markedly to what we observed elsewhere in the country.

"Really", said one zonal manager, "the main aim of the workshops is to get to know problems and to work together to find solutions." We would add that the workshops allow the participants to recognize the problems they have in common and, on that basis, to learn the potential of solving problems through group interaction. This involves discussion of existing solutions, other ideas, other examples, other alternatives. Ideas and alternatives are not pressed on people. The essence of Grameen Bank's attitude is that people must go through a process of integrating and understanding procedures and practices and new information which takes time. This process can be stimulated, facilitated and learned in stages, but it cannot be unduly accelerated.

Decisions are taken. As mentioned, each workshop concludes with a set of decisions formulated by the participants. On return to their homes and centres, the women are expected to implement these decisions. However, it is well understood that the best of intentions are inclined to dissipate and disappear in the face of every-day routines and the force of old habits. Neither the action decisions made in the vitality and unity of the workshop forum or the multiplier effect of training women are taken for granted Throughout Grameen Bank, checking, supervising and follow up are integrated into the work practices, and this applies to the workshop as well. Horizontal and vertical motivation and monitoring are part of the responsibility for each level of operations from clients to head office. Bank workers, branch manager, social development officers and programme officers are all checking on implementation of the decisions and keeping track of the progress of members.

Follow-up and checking. At the peer level, centre chiefs on return are expected to pass on workshop information and motivate their own centre members through house visits or mini-workshops. In the course of their routine house visits to centre members, bank workers check on the implementation of workshop decisions. In the regular visits to centres under a particular branch office, the branch manager will be watching for the centres' real progress in making their decisions a reality. He has a particular responsibility for motivating and encouraging the loanees. Their performance in terms of repayment and community improvement are considered a very direct reflection of the branch manager's own performance. At the level of the area office, the programme officers monitor the activities of randomly or selectively chosen centres as part of the overall assessment of the bank branches under their supervision.

Data collection - trainees. The workshops provide an opportunity to gather socio-economic data about the members. During lunch and tea breaks, the social development officers informally interview each participant using a standard questionnaire. There are usually two social development officers working together at a workshop, one of whom may be a trainee officer. The trainees participate in all phases of the work: planning and preparation, running of the workshop and follow-up in the villages.

PROCESS THROUGH THE JOURNAL UDDOG

A journal for internal use, *Uddog*, which means "Initiative" is the responsibility of Monitoring and Evaluation which sees to its publication under the overall editorship of the Managing Director. The first issue appeared in October 1982 and each subsequent year the number of issues increased. Now, Uddog is published monthly with a circulation of about 5 000 copies. Entirely in Bangla, Uddog is seen as a forum through which bank workers in particular can find expression. In practice, all levels of field personnel: senior assistants, branch managers, programme officers, area and zonal managers submit reports, comments or analyses of their work. Even staff posted at head office make contributions, but 95% of the content is comprised of submissions by field personnel. Uddog facilitates a process of horizontal information exchange and motivation.

Because it makes room for the personal, Uddog is a lively forum. Qualitative descriptions, analyses and vignettes of experience fill the pages. As an open forum for all field personnel, Uddog covers the full range of Bank activities taking place in the rural areas.

The information gathering and exchange of information has always been a dimension of Grameen Bank. From its inception as an action project, the Managing Director has encouraged informal and subjective reporting. Recognised as a valid and creative source of information in its own right, it was also a way of monitoring problems and waning motivation. Very early it became established practice that bank workers at any time could write and send their comments and ideas directly to the Managing Director. Some of the zonal managers now encourage the same practice. As the Bank expanded and certain processes required formalization, the subjective aspect was not discarded. For example, by incorporating a narrative statement into the branch manager's monthly statement, the important subjective dimension could still find a legitimate place for expression. To allow this process to continue for bank workers and others, and to allow for the exchange of an increasing amount of information, Uddog became the venue. It is now playing an increasingly important role in the relationship between Bank and staff members.

In the first half of Uddog, the articles tend to be relatively longer than those in the second half, with the subject treated in some depth. They may deal with any bank topic such as joint enterprises, fund management, workshops, role of Grameen Bank field staff, and various accomplishments of individual members or centres. What is noticeable about so many of these articles is the emphasis on what works and what doesn't, what proved problematic and what proved successful. The essential consideration is: What are the lessons learned. Uddog serves as a way to share this knowledge so it can be put into practice by others.

The last half of Uddog is reserved for regular, usually short items on the progress of Bank programmes and services. These topics include Growing Vegetables, Centre Schools, Marrying Without Dowry, House loans and Tubewells. Personal vignettes by field staff, general information on visitors to Grameen Bank, and news about social or religious celebrations often complete this section.

EXCERPTS FROM SOME ISSUES
In consecutive issues of Uddog, a senior officer is serialising at length the proceedings of a 7-day workshop which took place in Dhaka zone. In the sessions of the workshop set aside for discussing loan utilization, individual women recounted some experiences from their respective centres. Following are a few excerpts of these narrations documented by the author in Uddog No. 16.

"Rahela Begum described her experiences. A member from her centre took a first loan for paddy husking. It was 1 000 taka. On returning home, her husband demanded the money saying there will be no difficulty with repayment -from his business, he could easily return the money and pay the instalment. But our member had a strong will and she refused to give him the money. She said that she promised Grameen Bank before taking the loan that she would utilize it herself. She must keep her promise. Her husband was angry and said, "If you don't bring the money from the bank, you cannot stay in my house." In desperation, the woman went to her Father's house. Centre members kept up contact with her. After a while they made the husband understand the rules and regulations of Grameen Bank, its discipline and hopes. The husband understood his mistake. Then the wife returned to her husband's house and utilized her loan. Now they are leading a happy life together."

"Momtaz Begum told another story. Her centre's group secretary, Solaiman Begum, took a 4 000 taka loan for weaving. When she returned home from Grameen Bank, her husband forcibly took her money. He wanted to build a tin-shed house. Solaiman beseeched him to return it. She was unable to pay

উদ্যোগ

উদ্যোগ

UDDOG
ALSO
ON THE WAY
UP

*a journal of
increasing importance
in staff relations*

What's happening?
There are so
many vegetables
in the market!
And you have so many
in your basket?!

All the members of GB
buy vegetable seed packets.
So now I eat some
and earn extra
by selling some!

Come, young man,
I will tell
your fortune!

My Mother said,
"It's no use to rely on fate.
She has taken a GB loan.
We are getting ahead
in our business.
Everybody tells us that
now our fortune is good!"

Ho Ho Ho!
Just look at her!
What a circus!

Ha Ha

Say what you like.
It doesn't bother me.
I am a staff member
of Grameen Bank.
My loanees are
waiting for me,
so, I am in a hurry!

145

her instalment. Upon hearing everything, the members from her centre went to her house and pressurized Solaiman's husband to return the money. He returned the money and Solaiman was able to buy the thread and dye. Now she is working with her money. She is making nets and getting profits and regularly paying her weekly instalments."

Following this the women were asked how they went about verifying a loan request before authorising it. "Zahera Katun said that before giving a loan, we checked the loanee's condition i.e. if she applied for a loan to fatten cows then we checked whether or not she did this work before and whether she had a cow shed. If the loan is for husking paddy, then we check to see if the loanee has a husking pedal, if she is physically fit enough and where she can sell the rice. We see whether the loanee can use her loan and pay her instalment. For that we always tell loanees to take a small loan so that they can manage to pay. Somola, Kulsum, Helena, Firoza and Alima said almost the same thing."

To appreciate the personal touch of Uddog, we offer below a few excerpts from a selection of its issues:

A 300 arm's length long culvert in Mohacardi
by a bank worker in Botkajal, Baufal Branch, Patuakhali. (Uddog No. 12).
In Botkajal Baufal there is a women's centre which has five groups. Their centre house is near a major road. To get to it the members had to cross a dyked road through the paddy field. In the rainy season it became impossible for the members to cross it and reach their meetings on time. At last, in a special meeting, the members decided that they would construct a culvert to divert the water. Their husbands agreed to help them. They collected donations and made a 300 arm's length long culvert. Everyone in the village was surprised about this accomplishment.

She passed her School Certificate Examination with a grade of B
by a bank worker in Tangail, September 1985 (Uddog No. 16).
Samsunnaher is a member of Kilda Kalihati branch's Landless Women's Centre. When she appeared for her secondary examination, she achieved a second division. From her childhood, Samsunnaher wanted to study. But it was impossible for her old Father to bear the educational expenses. So she began to think how to earn money and continue her study. There was little hope. It was difficult enough for her Father to maintain the family. In Class 7, she was obliged to leave school. At that time she heard about Grameen Bank and sought information about it. She soon formed a group and once the group was recognized, she took a loan from the Bank and started earning some money.

146

Now she is a fifth time loanee. Her loan is 5 000 taka. She is carrying the responsibility of being the deputy centre chief. In between her work she continued her studies.

In 1981, when she became a member of Grameen Bank, she took a first loan of 2 000 taka. She bought a cow and husked rice. She paid her instalment from selling milk and rice and used the profit for continuing her studies. In 1985, she passed her examinations. She is very grateful to Grameen Bank. She wants to study more. Now she is a first year student of Alanga College.

Buy land for school and fish cultivation
by a bank assistant in Sehakati, Patuakhali, April 1985 (Uddog No. 15).
Tangail Landless Male Centre of Sehakati bought 21 decimals of land for establishing a school for their children. The price of this land was 5 000 taka. The members paid for it from their personal savings. They built the school by themselves, supplying bamboo and beams for the construction. To carry the future expenses of this school, the members leased a big pond for eight years. They dug the pond themselves and seeded it with small fish. They each took a loan of 150 taka and used some of the funds from their joint account to cover the costs. They have established the necessary committees to manage the enterprise.

Marriage between a male and female member
by a bank worker in Subidhakhali, Mirzagonz Branch, Patuakhali, January 1985 (Uddog No. 14).
The engagement between Razia Begum, a member from the Landless Women's Centre, Groalkhali Subidhakali, Mirzagonz branch and Ahmed Hakim of Ranipur Landless Male Centre was announced. This engagement was without dowry. When people heard about this, they were saying, "My God, what is Grameen Bank doing?" In their opinion, marriages without dowry would last only three days. When Razia and Hakim heard these rumours, they vowed that through their marriage they would prove that marriages without dowry between landless people would last forever. The branch manager attended the wedding and gave his blessing, wishing them a long happy life together. In this branch, this is our first marriage without dowry between members. We hope this kind of marriage will take place again and again.

Recovery of snatched away money
by Arun Kantishil, higher grade assistant, GB Cox's bazaar (Uddog Sept. 1992).
Kajli Acharyo, bank assistant of Jowaira Nala Ramu branch was coming from

the centre after collecting 5 500 taka on 7 January. On the way this money was snatched away by some miscreants. They started a cabbage business with the stolen money. Without realizing it, the criminal came to sell cabbages in front of the area office on 12 January. One member of Jowaria Nala Ramu branch informed us. Immediately the programme officer and I, with the driver, went to the bazaar and caught the criminal red handed. While we were coming towards the area office, the criminal tried to escape but was unsuccessful. We brought him to the area office and with the help of the head of the village, who is a Grameen Bank member, we were able to recover the money.

Poetry from Uddog (June 1992)
by Eren Chandra Das (Mita) Peon-cum-guard, Gopia Habigonj branch, Hobiganj area, Sylhet zone

Call for the landless

We all are landless,
how are we?
Everywhere you can hear
how we rejoice in Grameen Bank.
Men and Women all together
will run towards the bank.
In small groups, loans are taken
for business purposes.
We were landless before
but we are not now.
In time immemorial our names
will shine!
This is our prayer
to Allah.

I could not even hope for 200 taka
by Mali Ferozmia, bank assistant, Cronkakia, Compgonj (Uddog Sept. 1992). Lily Begum of Centre number 30, group number 2, exclaimed with joy "I can sign my own name, my signature!" to the head of the village. She and four other members were recognised on 24 November 1991 by the Bank and received loans. I (bank assistant) visited her house to look at how she was utilizing her loans.

Lily Begum is a widow 45 years old. Five years ago her husband died. Unable to sign her own name, Lily could not get a widow-card which would entitle her to many advantages from the Union. She requested a widow-card many times from the Union Chairman and its members but was refused because she could not write her signature. The head of the village interrogated Lily and asked how it was possible for her to sign her own name when her hand trembled when she held a pen. Lily answered him: "Outside the village there is a new bank named Grameen Bank. When I started taking loans the bank assistant taught me to sign my name."

Lily Begum took me into her house. When I asked her about her feelings regarding her loans, she replied that her God had seen her sorrows and when her husband died, she was in a desperate situation. My daughter "Pakhi" died for only 200 taka. Pakhi, aged 8 years, died of diarrhoea because Lily could not find anyone to lend her 200 taka. "In my village there are many rich people who will not trust me by giving 200 taka in loan". She went from house to house looking for money to buy some medicine for her daughter. If Lily had managed to get the medicine, Pakhi would still be alive today.

Lily Begum says that Grameen Bank trusted a beggar and included her in a group. She is able to sign her own name and in addition she received 2 000 taka as a general loan. Lily told me, "What Grameen Bank has done for me I cannot repay. If Grameen Bank had been there four months ago, my daughter would have lived. I feel such obligation to you for teaching me to sign my name."

Lily is an ordinary women. But this is how unaffected villagers express their feelings to us. I realize I am not only a banker. I am proud to say that it's not just a job we're doing; we are also trying to warm the minds and hearts of many Lily Begums.

Uddog's value is not only as a medium of information exchange among field personnel, trainers at the Institute draw on it in the course of their work with trainees; social development officers read from it to motivate participants in the workshops and to report and share with them the various Bank activities and experiences taking place in the zones.

PROCESS IN JOINT ENTERPRISES

The idea behind Grameen Bank is very simple: the poor are surrounded and oppressed by a monetary economy. Thus, they can improve their position only by being able to generate cash income and, above all, by being able to manage it well. In this way, the issue of conscientization of the poor is concretized, becoming the more practical issues of productivity, fund management or organization development and management. If members were to achieve more than poverty alleviation, the Bank recognized early the need for loanees to go beyond individual loans. But the challenging question was, and is: How to do that on a significant scale? One of the first approaches was through joint enterprises organized on the basis of a centre. However, by 1986, it was clear that many were not functioning as optimally as hoped and would not offer the major future direction for bringing the poor into the mainstream economy. Below, we describe the essential organizational features of joint enterprises as first practised and conclude with the learning acquired. We feel it is essential to understand this learning process experienced by the Bank and how staff persistently tackle the most intractable development issue.

THE FIRST JOINT ENTERPRISES

Loans for joint enterprises were usually from 50 000 to 100 000 taka, with a few approved for amounts up to 500 000. As mentioned earlier in this chapter, a joint loan is not an automatic concession. The loans were granted to centres which, over a period of three to four years, had demonstrated they are well managed, observe the Bank's rules and regulations and had accumulated a substantial fund in a collective Special Savings account. Most joint loans were given for agricultural purposes such as leasing of land for joint cultivation, investment in shallow tubewells or the purchase of powertillers. A few joint loans were made available for oil mills, rice-husking machines and aquaculture initiatives.

Management and accounting. Earlier and now, joint enterprises involving thirty or more members are managed through three committees: one for Management, one for Audit/Income and one for Finance/Expenditure. By separating the last two functions, opportunities to misuse funds are reduced. On a consensus basis, the centre selects nine people for these committees with three members per committee. The group chairpersons or centre chief act as the regular convenors of the committee meetings. The committees supervise the daily operations and review the economic situation in weekly meetings.

In the Bank's experience joint enterprises fail if well-functioning committees are not formed. Bank workers or branch managers introduce the concept of committees to centres launching into joint projects. However, by the time a centre decides for a joint enterprise, the members are usually well informed about the requirements and management of joint enterprises from their peers in other centres, and from the information through the workshop programme. Although the function of the committees is more focused, the members are quite

150

comfortable with the idea because it parallels their experience of working together in groups of five in a centre context.

As it was practiced, membership in a committee was four months in duration, after which the members rotateD to another committee. This rotation allowed for the internalizing of the entire committee process--all the selected members had an equal opportunity to learn what was involved in the management and accounting procedures. It also served to curtail the formation of internal constellations of vested interests. This is reinforced by the mandatory rotation of group chairpersons and centre chiefs. Overall, the rotation mechanism stimulates collective accountability within the centre. The main job for the branch staff was to train members to keep the daily income and expenditure accounts, inventories, general and miscellaneous accounts. Once the committees were in operation, bank workers kept a close supervisory check on their progress.

Vertical process. Whereas loans to more and more borrowers represent a horizontal expansion for Grameen Bank, joint enterprises represent a vertical expansion. Loan amounts for joint enterprises are considerably larger than those disbursed to individuals. Although the loan is granted to the centre, each loanee is legally responsible for the percentage of the total loan amount based on her/his membership in the centre. For example if a centre has 30 members, each individual loanee is accountable for one thirtieth of the loan. It has been estimated that the average loan size per loanee for a joint loan is 785 taka. This compares favourably with an average loan size of approximately 2 000 taka for individual loans. In other words, large joint loans do not necessarily mean an increased level of economic stress for the individual members.

Participation in joint enterprises offers an enhanced opportunity to accumulate assets and wealth. The original assumption was that centres engaged in joint enterprises should make themselves ineligible for future loans. Certainly they would no longer meet the loan criteria set by the Bank. The open question for the future was: Will the joint enterprises of centres retain their social and economic accountability when they become economically viable and no longer formally linked to Grameen Bank? Will they remain centres? This question is no longer relevant in light of the organizational experiments now underway. These initiatives are overviewed in a later chapter.

Mixed experience. Over the years the experience with joint enterprises has been positive and negative. The thinking in management and among the members seems to have evolved in two directions. Members have come to

151

realize that individual enterprises frequently give a better return on their investment and generate more easily the funds necessary for prompt repayment. Several activities such as operation of powertillers, threshing machines, power looms and also bee-keeping and nurseries have, contrary to the expectations, evolved into individual enterprises. Bee-keeping is one example. Centres have sometimes jointly bought a number of hives for coordinated production, but in almost all cases the centres end up distributing the hives to the individual members each taking over the responsibility for repaying the proportionate part of the loan. When more complicated technology or another level of knowledge is required for the enterprise and, therefore, demands the acquisition of new skills by the members, Grameen Bank has had to take over the management itself. As a learning organization Grameen has drawn its conclusions. Some types of joint enterprises do survive. Their characteristic is that they only involve skills already familiar to the members such as loans for joint cultivation, leasing of land, small fishpond leasing, livestock and trading in paddy. Other important factors are that the management of joint enterprises be confined to one or two groups, i.e. not more than 10 members and that the activity be located near members' homesteads for its easy monitoring. These two conditions contribute to good communications, transparency of operations and mutual accountability among the individual's concerned. Without the option of literacy as a resource and a controlling mechanism, people must be able to see the activity, physically handle it as necessary and talk about it easily.

An observer of the Bank notes: "Professor Yunus himself believes very strongly that joint activities should eventually form a major part of the members' economic lives, but as a result of experience over the last ten years he has concluded that this will only happen in the next generation, when the groups have become so strong through their savings and credit operations that they can move on to the next stage of joint enterprises. Both the "software" of the groups' solidarity and the hardware of technology will reinforce this trend, he believes, since people will want to engage in larger scale and more capital intensive activities as they become better off, and these will necessarily require more capital and more management time than one member can muster."

PROCESS AND WOMEN
The Women's Decade was instrumental in keeping alive the issues of women, equity and development at national and international levels. But the overwhelming reality is that poverty and exploitation of Third World women has remained untouched. Pleas for the "Integration of women in development",

calls for a "New Economic Order" that would recognize in cash or kind women's labour contributions, and petitions for governments to remove the legal and political constraints to women's participation, survive as well-written tracts on paper and not as viable projects in practice. Happily, the last fifteen years has also been characterized by more appropriate programmes for women which emphasize leadership training, business management and funding of small income-generating projects. With regard to leadership training, the question for what and with what resources? has often not been clarified. Many small to medium scale projects suffer by remaining small or never becoming viable profitable enterprises in the long-term. Markets, the local power structure, patriarchy, illiteracy, skill-training requirements, lack of start-up capital and the conservatism of women have all been identified as constraints at various times.

Through its credit approach Grameen Bank deals effectively with all of these. It adroitly side-steps the local power structure. It dismisses illiteracy and skill-training requirements as essential precursors to development. It tactfully perseveres in the face of conservatism. It ensures certain markets for women. It provides start-up capital. Its rules and regulations undermine patriarchy. In this chapter we have attempted to describe how this is accomplished. However, a few points should be discussed more fully for their profound implications for women and change.

In the Third World, small business enterprises for women have been beset by a series of problems. Some have been started without a proper assessment of the product's marketability. This has been the fate of many handicraft and sewing programmes. If an enterprise is lucrative, men seek to take it over. Others fail due to flooding of the market with cheap, imported manufactured goods. Safeguarding part of a market for the local production of goods by the poor would require an act of political goodwill by a government that is beyond imagination. However, Grameen Bank does exactly this for women in the course of its operations.

Earlier we pointed out the major role women play in post-harvest rice production. It is this skill they use most frequently with their loans from Grameen Bank. Individual paddy husking using a dheki, paddy husking and selling using the services of a nearby mill, or paddy husking with a jointly owned mill is the most common income-generating activity of women. Considering the limited options of women given their skills and restricted mobility, Grameen Bank allows only women to be issued joint loans for rice-husking machines. This serves to ensure a business activity for women along with a market which may fluctuate in profitability but less so in demand. Rice

153

is the most important crop in Bangladesh. With such protections women could enjoy the possibility of becoming significant actors in its processing and marketing on a large scale. However, in light of the limitations of joint enterprises discussed above, this is not a straightforward path. As it is now, seasonal and family loans accelerate capital accumulation and may diversify types of loan activity within the family unit. Since the loans are available mostly through women, their worth in the household is secured and likely their status is enhanced. These loans do not offer women, though, the same relationship to the larger economy as ownership of a higher-level productive investment. Perhaps this is too much to ask. In our experience, no development project has managed empowerment of women through ownership and management of medium-scale technology on a notable scale. If it is possible, the Bank will find a way.

Two small-scale homestead-based activities are, in practice, reserved for women: pigeon raising and bee-keeping. These activities can be located on or near a homestead. Since they are not labour intensive yet are highly remunerative, the activities are considered very appropriate for women. In Tangail, bank staff promoted them when women took house loans. In 1986 in Chittagong, one of the first skill-training courses arranged by the Bank was bee-keeping for women which now has spread to many other zones.

For women the issue of patriarchy and social justice are closely aligned. Internationally, the concern has been: How to bring pressure and changes in the policies and legislation of governments so women's rights could be expressed as real life options and, at the same time, guaranteed. Although necessary, this strategy has not led to grappling with the fundamental power structure of the family unit and the decision-making authority held by men within it. Grameen Bank does not work at the macrolevel of government; it concentrates on the microlevel. In and of itself, credit empowers women. Immediately, it grants them a resource. Control over that resource is ensured to a high degree in three ways: First, the rules and regulations of the Bank strictly specify that a loanee must utilize the loan her or himself. This is backed up by overlapping supervisory responsibilities of staff and members. Secondly, the existence of the group and centre mechanisms immediately provides a structural source of strength within the community itself. Throughout this chapter we have provided examples of this as a force for social justice for women and men. Thirdly, when necessary, the Bank as a recognized national institution can be called upon for legitimation of a woman's acquired investments and assets. Women receive loan repayment certificates and deeds for their houses. They must also have the land title for the house site in, or transferred into their own name. In summary, women find through their participation in the Bank, access to a resource, reasonable control of that resource and available to them, for the first time, a recourse to quick legal verification by a national body through the Bank's local branch office. However, patriarchy dies hard and, as the research indicates, even with this matrix of control mechanism, it is still a problematic area. (17, 18, 19).

A surprise dowry. The following story illustrates delightfully the vitality of centres to cope with custom and patriarchy. "In Tangail zone, a women's centre was looking forward to the marriage celebration of the daughter of one of its members. There was just one problem. The young bridegroom-to-be was demanding a bicycle as dowry. But this was against the 16 Decisions of Grameen Bank. At length the women tried to convince the Mother not to succumb to this request. Finally, the members took the matter into their own hands. Collectively, they purchased a bicycle. On the marriage day there is a stage in the closing ceremonies when the bridegroom's relatives cry, "Where is our son's wife?" "Now it is time to go to our own village." At this juncture, the centre members wheeled in the bicycle decorated and enrobed in colourful saris. In front of the relatives and guests, which included the branch manager and bank worker, the women said, "Here it is! You wanted a bicycle, not a wife!" The relatives felt quite ashamed. "We are giving you this bicycle", the women continued "not as dowry but as a gift you can use to help in your wife's work. She is going to husk paddy. Now you can carry and market it for her."

The two cultural issues that the Bank is managing to challenge are dowry and purdah. Dowry directly relates to patriarchy and a negative status for women. The limited physical mobility of women restricts women's entry in the area of trading which tends to be more remunerative than production and processing activities. Although the data and research show that change in these areas is slow, it is taking place. Marriages without dowry are occurring and women are engaged in trade. Contrary to popular assumptions, purdah is proving not to be an iron-clad constraint. Critical in this process is the factor of time. As more centres emerge in a village and surrounding villages, as the centres become more established, the social acceptance of new norms will be made easier and will be accelerated. We suggest that in areas where Grameen Bank operates, its approach will set in motion the elimination of dowry among the poor whether or not they are members of Grameen Bank. The centre allows women their own forum for discussion and decision-making. Perhaps not fully recognized is its potential significance for profound changes in how women will view and determine their role. Grameen Bank places women in a situation

155

which requires they take responsibilities in non-traditional areas and make decisions. The longer they do this, the greater the likelihood it will become second nature. What would make a difference for the future is if the women conveyed new positive attitudes about the worth and value of female children to their own daughters and sons.

Family planning. The historical origins of family planning are dubious, prompted as they were by the desire of the wealthy, educated class in the industrializing North of the 1850's and 1900's to control what they saw as the unbridled fertility of the lower and working class. (20) Concern for the health of women and children was really an ancillary issue in this debate. Today, the paranoia surrounding population growth persists and is cast into a North-South context.

The small family argument which has been the rationale for the development message in family planning, has fallen on deaf ears. Whatever the approaches and methods, whether liberal or coercive, family planning programmes in the Third World have been met with a dramatic, continuous and costly level of failure. It's interesting to note that as most Northern countries slash their aid budgets drastically, allocations to family planning suffer less than most other sectors. What makes us flog a dead horse?

The argument has been false, not in itself, but in its use in the contentious ideological context where it found refuge. High population density was and continues to be proffered as a root cause of poverty, and the argument for a small family is seen as a main solution to that poverty. It is not true that the message fell on deaf ears. The message failed because the ears that heard it knew three basic realities: (1) that the cause of their poverty was not because of the number of children they had (2) at least half of their children would die by the age of 5 and (3) their old age security was in their children. The real concern of the family planning campaigns has never been the urgent alleviation of poverty, but the long-term preservation of the existing economic order. What must be understood is that in the Third World children are resources parents cannot be without.

The acceptance of planning smaller families will not derive significantly from the arguments used in the Bank's workshop programme, but more from the credibility of the Bank as a long-term economic stabilizing factor in people's lives. Grameen Bank allows people to plan with a reasonable measure of certainty for the future. People find certainty in their assets, investments, personal savings, group fund, special savings, not to mention the possibility of

156

life insurance. The economic and social development programmes serve to create certainty and, on this basis, a future, to a significant extent, can be planned in many areas of a member's life. In this context, the small family planning argument falls comfortably into place for the first time in its history in the Third World.

PROCESS THROUGH OTHER ORGANIZATIONS
Grameen Bank is exploring various avenues of outreach to alleviate poverty in Bangladesh. Programmes in collaboration with other NGOs sharing aims, ideals and values similar to the Bank and which supplement, complement or extend its coverage offer such a possibility. An example is the pilot venture with the Centre for Mass Education and Science (CMES).

REACHING THE GIRL-CHILD
At 13 years of age, not yet quite marriageable, requiring diligent surveillance to ensure her purity, still needing a share of the family's scarce resources while seen as potentially devastating the fragile family economy through imminent dowry obligations, the girl-child is a social category fraught with conflicting emotions and perceptions. Certainly, the family may love their daughter, but as she grows into adolescence, so does the level of anxiety in the household.

Grameen Bank cannot address every social issue that accompanies the interface of poverty and culture in Bangladesh. If the Bank is to go beyond what it offers through its existing social programme, then it must link up with other organizations for innovation and outreach. Grameen Trust (described later) is a legal entity through which a variety of pilot initiatives may be launched. One of its collaborating partners is CMES, which is placing a special emphasis on reaching the girl-child in its overall educational programme.

The Centre for Mass Education and Science was born out of the concern of Dr. M. Ibrahim to bring science and technology closer to the lives of rural children. Launched in 1981, the programme is conceived as "life-oriented education" which addresses a rural reality where there are many more children than schools and where children due to poverty or ignorance do not attend school. In this context, the girl-child faces particular social isolation or early marriage which severely limits her potential growth to cope and contribute in society.

The CMES has prepared a plan of action with the approval of the Education Authorities to implement an educational programme designed to fill the gap at village level. It tries to equip children with a basic training in literacy and numeracy together with an orientation in life skills that would eventually help them to be productive members of their society. At a certain stage the children gain skills and knowledge in appropriate technology of crafts and trades which would enable them to generate incomes while living in their own environments. It will certainly help them to overcome their present economic and social disadvantages that have contributed to low self-esteem and self-confidence. It also seeks to equip them with social and communication skills.

Rural outreach. The educational programme is made available through two types of non-formal centres functioning as an integral whole, one of which is the Basic School and the other the Rural Technology Centre (RTC). One RTC serves a cluster of at least 20 Basic Schools. The school is conducted in the home environment of the target families. The RTC also serves as the Technology Resource Centre for the community. The students enrolled in both places are those who are not enrolled in the formal schools. It is ensured that 50% of those enrolled are girls. All books, apparatus and teachers' guides are provided by the Centre for Mass Education free of charge. The Centre even pays the salaries of teachers and provides in-service and refresher training to them. It also plans the examinations to be held centrally to students. Most of the children are from Grameen Bank families.

Subjects taught in the Basic School at the first level (1 to 2 years) are language, numeracy and environment and technology. For the purpose of introducing them to technology, children identify the tools used by farmers and artisans. At the second level (2 years), the same subjects are taught as for level one, with English being added to the list. The children will be gradually introduced to practical studies related to income-generating activities engaged in by their parents such as home-gardening, bee-keeping and poultry rearing. Children of both levels are taught art, music and games. After passing through the Basic School, a child can be admitted to Class 4 in a formal school. If she does not wish to do so, the child could go straight to the Technology Centre to continue studying.

The Rural Technology Centre is the venue for many of its own functions: the Technology programme of Basic Schools, training teachers for Basic Schools and training pupils in income-generating activities. A Workshop, Farm and Marketing Centre are available on site. Children completing the RTC course are able to enter the 6th Class in a formal school if they so wish. However the Centre provides those not willing to go to a formal school with three other options. They can enter a technical school, enrol as an apprentice in a crafts centre or a workshop or be self-employed.

158

Earn and learn. In 1991, the CMES decided it must focus on the social situation of the girl-child more actively. As the founder points out, people talk a lot about women and development issues, but very, very few see, hear or cater to the needs or potential of the adolescent girl. From Grameen Trust, funds and training were obtained so CMES could offer loan opportunities to adolescent girls in some Rural Technology Centres. Special teachers were appointed to implement and supervise the special loan programme. It is now operating in a few areas where Grameen Bank is present in Tangail and Rangpur Districts.

Improved self-esteem - a first step to empowerment. In the Rural Technology Centre at Deuti in Rangpur, fifteen girls who passed the Advanced Grade in the centre formed a group. They had received credit on the basis of 1 000 taka per person to be repaid in weekly instalments. An interest of 16% was being charged. A four-day workshop had been held prior to disbursing the loans in February this year for the prospective loanees in which their mothers too were requested to participate. The loans had been granted in July and on examination of the register it was found that the loan recovery rate was 100%. The activities for which loans have been given are: Sewing - 2; Paddy Husking - 6; Poultry - 6; Cows - 6; Total: 15.

We had a chance to interview a girl who was a loanee randomly picked from a group of seven present at the time in the centre. She appeared most confident and answered our questions quite positively. Fifteen-year old Machiara has three younger brothers and two younger sisters. They are all studying. Two attend the Basic School held at the GB Centre while two are in the Technology Centre. She said that her mother is a senior GB Member who had taken several loans to engage in income-generating activities. Having graduated from the Basic School to the Technology Centre where she specialized in dress-making, Machiara was anxious to purchase a sewing machine but did not yet have the capital for it. With her current loan for paddy-husking, she was determined to save enough to invest in a machine. She was also doing some hand embroidery that helped her to generate an extra income. Her monthly net income is about 250 taka. Although Machiara has not been to a formal school, she appeared extremely communicative and knowledgeable; she was even confident enough to answer a few simple questions in English and quite keen on following the English taught in the Centre.

Questioned about her future, Machiara said, "I will not marry until I am twenty years old." She was quite firm that she would choose her own partner and not let that decision be taken by any other person--not even her mother! We were amazed at her frankness and more so about her courage. We realized it was the education and guidance she received that fostered her sense of agency and self-confidence.

We met with Satar Begum, a teacher from a Basic School whose mother too was a GB loanee. Satar had completed the course in the Technology Centre and received training to teach the children in the Basic School at her mother's centre. Talking about the children of her school, Satar maintained that the children of the loanee members had a good standard of personal hygiene and were able to listen and concentrate better than those of non-members. This we felt reflects the disciplined life style that GB centres and groups have succeeded in creating through implementation of the social development agenda of the 16 Decisions.

Reaching out to include the adolescent girl has future implications for Grameen Bank which it may not yet fully appreciate. Youth are much more open to absorb technical skills, information and social messages than their parents. More saliently, they are likely to use such skills flexibly for the remainder of their lives. It may mean greater abilities to cope with more complex levels of management in joint enterprises. It would increase the leadership capacity of the girls. Among their own families, earning income would affect the girl's status positively. On entering marriage, the young woman would be regarded with some respect because of the earning potential she brings into the new household. Given that the practice of dowry is difficult to halt even among GB loanees, it is possible the girl's family may even use her income-earning capacity to negotiate lowering the dowry price. In the end the issue is whether such a programme can go-to-scale and be relevant for the 50 000 centres now in operation.

PROCESS IN JUST ANOTHER CENTRE MEETING

There are more than 10 000 centre meetings taking place every day which are serviced by staff who, together, walk or cycle about 40 000 miles to reach them. The meetings are very much alike and the process that takes place in them is the basis for all other participatory processes taking place in the Bank. What is happening is in some ways deceptively simple--and yet, makes a colossal difference in people's lives.

Early in the misty morning just before 0700 on 5 November 1992, we walked up to Centre No. 8 of Rajarhat Branch in Rangpur. We reached the spot through a narrow path. Perhaps it covered a distance of one-and-a-half kilometres or so. We could easily imagine how difficult it would be to trudge along its narrow slippery surface during the rainy season. Risky as it was, we also had to cross, twice, ravines on improvised bridges made from slim and shivering bamboo poles. It was an indication of the common obstacles there are for the bank worker to overcome in the course of his field duties. When we reached the spot, women had taken their places in the centre house.

Although it was a small shed, it appeared clean and dainty. The bank worker introduced us, the visitors, to the women, who were all looking at us with frank and open faces, some clearly with expressions of curiosity. Centre chief, Asma Khatun, a woman about 45 years, took over the responsibility of commencing the day's proceedings. She got up and saluted looking in the direction of the bank worker. Of course her gaze was on us too and we all promptly returned her salutation. Next she addressed the command to her colleagues who were seated on the floor. There were 30 women of varying ages who each responded in a different way. There wasn't exactly a military precision, but they were all serious about it: Stand Up! Attention! Stand at ease! Sit Down! After all, handling money is serious business, especially for poor women, and it is important to be in the right mood about it. After repeating the exercise three times, the women saluted us again and sat down in their squatting position. The day's bank business started in a very orderly fashion. The bank worker took over from the centre chief. Each group chairperson had, in advance, collected the passbooks and instalments from her members and handed these, in turn, over to the bank worker who processed one group at a time. These transactions took about 45 minutes. He had to count all the small notes carefully. The day's total turnover was 5 000 taka.

Having concluded this part of the meeting, the bank worker initiated a discussion focusing on the 16 Decisions. One loanee came out with a problem she had with her chickens and responding with a few inquiries, the bank worker promised to consult the Veterinary Officer of the area and visit her the next day. A number of similar practical questions came up and were dealt with. The women were talking in a sober and composed manner and really came out with their problems and issues. They communicated confidence, knowing they would be taken seriously. They were also invited to ask us questions, and did so with the natural curiosity always attached to facing foreigners. Where do you come from? Do you eat rice there? How many children do you have? What kind of houses do you live in? It was amazing to witness how women, quite recently condemned to passivity and relative seclusion, took hold of their own thoughts and their lives. Undoubtedly it is their participation in the organized process of the centre meeting which has given them awareness and strength to speak out.

Following this, the bank worker distributed packets of iodized salt, alum and vegetable seeds which the members paid for. He explained about their use. No one expected to get it for free. The centre has become a mainstay in the lives of the women. Involvement in the centre activities, the fact that all transactions are transparent and equal benefits accrue to all, has drawn them together so much. They trust the centre. They trust the Bank and they trust each other. When we asked them how they would feel having missed a meeting the women answered, almost in chorus: We feel very lonely and unhappy!

When the meeting closed, the centre chief repeated the exercises and the women recited their slogans. Selected by the women themselves, they vary from centre to centre. In Centre No. 8 that day the slogans echoing through the village were:

1. *Ukko, Karmò, Srincòla, Asi Amader path shola*
   Unity, hard work and discipline form the way for the Bank's success.

2. *Gràmeen Bànki Nàri Jàthi Shosse pole Buddhimati*
   We the Women of the Grameen Bank are intelligent.

3. *Gràmeen Bànki Esseche Bhùmi hein gegese*
   Grameen Bank came to awaken the landless and develop their economic status.

4. *Jòr bisti manbòna. Grameen Bank Shàrbòna*
   Grameen will protect us. We will not leave it.

5. *Grameen Bank Alo Gòre Gòre Jalo*
   The light of the Grameen Bank is focussed on every door.

6. *Jòr bisti manbòna, Kendror meeting shàrbòna*
   Whether there is rain or not, we will come to the centre meeting.

7. *Sele Meyar Lakapòra Shikàbo Shikàbo*
   We must do everything possible to teach our children

8. *Amader Kendragor Sela me der school gòr*
   The centre has its own school for children.

162

Salutes and slogans spark a worried look from foreigners as they visit the centres. Connotations of the military and subordination are what they interpret taking place. But let's look to the origins for explanation. Professor Yunus recollects how the two first female loanees started to bow submissively as they were about to receive their loans. Instantly he stopped them, instructing them to stand up and salute. At that moment he knew it was the right choice--while saluting, women stood upright and held their heads high.

PROCESS FROM THE CENTRE TO THE BOARD ROOM

"I always try my level best and always maintain the rules and regulations of the Bank," says Momena Begum, a member of the Board of Directors of Grameen Bank. Aside from divine intervention, these are the reasons she attributes to her successful election to the Board of Grameen Bank.

The Bank is serious about participation and decision-making by the shareholding members. It is not a token gesture. It is a principle view of the Bank that lack of literacy never stopped anyone from thinking or reasoning. In 1986, loanees held 4 board positions: 2 were filled by women and 2 by men. Currently, 9 members of the Board are women loanees, 3 positions are held by government and 1 by the Managing Director in an ex-officio capacity. Representation on this 13 member Board reflects the existing shareholding status of Bank members to government and women to men.

The electoral process. Grameen Bank's eleven field zones are divided into nine administrative units corresponding to the requirement for nine loanee board members. In this way, a representative base can be fairly established. The electoral process includes every single centre. Each branch office in one of the administrative units calls all the centre chiefs to a one-day meeting to elect democratically a representative for that branch. The area manager attending Momena's branch meeting urged the participants to have a group discussion and agree on selecting two candidates. Out of the 56 women who participated in Zhitka branch that day, Momena recalls that 10 to 12 had the courage to talk. Before the voting took place, Momena and the other candidate were obliged to give a lecture. Voting was carried out by a show of hands. The ten candidates from the ten branch offices then meet for a day at the area office for the same purpose. Two candidates are again selected. Here, Momena got six votes while the other nominee received four. In the next step, the ten candidates elected from the ten area offices proceed to the zonal office for a day and the final round of voting. Momena remembers the zonal manager saying to the contestants, "Choose who you want. I have no influence in these elections."

163

He suggested they form two discussion groups of five centre chiefs, select a candidate from each and then carry out the voting. In her acceptance speech, Momena said, "Thanks to all. I will try my level best to keep you with news and do something about my area." And she does keep in touch with all the area representatives.

Empowerment is being taken seriously. Are you really listened to? we asked Momena Begum earnestly, Do you ever disagree with the powers that be? With quiet candour, Momena replied, "I have no fear or else I would not go. In our last meeting we approved policy with regard to fisheries, deep tubewells, and the 20 storey building at head office. If the government representatives say no, we press vigorously and win." She gave the example of a Bank staff member who had requested two years leave. The government board members agreed to one year but the loanee members approved it for two. Certainly this staff member can be thankful to Grameen loanees for their sense of generosity.

The Board of Directors meet about six times a year and the term of office is four years. What will this experience promote in learning, perception and confidence of these nine members? What will be the effect on other women? Although not precisely measurable, these are open questions with positive vibrations. Just the idea of women representing women is a great source of strength and inspiration to the loanees. Now that the electoral process has been set in place, it could serve as the social infrastructure for all kinds of discussions and decisions by loanees on issues of concern to them.

In Momena's memory is her mother's life at the mercy of the moneylender. It's a hurtful image that doesn't let go. Joining Grameen Bank ten years ago has given Momena many more chances in life than her mother could dream of. What is empowerment in practice? Momena's mother barely survived, but Momena copes well. Momena's mother lived with the everpresent anxiety that her children might fall ill. Momena can pay for health care. Education was out of the question for her, but Momena's two sons go to school. Widowhood for Momena's mother would mean destitution, but Momena can carry on confidently. For Momena's mother, material security was a longing, dignity a dream; for Momena it has become a reality. Momena's mother feared the outside world; Momena holds her own in the boardroom of a big influential bank. In the context of Bangladesh, Momena Begum has arrived at the first stage of empowerment. So have one and a half million other female members in varying degrees. This has been made possible through an enabling organization that allows women through their own humble efforts to open the door of formerly inconceivable opportunities.

164

NATURAL DISASTERS
- INTENSIVE CARE

*"The issue was to recover
the people, not to recover
the loans (in the first place)"*
SHAH ALAM

Up to 1987, Rangpur was competing with Dhaka as the best performing zone
in the Bank with 77 050 members generating income and assets and ensuring
a repayment rate of 98%. From May until August that year there was a
colossal rainfall recorded of 2 423 mm--or more than 8 feet. With the average
height of rural houses being seven feet, there were not many roofs on which
people could take refuge. Rangpur is particularly vulnerable because the three
rivers Dharala, Tista and Bramaputra meet on its territory. Dams and
embankments broke. Depending on its elevation, the land was water-logged
from four to five days. The areas of Gailsanda, Aditmari, Pirgacha, Jaldhaka
and Kurigram were most exposed to the devastation. More than 50 000
members were affected while 43 000 of them lost their capital fully or partly.
Thirty-three thousand houses were similarly damaged. Nine thousand eight
hundred kitchen huts or cow shelters were destroyed. Cattle, goats and poultry
to a value of 26 million taka were lost. And worst of all, 34 members and 136
of their children were killed. Understandably people were reluctant to leave
their homesteads and assets. It was difficult to reach them with relief.
Robbery, theft and diseases spread in the villages. In this situation, the
Grameen bank workers remained on duty and endeavoured to get around on
floats made from banana trees. A group of four who failed to row their raft
against the current were swept away 45 miles and left stranded on the Rangpur-
Dhaka highway. It was difficult to find one's bearing as most landmarks were
flooded over. The rice crops were destroyed. The papaya and jackfruit

plantations created by members for additional profit were uprooted and floated away in the flood. People suffered greatly and could not even bury their dead because of the high water level. Loose earth had to be brought in. A smaller flood followed in 1988 and cyclones hit the district several times. The years 1989 to 1991 were characterized by the aftermath of disease, disorder and disillusion. Poisonous snakes took shelter in abandoned houses.

HOW DID GRAMEEN MANAGE TO COPE?

It should not come as a surprise that the normally efficient, organized banking operation collapsed for a while. In the Polashbari area alone, the number of weekly defaulters on loans rose to 4 000 and, in Rangpur as a whole, to 23 000. Attendance at centre meetings fell drastically but in varying degrees all over the district. Loanees who had taken loans a second or third time were affected, but showed some ability to recover. First time loanees, however, were more vulnerable. The bank workers took on their "lungis" so they could grapple with the mud and water-logged conditions of the villages, and went barefoot from centre to centre investigating the situation, trying to find out how they could help best. They worked day and night under great hardship. Mostly they were "met with joyous tears, but also with some bad eyes". Officers surrendered one day's salary for emergency relief. Adding its own funds, the Bank spent around 8 million taka to deal with the situation. Large amounts of special savings were withdrawn by the members. Loans from group funds were also disbursed, but sometimes with difficulty because the group members were scattered and the criteria could not be fulfilled. In all, 4.7 million taka was disbursed. Recognizing the health hazards, the bank workers were instructed to engage themselves intensively and they mobilized the health officers and organized the centres in a campaign for immunization and health education.

A survey documented it would be necessary to give 17 859 members house loans to rebuild their houses. In the months following the flood, the Bank managed to process full or partial house loans to 27% of its affected members and to disburse small loans for capital recovery to 41% of the members who had suffered losses. Given the extent of the damage or loss, this was far from enough. Members grew disenchanted with the bank. Emerging was a great need for rehabilitation. The Bank's principles and regulations sometimes hindered effective response and no clear policy and strategy had been forged to cope with such recurring and deepening disaster situations. This gap in policy and approach also contributed to worsening the loanee's situation. Although bank staff worked tirelessly to help alleviate the suffering of Grameen members, they were simultaneously under pressure to ensure loan repayments. As another zonal manager reflected, "The experience of both Rangpur and Tangail shows that it is far better to relax the recovery pattern of loans during a disaster. Insisting on recovery with fewer but larger instalments meant the loanees reverted to the moneylender and were deprived, thereby, of the capital to carry on with their income-generating activities. The zonal managers had pressurized the area managers and the area mangers, in turn, had reacted in the same way towards the branch managers who, in turn, had pushed the bank workers accordingly." Talking to a rickshaw driver on return from a centre meeting in Rangpur one cool morning reveals some of the stress that subsequently fell on its members. "Why did you leave Grameen Bank?" we asked him. "In my group, no one could repay his loans. So all the responsiblity to repay for my group fell on me. I couldn't take it. So I paid off my loan and left." After pedalling a little further down the road, he remarked, "But Grameen Bank is changing its policy now and I am going to rejoin." At that time, the safety net of the group and emergency funds could not handle the accumulating debt load of the centre members and the stress obviously fragments the group itself. If the instalment is the heartbeat of the Bank, the group itself is the heart.

In 1990, the zonal manager reported to the yearly conference the measures and approach he was taking and voiced expectations of improvement, but a year later this still had not happened and it was likely the Bank would face huge final losses. At the following zonal managers' conference in 1991, the grave situation in Rangpur came up for general discussion. Some advised that the zone should be divided; others recommended that the groups should be completely reformed. But there was general agreement that continued relief would not solve the problem.

It became clear that a special recovery programme had to be conceived and implemented. Rangpur should be considered an intensive care unit, exempt from many of the Bank's restrictions. Although the content of the recovery programme was not yet clear in detail, some decisions were in place. Firstly, the main policy principle was established: The primary issue was to recover people, so that they could recover their capital base and eventually pay back their loans. This would require the Bank to make fresh capital available for Rangpur, recognizing it as a high-risk venture that required bold action to get the economy of the members going again. Secondly, a new zonal manager was appointed towards the end of 1991 and given special powers. He declared immediately: No Grameen member and family shall go hungry. If they are hungry, they shall be given 300 taka in a food loan to be recovered by 1% weekly instalments. Such loans were issued in a total sum of 5.4 million taka to more than 18 000 people. But that was a stopgap only. A more comprehensive approach had to be developed.

FROM RELIEF TO DISASTER FUND
At quite an early stage after the flood in 1987, a consignment of World Food Programme wheat was allocated to the Grameen Bank (about 10 000 tonnes) for immediate distribution among its flood-affected members. Since it is the Bank's adamant principle that it shall not be connected with charity and free give-aways, it was decided that the bank workers should suggest to members to pay, voluntarily, the value of the wheat donation so it could be used as a fund in any future emergencies. Payment should be made after the harvest. As anticipated, most members responded positively to the suggestion. This was the beginning of the accumulation of monies in decentralized disaster funds. Subsequently, a centralized disaster fund was added. Members paid 120 taka for 31 kg. of wheat to the central disaster fund, 10 taka to their centre and one taka each for packets of alum for water purification or saline solutions against diarrhoea. Both at head office and in the zones, bank workers worked day and night to prepare such packets which were distributed in hundreds of thousands. The Bank's effective and reliable distribution of relief supplies was publicly praised both by international organizations and government agencies. On top of it, in Rangpur alone, 45 million taka was accumulated in disaster funds for future use. Seven other zones now have such funds. When a cyclonic storm struck the coast of Bangladesh in 1991, Grameen was prepared and could allocate its own funds for procurement of relief supplies which were again recycled into appropriations for future disasters. Again, it appears that Grameen's principled view led to organizational innovation that put other well-meaning, but unthought-out humanitarian efforts to shame. Especially in the field of relief, denigration of people's dignity is the hidden human cost overlooked in the total devastation.

RANGPUR : SPECIAL REHABILITATION PROGRAMME
But the ailing zone was in need of more ingenuity, a comprehensive and coherent effort addressing a variety of member needs. The zonal manager decided he must start with the grassroots to get a real picture of the situation. Re-establishing functioning groups and centres was the primary task. He embarked on a two-month intensive round of hearings. Members and staff at all levels were invited to come forth with their needs, problems and ideas for solutions. In January and February 1992, the zonal manager met with all staff area-wise and held four-hour talks with all centre chiefs in every branch office of the zone. Following this, he held a long series of one day "gotcha" or grassroots workshops with centre members. Relevant branch managers, area managers, officers and staff participated in the deliberations about what to do. The first session of the Gotcha workshop lasted from 0800 to 1400 and included taking lunch together. For the second session, from 1500 to 1700, spouses of

members were invited to participate in the discussions and tea was served for everyone. Listening first was the order of the day. To recover people, staff had to listen to them. Bank staff readily accepted criticism and elicited opinions and proposals. In this manner, channels of communication were cleared. People's needs and the Bank's possible responses to these were brought forward. A variety of practical loan types were discussed and solutions proposed. The outline of a special rehabilitation programme began to emerge having the following main features:

(a)   To re-establish themselves, the members required basic food security.
(b)   To recover their lost capital, members must have access to new loans and an appropriate scheme for settling old debt.
(c)   To get their economy going, they needed some inputs of appropriate and economically feasible technology such as treadle pumps and threshing machines.
(d)   There was need for schemes to recover lost livestock and land.

It was recognized that to retain the trust of the members, the Bank had to enact a recovery programme quickly. It had to be prepared to accept some risks and losses and to suspend, temporarily, some of its established procedures and principles. There was much to lose. Although some branches marginally affected by the flood still performed reasonably well, there were others where attendance in centres was as low as 10 to 20% with the weekly default rates soaring. Yet, it was clear in general that members felt bad about not paying their dues. They recognized it was important for the future of the Bank and themselves that as much money as possible was recovered. After some initial field testing, the special programme took the following form:

Food stock loan. To ensure a measure of food security for the future, it was necessary for members to keep a rolling stock of rice, wheat or other edibles. At the same time, it became clear that this stock could not be kept as a dead investment depreciating through exposure to insects and pests. It had to be made economically productive, adding to the family's income-generating base. The solution was to offer a special small loan for this particular purpose. This was done in collaboration with the Krishi Foundation which had food stocks available and thereby, also met some of its own needs for distribution and processing. Members were offered loans of 300 to 500 taka at the normal 20% interest to buy rice, wheat or other less-perishable edibles for processing and sale. On the principle of the loan, 1% percent should be repaid per week. After the difficult period has passed, the loanee is expected to pay back the balance of the principal plus interest. If there is a famine, repayment is conditional to the duration of the famine situation. It was the idea that purchases would be made in the low-price season, while sales would wait until market prices rose. It was further assumed that members, after a sale, to keep the stock rolling would reinvest the capital in a new food stock or they could apply for a new food stock loan. For example, a woman would get one maund of rice from the Foundation for 150 taka. After processing, it would fetch 210 taka in the market. She would earn 60 taka on each maund. With a dheki she could easily process five maunds a week. At the time of writing, 22 000 members have been given food stock loans and another 40 000 loans are proposed up to June 1993.

Capital recovery loan. Confronted with the fact that currently 55 000 out of 162 000 members, that is 38%, are defaulting on their loans, the Bank faces a potential huge loss unless an effective recovery strategy is adopted. Clearly, with accumulation of interest owing over two to three years, it would be impossible for loanees to repay their real dues. The most the Bank could hope for would be to recover the capital--and for the sake of principle--some of the interest due. At the same time defaulters need new capital to get started again. A capital recovery package is meeting these multiple needs by offering the following loan conditions:

(a) New loans upto 2 000 taka on nominal terms should be granted for purposes of capital recovery through an acceptable income-generating activity.

(b) The charging of interest can be frozen on old loans subject to the zonal manager's discretion. The loanee should be asked to assess what he/she felt capable of paying back of the remaining principal and interests accrued in a total amount.

(c) The Bank and the loanee should agree how much of that total amount the loanee could manage to pay in weekly instalments, the minimum being 10 taka.

It should be noted that the Bank prefers recovery of old loans in small weekly instalments. To push for repayment in big lumps would only result in members reverting to moneylenders to get the sum required and then use the capital recovery loan to repay the moneylender. It is better the member goes about her or his daily income-generating business without pressure and is able to put small amounts aside.

To be eligible for a capital recovery loan certain conditions apply. Recovering the people meant converting their apathy into a willingness to start again.

Having accomplished this, recovering their credit discipline was the next step. This required re-integrating members into Grameen's rules and regulations by re-establishing their credibility to each other and the Bank. This process begins with a 10-day training workshop in order to reconstitute the centre as a whole. Seven days of this period are set aside for repeating the regular introductory training obligatory for all new members while three days of training are devoted to their spouses or other close relatives. The formalities of new group recognition are carried out for each centre group. Then a loanee is expected to attend 17 consecutive centre meetings regularly. Each week she or he must pay one taka as the instalment on the owing principle and one taka as the common group tax. It is also a requirement to start using their group fund for loans. Members who receive a capital recovery loan are given first priority for all other recovery options in the special programme. After two years the debt will have been paid and the member again has the opportunity to take out general loans. So far, about 6 000 members have been granted capital recovery loans and the zone plans to include another 36 000 by June 1993.

Treadle pump loan. Small-scale irrigation is required for productivity on the very small land holdings available to loanees, especially for income generation by horticulture or tobacco, but also for paddy. Where the water table is suitably high, very simple treadle pumps can be used much more efficiently than irrigation by hand and bucket. Treadle pumps are adequate for half-acre plots. The Bank purchases large numbers of such pumps for 240 taka each and the loans are given in kind on these conditions: The cost to the borrower is 270 taka. It is to be repaid over two growing seasons. After the first harvest, the instalment is 170 taka. After the second harvest the balance of 100 taka is paid and the pump becomes the property of the loanee. The 30 taka retained by the Bank covers transport and service. Five thousand treadle pumps have been distributed and another 17 000 are projected by June 1993.

Threshing machine. Processing of rice is extremely labour-intensive and members can greatly enhance their productivity through the use of machines. The Bank makes available on loan a new, appropriate and well-tested manual threshing machine driven by a pedal. The loan value is 2 200 taka and repayment is staggered over 4 harvests at 550 taka per harvest, after which it becomes the loanee's property. The loan is interest-free. By nature this loan is suitable for a more limited number of loanees. Potential loanees are very thoroughly evaluated.

Livestock recovery loan. During the flood, the massive loss of small livestock confronted the Bank with another practical problem demanding their ingenuity.

THE TREADLE PUMP

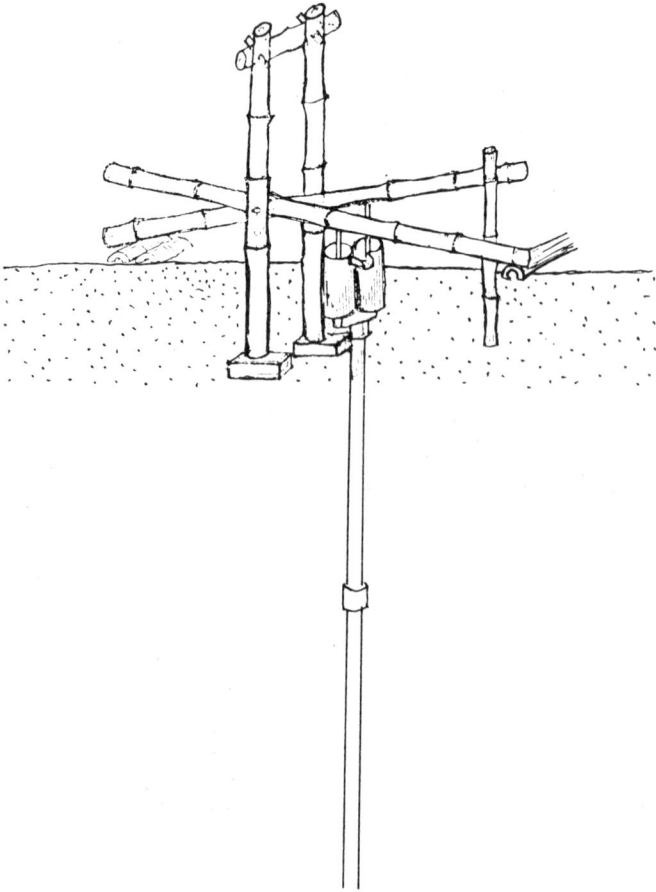

is a good example of labour intensive appropriate technology that can immediately increase productivity among the landless. It is low cost, easy to operate, simple to maintain and repair and spare parts are available. Water output is as high as 2 litres per second and lifting capacity is 22 feet. It is therefore both efficient and productive.

The goat-loan was invented. The arrangement is simple. Members who qualify due to earlier loss of livestock and by regular attendance in centre meetings may be selected for the loan. It is the centre which decides who is in greatest need. The selected member receives a she-goat, preferably pregnant. After six months when the first kids are born, one has to be returned to the Bank. When the second batch is born the following six months, the member has to repay with another kid. If the kids repaid are female, the Bank hands these over to other loanees while male goats are sold on the market. Upon this second payment of a kid, the Bank issues a deed of ownership to the loanee.

At the time of writing, the Bank has issued 10 000 goats and intends to issue another 50 000 by June 1993. The basic premise of the scheme is to assist people while regaining the capital investment as a minimum return. Currently, a she-goat costs 500 taka at the local market while two kids will sell for 300 each, a total of 600 taka. This would leave the Bank with a "service fee" of 100 taka for administering the scheme. Under normal circumstances, only 1% to 2% of the kids would die. If the goat dies, Grameen replaces it. If it is stolen, it is the loss of the loanee. Members have reacted very favourably to the scheme since, in traditional share-cropping of goats, landowners always demand only she-goats in return.

Land recovery loan. During and after the flood emergencies, many members had to mortgage their plot of land to the moneylenders and were incapable of paying their dues. This was one of the reasons for the high default rate in many branches. Together with Krishi Foundation, the Bank has surveyed the situation. The cases are categorized and, starting with the most needy, they implement a systematic scheme to redeem the land. After agreement with the member, the Bank/Krishi arrange to buy out the moneylender and take over the mortgage. The amount may range from 5 000 to 12 000 taka. Then the member is obliged to cultivate the land on a share-cropping basis with the Bank. Repayment is to be made over a period of three years, sometimes more. Each case is judged individually. The Bank/Krishi does not aim at profit, but at breaking even by covering its service costs. There is a plan to redeem 105 000 acres up to June 1993 and much more in the years to come, if the investment capital can be made available.

As part of the capital recovery package, the Bank also has a scheme for distributing beehives.

Is recovery succeeding? The flood demonstrates the Bank's vulnerability, a vulnerability it shares with most other development efforts in Bangladesh under the repetitive onslaught of natural disasters. The Bank's strength is the tightly organized branch operation with its disciplined centres and as aptly remarked, the weekly instalment is its heartbeat. This is, in a sense, also the weak point. In emergencies the physical conditions prohibit weekly centre meetings, the moral communal support members enjoy in the centre disappears, income generation from production or trading falters, and the group and the centre unravel as social units. The immediacy of personal and family needs starts overruling social and economic accountability. Aggravating the situation was the fact that Rangpur is a very depressed area. Eight percent of the population own practically all the cultivable land. Ninety-two percent have only a homestead or no land at all. Much land lies fallow. There is low cash flow and few income-generating opportunities for the poor.

Given this background, Grameen appears to have approached the recovery programme in a very insightful way. It is coherent, comprehensive, foresighted and based on a masterly situational analysis and grasp of detail. The primary task was to re-establish regularity of attendance at centre meetings and to revive the trust of members. It was not an easy task, considering some of them had abstained from paying instalments for two to three years. To get them back to the fold is a major feat. The response to the special recovery programme is very encouraging. The performance of Rangpur zone is now improving week by week. Within one year, the zonal manager hopes to declare Rangpur as a regular zone, not a problem one. Considering that originally 85 million taka was overdue, it will be a slow process. The zonal manager, though, is confident he will succeed, forecasting that he should be able to recover about 40% per year in 1993 and 1994, with the last 20% the most difficult hurdle. Over such a long time people have moved or died. There is bound to be a small loss at the end. The main achievement will be that people, not money, have been recovered for productive work in the future. Rangpur is a valuable case study providing food for thought for organizations who dabble in relief and rehabilitation. However, it may serve a greater good in showing us a way to initiate programme strategies for rural areas and regions of the world characterized by the most marginalized and depressed poverty. Parts of rural Africa come to mind where, for a variety of reasons, people face conditions of scant rainfall, fragile soil conditions and a minimal crop and product diversity.

The following sequence of photographs illustrates the flood devastation. The Bank employees went all out with an emergency response that catered for both health and housing. Food, alum and saline solution to prevent sickness, and temporary shelter were mobilized and finally help to reconstruct homesteads.

175

CONGLOMERATE GROWTH
- GRAMEEN FAMILY
OF ORGANIZATIONS

*"We do not want
to eat bitter rice"*
JOBRA FARMERS 1976

*There is no need
to be afraid of errors,
there is need to be afraid
of repeating errors.*
MUHAMMAD YUNUS

Realize that the organizational growth of Grameen into ever new specialized institutions is not a haphazard process, but systematic response to major experiences gained through the work of Grameen Bank as a learning organization. It is a series of products of the learning process approach. The purpose is to create enabling institutions. Yunus' vision is crystal clear and explicit when he says, "Our dream is to get control of mainstream economy, to connect the marginalized with major economic endeavours. There are a lot of unused land, fishponds, deep tubewells, capital equipment and people. Management is the key factor in making it work. Grameen members have lifted themselves out of dire poverty, but they are still marginal to the economy as a whole. The principle to follow in this process is to stick to activities that people already have a lot of knowledge about." In another context, Yunus states his intentions even more strongly, "Either I am mad--or I am going to change the economic structure of this country."

His focus is that this must be done from the bottom up, through a "gram sakar", an organizational framework at village level in which people can organize themselves and community resources to solve their own problems. These are wild and beautiful dreams from a Bengali boatman, a *Bhatiali* song where head and heart flow together throughout the land.

This chapter overviews these experimental organizational approaches to poverty eradication in Bangladesh and beyond.

KRISHI FOUNDATION

BACKGROUND FEATURES

An outline of a few characteristic features of agriculture in Bangladesh and particularly in Rangpur is helpful in understanding the need for an institution like the Krishi Foundation. Ninety percent of the land is in the hands of bigger landowners and remains underutilized while huge tracts of land including that owned by government lie fallow. Landowners tend to under-report their holding and how they are using it, for fear of land reform legislation (21). Most of the rural poor are under-worked especially women. There are very few employment opportunities beyond cultivation. Much land therefore is cultivated by share-cropping. The share-cropper who usually gets 50% of the harvest and bears almost all the costs of production generally loses on the transaction because he does not calculate his and his family's labour as a cost. He treats share-cropping as profitable compared with the situation of not having any work at all. (22)

Generation by generation, the land becomes more and more fragmented. Many holdings are too small and inconveniently composed to be economically viable production units. Access to water is a constant source of social conflict. Tubewells, capital equipment, agricultural research institutions and extension services are frequently underutilized due to poor management. The farmers are skilled at the techniques of growing rice and prefer doing that in their own way. The new High Yield Variety (HYV) technology, a package of inputs such as fertilizer, seeds, insecticides and water is rarely applied in share-cropping situations as the share-cropper cannot afford the high costs of the package.

Crop diversification is necessary both for nutritional and economic reasons. Sugarcane, maize, potatoes, wheat, mustard, soya beans, pulses, banana or vegetables have the potential for better soil utilization and general profitability. Although crop diversification faces many problems, they can be overcome. While marketing systems for rice are in place, marketing of other and especially perishable crops is difficult. Non-rice crops cannot easily be grown on a large scale individually. Bringing a new plot under non-rice cultivation means the rice area has to be decreased. An isolated plot of non-rice crop will easily be submerged by water from the surrounding rice fields, and the soil will have a too-high moisture content for several types of crops. This is a water management problem that must be resolved. Similarly, studies show that management is the critical factor in irrigation schemes. The rural elite use irrigation to reinforce their relative advantage by strongly influencing decisions on how scarce water is allocated and how turnouts are relocated to better serve

178

Certificate of Incorporation

No...*त্মাটি৩ ২৩৫(০৭)/৯১*...of 19~~—~~ ~~19~~

I hereby certify *that* GRAMEEN KRISHI

FOUNDATION.   x

....

is this day incorporated under the Companies Act (Act **VII**)

of 1913 and that the Company is Limited.

Given under my hand at Dhaka

this Tenth *day of* December

One *thousand nine hundred and* Ninety. one.

Registrar of Joint Stock Companies
Bangladesh.

Like the Grameen Krishi Foundation, all entities in the Grameen family of organizations are or will be registered as independent companies. These collaborate closely with Grameen Bank, but the Bank is not, economically or otherwise, directly liable for their actions.

179

their own land. (23) Conflict is unevenly distributed. The data indicate that farmers at the midstream position of the distribution system experience more conflict and problems than others. Farmers with "low" level of water adequacy for cropping have more conflict than farmers who have a "high" level of water adequacy. It is clear that successful irrigation schemes ultimately depend on their social acceptability and participation by the farmers, which again is an issue of organizing, facilitation and management skills.

Although share-cropping is an exploitative system, it is a tested one that may be justified in a labour-surplus economy like Bangladesh. The issue may be not to scrap it for some unproven ideology, but to look at the terms of share-cropping, to reduce suspicion and conflict between share-croppers and landowners and to create a condition where both share-croppers and landowners have a vested interest in increased productivity.

LONG HISTORY
The Krishi Foundation was registered under the Companies Act in December 1991. It has a long history starting with Yunus' experiences in Jobra Village in 1976. In an attempt of joint cultivation around a tubewell, the farmers had continuous fights over management of water and crops and refused to collaborate further because they did not want "to eat bitter rice"! In response to this emerged the idea of the three-share-cropping system and later the concept of *the Primary Farm*. Originally Yunus launched the idea in Jobra as *Nabajug Tebagha Khamar* (NTK) the *Three-Share-Farm*. It aimed to effectively utilize land in the *Boro* season, the cold winter months when land is usually left idle by the farmers. This was a major factor contributing to an annual, or local food deficit. The principles of the three-share farm were: a Management Committee responsible for all inputs of water and fertilizer is entitled to one-third of the crop; the farmers undertake all pre-harvest labour and get one-third; the landowner provides the land and receives his third for that. The basic intention of these approaches is to relieve the farmers of the direct management problem until they are practically capable of handling it. In the years that followed, Grameen Bank developed these and related ideas under its SIDE programme. Both its Research and Development and its Technology Project Departments were involved in exploring and testing inputs, technologies and methods within agriculture and fisheries. Increasingly, Grameen took over mismanaged fish farms, deep tubewells and agricultural projects from Government. This led to the formation of the Grameen Agricultural Project, GAP. In 1986 the Bank decided to buy and manage several deep tubewells, DTWs, in Tangail. GAP operated in two of the most depressed areas of the country. Northern GAP focused on Rangpur, Dinajpur, Rajshahi, Sirajgonj and

180

Tangail and Southern GAP in Patuakhali and Barisal. The Krishi Foundation comprises only the Northern GAP locations, some fisheries and other projects. The intention is to evolve it into a national foundation. Now it is a non-profit organization with a broad mandate in the field of agriculture and, as stated in its memorandum of agreement, "organized and established for helping the poor, the landless and the asset-less and poor women in order to enable them to gain access to resources for their productive self-employment, to encourage them to undertake income generating activities for poverty alleviation and for enhancing their quality of life". (24)

ISSUES AND OBJECTIVES

Having evolved an insightful analysis of the problematique of agriculture in Bangladesh, the Bank has developed the necessary expertise in dealing with its many aspects. This has now come to fruition through the organizational frame of the Krishi Foundation headquartered in Rangpur. Largely funded by foreign donors, the Foundation is an independent economic entity which collaborates closely with the Bank's operations. Thus, it is another essential element in the Bank's Food Security Programme for the poor of Bangladesh. Food security has two vital dimensions: one is producing enough food to go around and the other is creating purchasing power, income for the poor to have access to the food. By attacking the problem through this complementarity, Krishi is probably the first institution in the world that has a practical approach to the realization of the concept of "food-entitlement" for the poor. Food grain production is lagging behind. Bangladesh has had a food deficit since the late 1950's. There is a clear link between irrigation and growth rates of cereal production. Water resources are available. The critical input factor is deep tubewells and management is identified as one of the key problems. The policy is to sell water to the farmers in return for a share of the crop. The farmers generate cash income and the landless are employed in the process. For food security, Krishi stores its own share of paddy for the duration of the monsoon. If there are disasters, the grain is sold to members on credit. This is presently practised in Rangpur through the Food Stock Loans. Otherwise, the grain is sold on the open market when prices are favourable. Regular water supply is a gateway for farmers to adopt modern agricultural techniques and inputs such as high yield seed varieties, and fertilizers. Currently, one-fourth of cultivated land is irrigated. Even in 1986, the National Waterplan of Bangladesh pointed out that it was technically feasible to expand the irrigated area from two million to seven million hectares.

Given the existing socio-economic structure in rural Bangladesh and the fragmented landholding structure, Krishi accepts, *à priori*, that water cannot be

181

managed selectively only for the poorest. The challenge is to forge an operational unit out of the existing mix of interests. Therefore, it established as a principle that the beneficiaries of its irrigation programmes would be all categories of farmers: marginal, small, medium and big landowners. The attractive point is that access to water will be managed in a more equitable manner than in the past and costs for the necessary inputs will be borne more equitably. No cash is required; participants pay Krishi a share of the crop for water and other inputs. The objectives in Krishi's work can be summarized as follows: achieve self-sufficiency in food production and food security for the poor, including food-storage facilities, provide a built-in insurance programme, enable ownership of agricultural equipment by the poor, enable an equitable partnership between the poor and the landowning farmers, introduce crop diversification and effective utilization of underutilized land and other agricultural resources, generate rural employment opportunities, especially for women, solve the problems of agricultural credit, protect the environment and build local pride and a sense of responsibility.

Taking the risk out of the farmer. The fear of disasters, the need for irrigation and agricultural inputs combined with all the social conflict over its management has understandably made the rural population averse to risk-taking. Prevailing is a psychology of inertia and resistance to change: People prefer the old, and in their view, tested approaches to agriculture. The cost of sinking and setting up an operating deep tubewell is in the range of 200 000 taka. Such a well can irrigate 50 acres--or around 200 acres over three seasons--but it is a high-risk capital investment for an individual farmer. Further risk is connected with the financing of other inputs such as equipment, seeds or fertilizers. Collective ownership has a better chance, but the management experience implies a social risk, with a few appropriating for themselves more than their share of benefits. By taking over the financing and management for a period of operation, the Krishi Foundation literally takes the risk out of the farmer and eliminates the risk-aversion factor through a built-in insurance programme.

The Foundation practices two types of share-cropping systems, depending on the participants' needs and desires. Under the one-fourth system, the farmers pay for water with a one-fourth share of their crop. Under the one-third system, the farmers pay for water, seed, fertilizers and pesticides with a one-third share of their crop. In this way, Krishi shares in the farmer's risk because the payment is a function of actual production. Under other share-cropping systems, the farmers would have to make investments by cash or credit for such inputs--and these payments would have to be made irrespective of actual production. In years when harvests are good, Krishi will recover its costs or make a profit. In years when harvests are bad, it too will make a loss. It cannot insure completely the farmers from crop losses, but Krishi as an institution can lessen the negative impact of loss. It will be able to absorb losses which, for an individual share-cropper or marginal farmer, would mean disaster. The Bank's establishment of disaster funds will provide a significant buffer in such high-risk activities. Overall, this is the planning assumption of the Krishi Foundation. It is important to recognize that Krishi itself did not decide on the appropriateness and priority of DTW irrigation in Bangladesh. The fact is that thousands of DTWs already exist scattered throughout rural Bangladesh; but this heavy capital investment by Government is either unutilized or underutilized. Krishi Foundation is inheriting what others have left, endeavouring to make economic sense out of the remnants.

THE PRIMARY FARM - A BASIC CONCEPT

In the Krishi view, modern irrigation has been too technology-centred. No government project has ever considered the involvement of the farmers. Practical operational questions are: What is soil type and quality? What crops do you diversify in? How do you distribute water for which crops? What seeds, fertilizers and pesticides should you provide, in which quantities and when? And above all: How do you organize 100 to 150 farmers around a tubewell, establish a trusting relationship with them, communicate all essential specialist agro-information to them and finally elicit their agreement in and commitment to a joint action plan? It is a momentous practical task requiring a variety of skills, knowledge and experience and capacity for facilitation.

A Primary Farm (PF) consists physically of the land serviced by a deep tubewell which is around 50 hectares. It corresponds to the command area of a pump station. The farmers involved are usually a mixed group of people. It may be a big landlord with a total holding of 2 000 acres, but who has 15 acres within the PF, a couple of medium holders of up to 10 acres, several marginal farmers with an acre or two, and a larger group of landless who have up to 0.5 acres or nothing, this last group being the share-croppers. Thus, the social organization to be formed for collaboration and collective decision-making within the PF is totally conditioned by the incidental physical layout of the land holdings around the pump. As an operational unit, the Primary Farm corresponds to the centre with its groups in Grameen Bank, but whilst the centre is psychologically and socially homogenous, studiously composed as it is by like-minded people in self-generated groups, the collection of people in a Primary Farm is highly heterogeneous. They are brought together by the incidence of the land layout, are of different, traditionally-opposed socio-

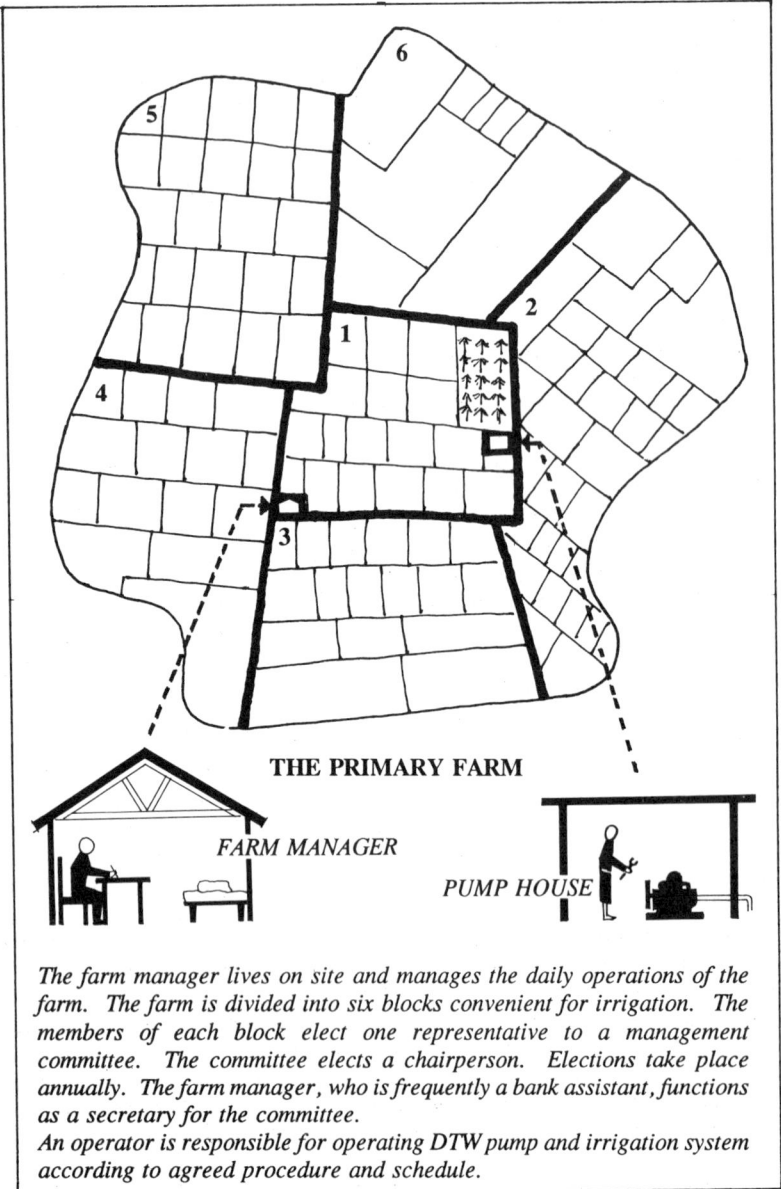

THE PRIMARY FARM

FARM MANAGER

PUMP HOUSE

The farm manager lives on site and manages the daily operations of the farm. The farm is divided into six blocks convenient for irrigation. The members of each block elect one representative to a management committee. The committee elects a chairperson. Elections take place annually. The farm manager, who is frequently a bank assistant, functions as a secretary for the committee.

An operator is responsible for operating DTW pump and irrigation system according to agreed procedure and schedule.

economic status and hold particular vested interests with frequently hidden social agendas. This feature of the Primary Farm is the weakest and likely the one that will cause much headache in implementation. However, there is a firm belief in the Krishi Foundation that in the long run the landlords will not be able to resist its propositions because it is for the wellbeing of everybody.

The Primary Farm is managed by a farm manager. Currently, most of them are apprentices. A farm manager corresponds to a bank assistant in Grameen Bank and so far it is bank workers who fill these positions. Krishi has developed a special training programme with 226 candidates under training. Another 600 farm managers and 100 unit managers will be trained in 1993. The farm manager resides on the farm in a modest shed set up for that purpose, usually close to the pumphouse. His physical presence day and night on the location is of major importance for water management and general operation-- and not the least for the development of trust with the farmers. Government officers do not live on location. The message is, Krishi Foundation has come here to stay! There is also a pump-driver. The farm manager supervises all activities, financial, technical, agricultural, selection of land and contact with the individual farmers. Over three seasons upto 200 acres may be under cultivation if cropping intensity is high. Within his command area, the farm manager establishes a list of farmers and share-croppers who want to participate in a season's cultivation. At times, some farmers will prefer to lay some land fallow.

ORGANIZATIONAL SUPPORT SYSTEM
The farm manager is supervised by a Unit Office catering for, ideally, 10 Primary Farms. The Unit Office is supervised by a Regional Office which, in turn, reports to Krishi Foundation Head Office in Rangpur. At the time of writing, there are 592 Primary Farms in operation, 91 Unit Offices and 7 Regional Offices which supervise 10 to 15 Unit Offices each. A Regional Office has a Regional Manager, a technical specialist, an accountant and two to three programme officers who supervise the production of various crops. A Unit Manager corresponds to a Branch Manager in Grameen Bank. Including the farms, a Unit Office will have about 15 staff members. There are three Service Centres located and operating in the area which maintain the technology and produce simple equipment such as treadle pumps. This system of organizational support is built up very much on the model of Grameen Bank proven so well in practice.

OPERATIONAL MODES
Although quite extensive, the operation must be characterized as being very

much in an experimental stage. The basic concepts of the work philosophy are in place while a variety of practical modalities and procedures are being tested. The farm manager holds individual, informal talks and formal meetings with the interested farmers and share-croppers in his command area. After negotiations, he develops a complete tentative annual crop production plan and budget proposal for three seasons. These proposals are accepted or modified by the Unit Office, consolidated, and sent on to the Regional Office. After further consolidation, the Regional Office obtains final approval from the Krishi Foundation in a meeting of all Regional Managers once a year. The farm manager holds a formal meeting each season with all participants for signature of the crop production contract. He maintains running estimates of potential income, based on market prices and similarly estimates all expenditures. In addition, he keeps accounts of the same. He is responsible for the timely provision of all agreed inputs. The participating share-croppers negotiate individually with the landholders or, in some cases, Krishi leases land from the landholders for use by the landless.

Several models are being tested depending on the practical circumstances. Ownership within a Primary Farm is fairly constant, but share-cropping arrangements may change. Particular care is taken that landless Grameen Bank members are given employment at fair daily rates. In reality, the Primary Farms are being operated by the Krishi Foundation through the farm managers. This has been the basic planning assumption from the outset. But experiments are going on in the formation of management committees in nine Primary Farms. These are constituted by landless Grameen Bank members in an entity similar to a centre. This is to ascertain if Primary Farms managed by such groups in accordance with the Grameen work philosophy will be profitable. While the results so far have been encouraging, it is too early to draw conclusions. Fifteen other Primary Farms have management committees of a mixed composition. The command area of the farm is divided in 6 blocks and all participants elect by consensus a representative from each block. The blocks are designed on the basis of land topography, not on the socio-economic status of ownership. Membership in the management committee is by rotation on a one-year basis. One of the members is chosen as chairman. The farm manager is a secretary member of the committee. The efficacy of these committees is also under testing and assessment. Those who are better educated, most vocal and of higher socio-economic status generally take the lead. The prevailing view in the Krishi Foundation is that there is a long learning process ahead before true participation and ownership can be realised. In the meantime, it is an overriding concern that the Primary Farms be made profitable so that an economic base for participation is ensured.

AN UPHILL BATTLE ON FLAT GROUND

Travelling and interviewing Krishi workers in the rice fields leaves no doubt that it is a daring attack on poverty. Progress is being made, but the practical obstacles are many and the battle is heavy and uphill. Landowners do not easily accept to lease out their land. Some insist on growing only tobacco which is not acceptable. Others insist on laying some land fallow. Many own land outside the command area of the Primary Farm, and have diverted deliveries of inputs such as fertilizers there, instead of on their land within the Primary Farm, and thus lowered the potential yield. In such cases, delivery of fertilizers had to be discontinued. Many of the DTWs taken over were sunk in unsuitable places, for example on land with a rugged terrain, which has increased the preparation cost for irrigated cultivation. Much land was also too sandy and unsatisfactory for cultivation in the Boro season. On the other hand, farmers have been more interested in producing Boro rice and Krishi has had to bear the cost of unprofitable investment in that season. Some crops have been lost each year to drought, flood or pests. Soya bean cultivation has not caught on. Many cultivators are not interested in the highly profitable sugar cane because they feel input costs of fertilizer and water are too high. The idea of a rotating cropping system has not yet been widely adopted. Production in Thakurgaon district with 174 DTWs has encountered many difficulties.

Although Krishi provided all inputs against one-third of the produced paddy, the farmers did not exercise necessary care. They did not cultivate properly, did not apply the inputs properly and did not pay their due share of the harvest in time. The DTWs in this area are driven by electricity. But during the Boro season there was load shedding and electricity was available only 3 to 4 hours a day and sometimes entirely cut off for several days. As a consequence, the crops suffered from severe drought. This power problem is likely to remain in the foreseeable future. Moreover, the sandy soil in Thakurgaon makes it very expensive to produce Boro rice due to its high irrigation requirement. Water loss is too heavy and hinders profitability. To equip DTWs with buried pipe is a heavy investment solution under consideration because it may expand the common areas upto 28 hectares. A plan for crop diversification is the other solution, but very difficult for the farm manager to elicit its acceptance. The availability of improved seeds is unreliable and Krishi Foundation must undertake its own seed production programme. Excessive dependence on paddy cultivation has negative environmental consequences. The necessary input of agro-chemical fertilizer leads to aquifer pollution and has adverse effects on the micronutrient concentrations in the soil. More use of compost and green manure is necessary and must be organized. Integrated Pest Management (IPM) is also an important element to introduce.

To supplement or replace DTWs, there is a plan to install 2 000 Shallow Tubewells (STWs) in the next five years. An STW covers 10 to 15 acres of land. Three STWs can service a Primary Farm. The investment is limited to 35 000 taka each year. Maintenance is much simpler. Efficiency is higher and water loss is much less. A single pumphead can be detached and used on several wells as required. While the operating costs for a DTW is 150 000 taka per season, a STW requires only 25 000 taka.

PROMISING FUTURE

The Primary Farm is an approach to solving the problem of increasing land fragmentation and the deteriorating social conflict that follows in its wake. It counteracts fragmentation by creating larger, more effective and profitable units of production. It is, in a sense, a way of carrying out land reform without doing it. Although latent, social conflict is defused through the common need for water and its effective management. The need for credit is eliminated; employment is created for the landless. The Krishi Foundation endeavours to improve the overall economic environment of the poor, thereby indirectly improving the economic opportunities of Grameen Bank members and the profitability of the Bank itself. That the Primary Farm approach has potential, is demonstrated by numerous examples. In Lalmonishat, a Primary Farm of 35 acres cultivated 5 acres of sugar cane with all inputs. The output of cane was 44 tons per acre compared to 15 to 20 tons normally achieved in the area. A Primary Farm in Polashbari achieved 50 tons! By use of the Space Transplantation Method (STP) two feet between plants and three feet between rows and transplantation in bundles of three, as much as 60 tons have been achieved. Sales value of such a production of sugar cane is presently 56 000 taka, the cost of inputs would be 20 000. With 50/50 share the net income per acre is 18 000 taka for Krishi Foundation and landowner respectively.

A Primary Farm in Rajharat increased its production of Boro paddy from 1.5 to 3 tons per acre. Abul Kalam Assad in Rajharat used to cultivate paddy, pepper and pulse and had an average income of 8 to 10 000 taka per acre. Now, having diversified his crops in sugar cane, maize, banana, potato and mustard, his average income per acre is 20 to 25 000 taka. He feels he did many things wrong before, for example, planting at the wrong time and applying wrong doses of fertilizer. He values greatly the advice and collaboration he gets from the farm manager. Mumtazo Uddin, a landless labourer at the same farm and member of Grameen Bank, now has regular employment at the farm 30 days a month for 25 taka per day. In the harvest season, he receives as much as 35 taka per day. The common local rate is 10 to 12 taka and there is little work available. Any number of such examples can

189

be given. At the time of writing, the Krishi Foundation has had 805 DTWs transferred to it of which 592 are operating. An additional 124 STWs are in use. In total, it has roughly 30 000 acres under cultivation with 28 000 of them in Boro, Aush or Amon paddy and 2 000 acres in wheat and other diversified types of crops. In terms of crop diversification, it still has a long way to go.

In the difficult Thakurgaon and Birganj areas of Rangpur, there are plans for a total acreage of 14 000 in the year 1993 with more emphasis on diversified crops such as wheat, sugarcane, banana, corn and vegetables. The Krishi Foundation is currently operating with a loss and it is far too early to expect anything else. This is particularly so when indirect costs such as depreciation of equipment are considered. If only direct costs such as input costs of water, fertilizer and labour are calculated, the picture is brighter and profits are registered at several individual Primary Farms. In two to three years time overall results are likely to be even more positive. Now this is a time of gestation before horizontal and vertical growth. The organization is challenging itself and learning to set solid roots and sprout. But most important is its spirit of vitality. We have no doubt it will succeed. Fertile ideas are being tossed around in discussions. One is to form crop groups of five, a soya bean group or wheat-group to develop knowledge and skills in a particular crop among the members.

FISHERIES FOUNDATION

BACKGROUND FEATURES

Already in 1986, Grameen Bank involved itself in fish farming by taking over the Joysagar Fish Farm from Government. Under the GAP project, similar enterprises were later added, Dinajpur Fish Farm, Ghokaria Shrimp Farm, Satkhira Shrimp Farm, several fish fingerling farms and numerous single fish ponds. These enterprises have been managed in various ways, partly by departments within Grameen Bank, partly by the Krishi Foundation. Many Primary Farms actually include a fish pond. In view of the stated intention that a Fisheries Foundation will be created when the time is ripe, we think it is appropriate to place the major fish farming initiatives under this heading.

Fish ponds are an old tradition in Bangladesh. Effectively operated, fish ponds are very lucrative. According to a BBS survey in 1987, (25) the area covered by fish ponds is vast, 151 925 hectares is estimated while 129 000 of these are cultured or considered cultivable. The average yield on the total area is assessed to be 0.716 tons per hectare. However, in China, average production is reported to be 2.5 tons per hectare with an achieved maximum of 7.5 tons in some ponds. Corresponding figures for other countries are: Indonesia 2.25 tons, Malaysia 1.31 tons, Singapore 1.89 tons and Thailand from 4.3 to 5.8 tons. A study of 180 ponds in Bangladesh revealed that under intensive culture 9.0 tons of carp and tilapia species could be achieved per hectare. The potential for the development of such enterprises in Bangladesh is clearly enormous. Productivity is, in practice, impeded by several problems. As perceived by the farmers, the foremost problem is the multiple ownership pattern which results in management complications. Rated second are the farmers poor financial ability, that is the need for credit and the unavailability of quality fingerlings. Other problems are lack of awareness of what can be done with fishponds and lack of knowledge about how to do it. Theft is also a frequent problem.

At one time, fish was a cheap source of protein in Bangladesh, but as the population grew it became a luxury, especially for poor people. Not enough fish is caught. Fish prices have risen beyond reach and fish consumption per capita has fallen from 33 mg to 21 mg over the past 30 years (26). Part of the cause is to be found in the revenue oriented policy of government which auctions off and grants fishing rights to the highest bidders. This policy favours the cash-rich middle men and local elites and blocks the poor from access to water resources. It is also a policy that discourages good management and conservation of water bodies. Government attempted to do something about the issue in the Neemgachi Fish Culture project in Rajshahi. After five years of operation, however, the yield was abysmally low, not more than 0.44 tons per hectare. It appeared the project was systematically plundered by officials and local middlemen. In spite of heavy donor funding, it never produced a net profit and Government felt compelled to divest itself of the project. The whole enterprise was subsequently offered to Grameen Bank.

500 GROUPS OF FIVE

With characteristic valour, Grameen has taken on this challenge of involving the poor in profitable exploitation of Bangladesh's abundant water resources. Neemgachi was renamed Joysagar Fish Farm (JFF). For the benefit of the reader, we shall limit this description to Joysagar where the realization of the Grameen ideas is most advanced. The first essential task was to learn the professional tricks of fish culture such as induced breeding which is very technical. (27) The second task was to establish a farm, a geographically spread-out product base, giving a substantial number of landless an opportunity for participation in the venture. A small team of trusted officers were sent to reorganize and restore the project and the initial three years were spent doing just that. Amazing all experts, they quickly acquired the necessary technical skills. More complicated was the process of actual takeover of the ponds. The project comprised a total number of 808 ponds with a total water area of 716 hectares. The ownership of many of these ponds were in dispute. Various representatives of the local power-elite claimed various degrees of ownership and the project had to start a long-winded, cumbersome process of establishing possession through persuasion, documentation or litigation. At the time of writing, around 75% of the ponds are fully possessed by the Bank and the process proceeds.

The Joysagar project is run by a farm manager. The entire farm area has been divided into 4 blocks, each headed by a block manager. Each block is divided into 4 units headed by a unit manager. Each unit has a number of unit workers. Until now, the farm manager has been supervised by the Technology Project Department at Grameen Bank head office.

The involvement of the landless is quite far advanced, while legally, JFF retains the possession of the ponds and bears ultimate responsibility for their economic management. About 500 groups of five, called Fish Farming Groups (FFG), are consolidated in centres and operating. Each centre is given responsibility for a pond. The group formation process follows the model of the Bank, including knowledge of the 16 decisions. But in this case, extensive training related to fish culture is also given. Most participants are illiterate and it may take a month's training or more before they all understand what JFF is all about. Discipline is tough and participants who are lax in attendance or do not show necessary group spirit are expelled. When a group's understanding and commitment is judged satisfactory, recognition is given. The members are then asked to elect among themselves a group chairperson and a secretary for a one year term. Subsequently, these group chairpersons elect from among themselves a Centre Chief and an Assistant Centre Chief for a period of one year. When the centre is thus fully prepared, JFF signs a one-year renewable agreement with the centre allowing it to participate in joint fish farming. The agreement is signed by all centre members. For the sake of smooth management and communication, a five-member management committee is set up. It comprises the unit manager, the unit worker in charge of the centre, the centre chief and two group chairpersons. Meetings of the centre are held every fortnight. All members are required to attend and indiscipline is penalized. At these meetings, issues related to fish culture and practical operation of the ponds and other matters are discussed and decided upon. A unit worker is present. Normally, test netting of the pond(s), which is managed by the centre, is carried out at the day of the meeting to check health and growth of the fish and determine what action to take next. A compulsory two taka personal savings are collected at each meeting and deposited with Grameen Bank. If appropriate, loan proposals put forward by members for an individual or collective undertaking are discussed and approved.

The particular way Grameen Bank has developed its organizational structure for managing the fish farms differs in some respect from the standard Bank model. Since it is of general interest for poverty-focused projects where participation is an issue, we describe it in greater detail.

RESPONSIBILITIES AND BENEFITS
With a few exceptions, all of the culture ponds under JFF are now operated through the fish farming groups. It is a joint venture where responsibilities and benefits are clearly defined and shared. This is how it functions:

The fish farming group provides labour for excavating and rehabilitating the ponds, collecting and preparing organic fertilizers from cow dung and water-hyacinth compost. They transport and apply the feed, medicine and other inputs. They guard the ponds--on an average a member devotes 50 days and 100 nights a year. They carry out test netting and harvesting as required and generally look after the ponds and the state of its fish population. They are particularly instructed to follow the prescriptions of advanced scientific fish culture and are not allowed to undertake any other activities in the pond than fish culture. Members are obliged to follow the centre rules and attend training being offered. In addition they grow vegetables and fruit on the embankments of the ponds. They are responsible for repaying and recovering loans taken from group or emergency funds and save as required. The groups share income from sale of fish on a 50/50 basis with JFF and the group distributes its share equally among the members. The group chairperson's responsibility is to collect and deposit savings, to maintain regular contact with the centre and the JFF unit officer in charge, and to manage the group fund jointly with the secretary.

The centre is obliged to develop a permanent and effective mechanism for mediation and settlement of disputes and misunderstandings among its members. It supports the JFF management in its endeavour to achieve a smooth, effective operation and higher fish production and sales for the benefit of everybody. The centre chief conducts meetings, maintains a cooperative spirit and a sense of responsibility, keeps regular contact with JFF management and administers the emergency fund jointly with the assistant centre chief.

194

The management committee decides work schedules and distributes the work among members. It decides on the harvesting schedule, the sales price of the fish and marketing strategy. This is subject to approval by the top JFF management. It settles disputes.

The JFF project retains the legal possession of the ponds and consequently bears the ultimate legal responsibility for management. It makes the technical decisions on fish culture, selection of species, release of fingerlings, time of harvest. It provides all equipment and inputs: fertilizers, feeds, medicine, predator killers, fuel and the necessary hatchlings such as fry or fingerlings. It provides free-of-charge all training to centre members on fish culture and social development matters. It pays for cow-dung collected by the members and for all taxes levied on ponds and facilities. In return it receives 50% of the proceeds. In this organizational adaptation, interesting modifications have been made in the 16 Decisions, reproduced in full on the following page, and in the group and emergency funds.

The group fund has five sources of inputs. First there is the 2 taka fortnightly personal savings. Then there is a group tax which consists of 5% of the individual member's income from fish sales or other group activities. Group tax 2 consists of 5% of a loan taken from the group fund itself. The group fund benefits also from fines paid by undisciplined members and from interest paid by Grameen Bank for the deposit. All members have equal rights, but if one leaves the group only the fortnightly personal savings can be withdrawn. The primary objective of the fund is to encourage investment in economic, preferably collective, activities. Maximum loan allowed is 50% of the fund. The group has to agree on the terms and conditions of all loans and it may or may not charge interest. If interest is charged, the rate must be the same for each member's loan. Interests paid are entered as income to the fund. The group itself is responsible for recovery of the loan and no new loans can be sanctioned before recovery is complete.

The emergency fund. Sources of this fund are 2.5% of income from fish sales and other centre incomes and the interest paid by Grameen Bank on the funds deposited. The fund belongs to the centre and is jointly managed by the Centre Chief and the Assistant Centre Chief. No member has any personal right over this fund and thus may not claim any part of it. The fund is meant for contingencies the landless are exposed to: illness, injury, death, loss of property through theft or disasters. Also, it is for joint initiatives of various kinds such as sinking of shallow tubewells, leasing land for cultivation or starting a rice mill. Any number of members are able to take a loan from the fund with the

THE JFF 16 DECISIONS

1. *The four principles of JFF - discipline, unity, courage and hard work - we shall follow and advance in all walks of our lives.*
2. *Prosperity we shall bring to our families through fish culture.*
3. *We shall not leave any ponds unproductive. We shall increase fish production at the earliest.*
4. *We shall grow vegetables on the embankments all the year around. We shall eat plenty of it and sell the surplus.*
5. *We shall culture fish all the year around. We shall increase fish production, increase fish consumption and eliminate poverty by selling fish.*
6. *We shall plan to keep our families small. We shall minimize our expenditures. We shall look after our health.*
7. *We shall educate our children. To ensure continuous education of our children, we shall produce plenty of fish.*
8. *We shall always keep our children, the environment and ponds clean.*
9. *We shall build and use pit-latrines.*
10. *We shall drink tubewell water. If it is not available, we shall boil water or use alum.*
11. *We shall not take or give any dowry in our children's marriage. We shall not practice child marriage.*
12. *We shall not inflict any injustice on anyone, neither shall we allow anyone to do so.*
13. *For higher income we shall collectively practice advanced fish culture.*
14. *We shall always be ready to help each other. If anyone is in difficulty, we shall all help him/her.*
15. *If we come to know of any breach of discipline in any Centre, we shall all go there and help restore discipline.*
16. *We shall introduce discipline in all our Centres. We shall take part in all social activities collectively.*

consent of other members. Otherwise, the rules are the same as for the group fund, except that no deductions are made from the loan.

Like in Grameen Bank, the organizational framework and procedures in JFF display a subtle balance between demand and obligation while offering an opportunity for individual action. Evidently, discipline is a core factor in an operation which depends so much on a technically, very finely-timed series of inputs. All transactions are conducted in the open. Fish harvest is allowed only after sunrise and before sunset. When harvested, fish are weighed and sold on the pond banks in the presence of JFF staff. The group's share is distributed equally among its members on the spot. Under no circumstances are members allowed to sell fish in the absence of JFF staff. Conversely, when JFF harvests and sells fish on its own, group members accompany the consignment of fish to the market and monitor the sales. Nevertheless, it takes time to shape the foundation for trust in people. Members have been expelled for poaching fish, although external poaching is practically eliminated.

ONE MEMBER PER BIGHA

An ambitious goal for involvement of the landless was set and is close to being 100% achieved. The water area of the presently cultivable ponds is 2 820 bigha or 380 hectares. It was decided that 2 820 members should be involved. By July 1992, members had increased to 2 301 distributed on 497 groups and 145 centres, that is 82%. All ponds except four were under joint management. Since then even further progress has been made. Joysagar Fish Farm demonstrates the potential for progress that can now be expected within the Krishi Foundation if it is given the necessary time and patience. The JFF project has taken eight years to arrive at this stage of technical and organizational competence. Fish production has, in the meantime, been continuously increasing, in spite of setbacks during the exceptional floods in 1987 and 1988. Ending June 1992, a total of 503 tons of carp was harvested, which corresponds to 1.3 tons per hectare. This is due to the introduction of intensive fish culture but also very much to the involvement of the landless. Intensive care of fish and ponds in a project scattered over a wide area can only be realistically achieved by the people living in the immediate vicinity of the ponds. It could not have been done by JFF staff members alone. A sense of ownership is building up: This is "our pond" and a sense of pride in good care and production. Contributing to that is certainly the good extra income. The average in 1991 was 1 850 taka per person with the most successful group earning 6 100 taka per member. This says something about the potential--and it is a substantial amount of money for members who otherwise may earn a total of 4 000 to 8 000 taka per year on arduous agricultural labour.

At this stage, the fish farming groups are predominantly male. Many new opportunities for women have been opened up in the form of labour or entrepreneurial activities that spring from the needs of the fish farm itself. In terms of community development JFF takes its social development task seriously. It has built two trunk roads over 22 km costing 20 million taka and some forty schools for the local communities. People are improving their diet, housing standard and sanitary conditions. A new self-confidence is noticeable among the people. We have managed to do it--against all odds!

At the time of writing it is said that a Fisheries Foundation will be established in June 1993 under the name MOTSO.

GRAMEEN TRUST

RATIONALE

"You may lead a horse to drink water. You may be able to make him drink water. But you must have the water." By "water", Professor Gene Octavio, Managing Director of a GB replication in the Philippines, means the necessary start-up funds, the seed money, to launch an action-research project on the lines of Grameen Bank. Since most donors do not wish to fund a project until it can show concrete, positive results, good projects tend to remain good ideas only. At the same time, the astounding success of the GB approach to credit for the poorest has generated a wide international as well as local demand for its services in training, expertise and seed capital. On its own, however, Grameen Bank could not possibly respond to the extent and range of requests it receives. Already, its staff work at a demanding pace to maintain the Bank's viability. For reasons of clear financial accountability to its donors and members, it was best not to extend the mandate of Grameen Bank itself. Instead, in order to meet such increasing needs for its services, Grameen Trust, a separate legal entity, was added to the family.

A TRUST FOR A CHANGE

Grameen Trust is a non-governmental organization dedicated to the eradication of poverty in Bangladesh and the rest of the world. In its Memorandum of Association and Memorandum of Articles, the Trust declares a very broad scope for supporting social and economic initiatives for this end. Aside from sponsoring replications, the statutes of the Trust include making funds available for a range of research and experimentation directly relating to issues and conditions of poverty. Thus, a certain provision for creativity is ensured, allowing for the consideration of a variety of programme approaches to poverty which may be launched and tested in practice through the organizational entity of the Trust.

AWARENESS, ADVOCACY, DIALOGUE

Credit is becoming recognized as a major way of addressing "entrenched" poverty. More and more individuals, organizations and governments are interested in its potential, but they need information. Those already launched on a credit programme inspired by Grameen Bank need especially to share experiences that are as close as possible to their own. *Grameen Dialogue*, a newsletter covering the international experience in credit modelled after Grameen Bank, is published by Grameen Trust for this purpose. The first issue appeared in September 1989. Now, *Grameen Dialogue* is published quarterly and has a growing distribution worldwide. Articles, exchange of practical information, personal comments and experiences, project reports of progress and problems, critiques, letters of encouragement and hope emanate from all continents and from South and North.

The *International Dialogue Programme* is a series of workshops funded through Grameen Trust. They offer potential replicators an initial exposure to Grameen Bank methods and principles. The format of these twelve-day workshops follow the pedagogy of all Grameen Bank training: Experience rural reality and poverty in person, then reflect upon it. So, participants spend the first day at Head Office for an introductory briefing, immediately proceeding on the second morning to a branch office where they stay from three to five days. This immersion gives them the concrete experience of the branch staff's daily procedures and routines and one-to-one contact with centre members themselves. On return, they share and discuss experiences, air confusions, and clarify and refine insight and understanding with senior staff. Generally, a group exercise follows this to identify the "Essential Elements of Grameen" which account for its success. Other countries which have replicated Grameen present their own account of successes and constraints. The final days of the workshop concentrate on significant elements in project design and the preparation of replication proposals. By end of 1994, Grameen Trust will have sponsored eight International Dialogue Programmes with an estimated participation of 175 people.

SUPPORT TO REPLICATIONS OF GRAMEEN

Organizations whose project proposals are accepted by Grameen Trust are eligible for staff training in Bangladesh, seed capital and essential technical support. The Trust anticipates that "around 200 persons will be provided with training, and US$1.5 million will be made available as grants/loans for start-up capital to fund 30 replication projects. " (28) While the Trust bears the cost of some staff training for replicators, the *International Training Programme* of Grameen Bank includes the participants in its on-going programme. During 1992, fourteen project proposals had seed capital approved by the Trust. The submissions came from Nigeria, Philippines, India, Vietnam, Lesotho, Nepal and Tanzania.

OTHER FRONTIERS
While a principle decision of Grameen Bank was to address poverty in the rural areas, the Trust can take on other challenges. The urban poor, the people in the Hill Tracts of Chittagong and certain corridor areas with India pose problematiques such as isolation, difficult terrain, unsettled or migratory populations. Can Grameen Bank be replicated faced with these conditions? The Trust is attempting to do this through other interested NGOs and has started an In-country Training Programme specifically for their staff. One NGO has been successfully disbursing credit modelled after the Grameen approach in a Dhaka slum area since about 1986. Analyzing credit as a tool for uniting people and creating an organization so people can participate in solving their problems, the General Manager of Grameen Trust feels this will counter factors inhibiting social cohesion.

The fragile economy of the poorest is capsized by short-term illness and devastated by long-term illness or disability. And it is the women who bear the brunt of any illness in the family. This has been recognized by the staff of Grameen Bank for a long time. Grameen Trust is taking up this challenge by a call to concerned physicians and NGOs to help them design an appropriate health scheme for Grameen Bank borrowers.

A research initiative now underway by Grameen Trust is a study of seven of the earliest replications based on the Grameen Approach in five countries in Asia and Africa. This study will allow an analysis of the kinds of problems being experienced by replicators which can be shared immediately and guide future replicators. Also, the study will lay the necessary base-line for subsequent impact evaluation to be carried out in three to five years' time. This research is needed to enable policy makers and donors to commit the funds required for both sponsoring and scaling-up credit programmes directed to the poorest. The study is asking the overarching development question: Is credit to the poorest of the poor a major way to address the issue of poverty in the world?

NETWORKING AND COLLABORATION
The newsletter, *Grameen Dialogue*, promotes networking, but Grameen Trust

also extends collaborative support to networking among organizations directly engaged in poverty alleviation. One outcome of this is the Asian and Pacific Network for the Eradication of Poverty through Credit and Savings. Called Credit and Savings for the Hard-Core Poor, CASHPOR, the network office is in Malaysia and the membership constitutes eight replications in the region. The creation of an African regional network with the aims of advocacy, lobbying for funds and sharing ideas and information is being advanced.

A Memorandum of Understanding has been signed between Grameen Trust and the Asia and Pacific Development Centre to work together to promote the Grameen Bank Approach in the Asian Region. Four projects in India, Nepal and Vietnam will be co-financed under this agreement. Response to the Trust has been good with a number of donor agencies contributing funds for replicating the Grameen Approach to credit.

OTHER FOUNDATIONS

THE VIGOROUS VISION

To understand the Grameen movement as it now emerges, one must understand not only its organizational talent, its banking craftsmanship, or its mastery of sophisticated modern technique, one must understand also its depth of feeling and its capacity for long-term vigorous vision. Set on its goal of eradicating poverty, it is intensely scanning the horizon for new opportunities, new directions, new ways of reaching that goal. A health foundation and an urban foundation have been mentioned earlier as some of the options that are considered, on and off. For example, Grameen Trust is able to act as a channel for the unharnessed creative energy and goodwill available in Bangladesh which can be mutually interchanged on behalf of the poor. In essence, the borrowers would contribute to a Health Fund and Grameen Trust would ensure all health costs, medicine and X-rays. An experimental programme is about to be launched in a branch office in Norshindi in Dhaka Zone. But the eyes are also set in other directions. A dairy trust is one possibility. There is, as mentioned, a vision of doing something about alleviating the much neglected situation of the hill-tribes in Chittagong District. Time will show when, how, and in which order, such visions will be realized. The intent has been clearly stated for a long time. In the preparation report for the period 1990 to 1993, this is explicated under the "Future role" of Grameen Bank: "..... Grameen is committed to the alleviation of poverty and hunger from Bangladesh. Ten years from now it would like to see that it has made sound institutional preparations to make it happen. Credit for the poor should become a reality in all villages

GRAMEEN FAMILY OF ORGANIZATIONS

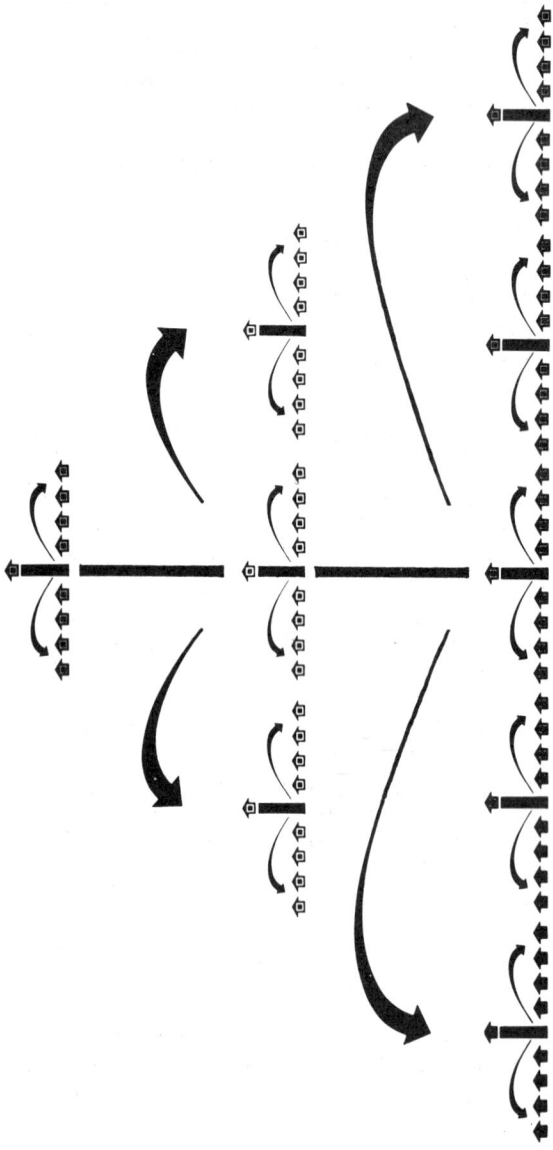

- a process of horizontal, vertical and conglomerate growth in Bangladesh - and maybe even beyond its borders? Whatever their individual trademarks are, the members of the family share the same visions and carry the imprint of the mother organization.

of the country. Grameen Bank can create affiliated institutions such as Grameen Agricultural Trust, Grameen Fisheries and Dairy Trust and Grameen Management, Information & Research Trust, etc. Like Grameen, each Trust will aim to organise landless persons to share ownership and management responsibilities in all its activities. The advantage of the Grameen Agricultural Trust is that its activities can be divided into many bite-size segments so that landless groups can find it easier to take little steps and prepare themselves to take bigger steps leading to the gradual taking over of ownership and management responsibilities, with Grameen Agricultural Trust holding together the macro framework."

CONGLOMERATE GROWTH
An interminable drive and optimism is now taking Grameen Bank from a process of horizontal and vertical expansion into a process of conglomerate expansion and growth. The analysis of each distinct development problem area, as it has emerged in the Bank's experience, evolves into a specialized organizational entity to cater for the solutions required.

Within each organizational entity there is a process of horizontal and vertical expansion. The conglomerate as a whole germinates, ferments and expands horizontally and vertically in an almost unlimited process. Peaking the conglomerate process is a foundation for the refinement of *management and organizational development competence*. The ultimate dream is to replace an incapable governing system and build a society of new enabling institutions for the poor. In this the Grameen movement is as transparent as a sunny day. It is all there for the seeing. It is driven by a defiant dream of social change, not by revolution, but by managed evolution, not by force, but by better performance. What a wild dream it is--and beautiful.

The process of realizing the dream is, as we have seen, far advanced. Therefore, we should not doubt what is going to happen in the future. The Grameen movement may become one of the most herculean and profound social and economic development efforts the Third World has ever witnessed. If we listen carefully, this is what is being said with pain and anguish, with defiance and determination: Our State of Bangladesh has forsaken our people to endless suffering when what they deserve is a simple, decent life. The organizational framework of the State has disproven its claim to be the instrument of social and economic development. A new form of enabling statehood must be created. Although at all times deliberately fully transparent, it will take time before the Grameen movement is recognized for what it really is. It is the seed of a new type of social activism that will come to fruition in the 21st century, an activism

203

that has learnt from the experience of the last fifty years recognizing that eradication of poverty and realization of human rights is a matter of applying professional proficiency, believing that revolution is not achieved by destruction, but through a process of insightful construction and more competent performance. As for the sincerity and depth of feeling these are excerpts from a Yunus speech published in *Digouto*, the Grameen newsletter in Rangpur zone:

"The aim of Grameen is to challenge and achieve. To make the impossible possible is our characteristic. The people of our country have tremendous strength. The young can make the impossible happen. Poverty is a professional challenge. We will fight and win over poverty, get rid of hunger and malnutrition. We are all freedom fighters. We will keep on fighting till we win this war. You can be the teacher and teach mankind. Be creative, keep on thinking for yourself and generate new ideas. Political commitment is a precondition for eradicating poverty. We want to rebuild our motherland as we have dreamed. We do not want ourselves to be seen as beggars in the years to come. I do not want the fate of my nation to depend on the mercy of others. Every citizen has ownership and equal right to this country. Half of our population are women, so half of our country belongs to women. The rich do not own our country, the powerful have created barriers in our social and economic structure so it is impossible for the poor to ask questions. If collateral is the basis for loan transactions in our financial institutions, it is just to say that those institutions are just making the fat man fatter. The way they have seen the world, the poor have thought that this was the rule of the universe. The poor have not thought that they had a right to their own share. If a poor person is afraid of me, it means I am guilty. We cannot trust the law, the law is for rich people. We must trust our own capacities to regain our devastated economy. We must build up our agriculture to the level of the modern world. We must overcome the crisis of *Kartik* and *Agrabayan*."

And Yunus insists: "A large portion of our total national income is constituted by the contribution of the poor. Credit is a strong economic weapon. To demand collateral is only a technique used to cheat people from participating in progress. Credit increases control over resources. It is not true that the poor are unable to earn money. Women think more about the future than men. The way to alleviation of poverty is to give credit to women for income generation. To give credit without collateral is to fly without wings. We have managed to do the impossible!!" So, dear reader, do you understand also with your heart? This is not about money or the pre-eminence of organizational talent. It is about the importance of dignity for human beings, about taking pride in being a Bengali.

THE BANK'S GROWTH SPURT
- EFFECTS AND CONSEQUENCES

Today I can enjoy
the fruits of my labour.
I am really confident.
I know there is nothing
I am not able to achieve
by hard work, unity,
discipline and determination.
ASMA KATHUN
Chief, Centre No. 8, Rajarhat

In our visits to Grameen Bank since 1985 we have interviewed hundreds, if not by now, a thousand women, individually, or in centre meetings. We have witnessed their material and spiritual progress. We believe "spiritual" is a more apt rendering than mental or psychological. There is such a dimension to the work in Grameen Bank. Defiance, dedication, a belief in one's own capability, a feeling of agency, permeates the organization and is weekly enhanced through the ritual of the centre meetings. What Grameen does for people's self-image may be as important as what it does for their stomachs. There is more to it than the quantitative measurement of effects. We shall endeavour to convey some of the qualitative aspects of Grameen's influence on people's lives along with other consequences.

A SHOWCASE ON MICROLEVEL
"Now I know I can do!" says Asma Kathun, much in contrast to the timid anxiety she felt when she took her first loan of 1 500 taka in 1986. It was for a milch cow, she recollects, and she was worried it would get sick and die, leaving her with a lost investment and incapable of paying back her loan. She talks about the hardships of her early years. Her father had to sacrifice his plot of land to pay dowries for his daughters. They did not even have a proper house to sleep in and suffered much from colds.

205

Asma is a woman of 45 years of age, strong and matronly looking. Her husband appeared quiet and retiring. Both had attended school up to Grade 5. The husband had casual work as a labour supervisor for Government. Of their five children, two were at home. They all came smilingly to the doorstep to receive us. Asma was brimming with happiness to show us her new house and other possessions. The family seemed closely knit and united. Although rare in Muslim culture, here the woman appeared to play the main role in the house.

Asma Kathun continued to take a loan every year and, by 1989, the loan size had increased to 5 000 taka. She invested in paddy and wheat trading and put some money aside. In 1990 came a turning point, she took another loan of 5 000 taka and rented a small shop in the bazaar, intent on tailoring and selling saris and lungis. It appears the husband is more heavily involved in the loan utilization than the Bank's records may reveal. He took care of much of her paddy trading and now the shopkeeping. In 1991 another loan of 5 000 taka enabled the family to invest in a sewing machine for the shop. Her eldest son of 25 is taking care of the tailoring and recently an extra tailor was appointed who is paid 40 taka per day. With the shop lucratively established, Asma returned to the paddy business and milch cows. In 1992, she took a general loan of 5 000 taka and added two seasonal loans over 6 months. Total loan amount that year was 7 700 taka. She leased one acre paddy land for seasonal cultivation and invested in fertilizer and water.

New house inspires family. On their way up other things also happened to Asma and her family. In 1987 she took a housing loan of 10 000 taka. Adding their savings and free labour, the family invested a total of 18 000 taka. It is the more prestigious model called "Chouchala", says Asma guiding us around with an obvious expression of well-being in her face. And her house is nice, indeed, built on a high strong plinth with concrete columns and roof of corrugated iron sheets and with walls beautifully patterned and crafted from bamboo reeds. Two big windows give plenty of light and ventilation inside. The house has two large rooms and a separate kitchen. A latrine and a shallow tubewell have been installed. Asma also added a storage house which was packed to capacity with rice, wheat and flour for trading, consumption and food security. But the centrepiece of attraction was, in Asma's eyes, undoubtedly her showcase--a well-crafted and varnished wood cabinet with double glass doors, lock and key! In it, she displayed her six decorated enamel plates, teacups and saucers, silvery shining aluminium jars, an embroidered tablecloth and other household objects of pride and utility.

206

Asma and husband were anxious we were served tea as proper and recounted their story with little prodding from our side. Mostly Asma spoke with nodding secondment from her husband, " People talk well about us now. It never used to be like that. When a few of us became members of Grameen seven years ago, some well-to-do people in the village were not much in favour of women joining in. We discussed among ourselves and agreed that if they should feel happy we would have to starve. Their words and threats were empty and they would never help us in any way, so we decided to join the bank in spite of criticism. My husband encouraged me to join after we had discussed the issue and I encouraged other women to join. Looking back, none of us regret that decision. The success we have had in my family is due to the open discussion I and my husband had together with our children. My husband does not dictate to me. He collaborates in my endeavours. He owned the land for our homestead, but transferred it in my name so that I could get the house loan. He is so supportive and facilitates both my work and that of my son." Asma gives the clear impression of being the one who manages the family finances. It seems her inner strength has found a real opportunity to manifest itself.

A united centre. "The members in my centre are a united lot. When someone gets a house loan, we help each other constructing the house. Grameen is our saviour. We do not only get the credit. The bank assistants work closely with us to plan, organize and implement our projects. We discuss important things with them in the meetings. I am grateful for the Bank's idea of forming groups where we support each other."

Assets and debt. "My husband does not earn much as a seasonal labour-foreman for government--only 50 taka a day when there is work and that is not often--so he is mostly in the shop. We sell for about 5 000 taka a week, but the expenses are high. We pay salary and food for four employees and my son receives a monthly allowance of 1 000 taka. We estimate we have a profit of 10 to 12%." Asma says if she trades paddy for 2 500 taka she has a "profit" of 1 500 taka, but then she does not calculate the costs of her own labour. To get an exact record of people's income is difficult, partly because they do not look at their own labour input as a "cost" in the production process and partly because this is, after all, a matter of privacy and people are reticent about divulging their real earnings, at least until a longer-term relationship of trust is established. Asma said she had no problems repaying her debt which was, at the time of our visit, 7 782 taka. A lucky circumstance that likely influenced the steady growth of the family economy is the high elevation of the homestead land. Because of this, the family was not seriously affected by the floods in Rangpur. After thorough deliberations, Asma and her husband specified their

	Taka
Sales value of house	35 000
40 decimal land	80 000
3 sewing machines	7 500
1 treadle pump	250
4 chairs, 1 table, 4 beds	2 800
Showcase	2 500
3 clothes stands	1 000
1 storage bed	1 500
Dressing table	3 000
Bicycle	1 500
Family clothes	4 000
3 wrist watches	1 400
2 milch cows	7 000
10 ducks, 4 chickens	700
Pigeons	350
Food stock	1 000
Stock in shop	70 000
TOTAL ESTIMATED VALUE	**Taka 219 500**

ASMA KATHUN'S SHOWCASE

208

assets. It is a great achievement from having nothing seven years ago. By the way, Asma's other son has just passed first division of his Secondary School Certificate. But there is also sorrow in the family for one young daughter is deaf.

TOWARDS THE MACROLEVEL EFFECT
In an economy of poverty it is the growth in assets which is important and which must be conspicuous! The growth spurt Asma Kathun and her family has experienced in accumulation of assets is psychologically strongly correlated with the development of a good self-image. To feel good about oneself: We have done it! We can do it! People talk nice about us! is an asset of great emotional and psychological value. If such motivation spreads to a whole nation of poor, it can work wonders.

Although it's given that *Purdah* restricts Asma's physical mobility, credit has helped her transcend it considerably. The pattern of Asma Khatun's development can now be multiplied in the hundreds of thousands to members who are in their 7th, 8th, 9th or 10th year of loans. Not all of them are equally successful due to a number of factors. In Asma's case, her husband is supportive and their educational level is probably an advantage. They were spared from local natural disasters and any major setbacks because of health crises in the family. Thus, their economic progress was able to continue in a paced manner over the ten-year period. Access to the Family Loan has meant her husband and son could extend family business in larger, more complex investment activities. The popular Seasonal Loan has facilitated the ongoing leasing of land which is so remunerative. It's important not to forget that the venue for this family success story is Asma Khatun.

Over the years, several researchers have looked into the effects of Grameen Bank on the lives of its loanees and on the wider context of the rural economy, notably Dharam Ghai (29) as early as 1984 and Mahabub Hossain in a series of studies, the latest in 1988. (30) The findings are striking and a variety of considerations for the management of further growth are raised. The studies confirm that the most direct effect is the accumulation of capital by the poor. The amount of working capital employed in members' income generation increased by an average of three times in little more than two years. Investment in fixed assets is about 2.5 times higher for borrowers with more than three years' membership than for members in their first year. One-third of the members reported they were unemployed before they joined the Bank: 7% of the men and 50% of the women! An indepth study of households in five Grameen villages and two control villages found that members had an income about 43% higher than the target group in the control villages and about 28% higher than the non-members in Grameen villages. And this very positive income effect derived from income generation based on the Bank's loans is highest for the absolute landless. Also, there is a wider effect on the rural economy--average household income is about 16% higher in Grameen villages than in the control villages. By creating their own employment, Grameen members withdraw their services from the agricultural labour market. This has an indirect positive effect on the employment situation in the area and, consequently, on the earnings of those agricultural labourers who have not joined the bank. The daily rate for casual labour is pressed upwards. A Midterm Review report estimates increases by as much as 55 to 80% in such daily wages across different seasons or activities. (31)

Socio economic impact. This report from 1992 points to a dramatic average income increase of 53% in real terms over three years. Other significant socio-economic impacts include: The food and nutrient intake per capita is 9% higher in Grameen households than in comparable households over three years and there is an increase of 18% in proportion of total expenditure in satisfaction of non-food basic needs such as clothing, education and health. Greater occupational mobility is another effect of the Bank's presence. Men engaged in agricultural labour decreased from 8% to 5% and women engaged in domestic services from 46% to 8%. Households engaged in trading or business increased from 40% to 70%. There were similar significant changes in people's capital situation. 64% increase in average amount of working capital invested per borrower per year and 62% higher average amount of fixed capital invested by borrower households than by comparable households. In the same vein, Grameen mobilized nearly four times as much total savings as five commercial banks mobilized in 20 districts. In general, poverty was reduced. The concentration of households in low-income brackets was 62% in Grameen villages while 80% in the comparable control group.

The impact of a social nature is similarly significant. Grameen borrowers rank higher than control groups on indicators of clearer self-perceptions. 93% as against 50% of husbands now think of their wives as equals. 75% of female members report about increased affection from their husbands after taking Grameen loans and these women have more influence in family decision-making. 53% of them use contraceptives as compared to 36% among comparable women. The dependency on the local elite is reduced and participation in the political process is increasing. Grameen members vote higher than average in local elections.

More recent research by D. Gibbons and H. Todd confirms the socio-economic impact summarized by the Midterm Review report. Sixty-four households in Tangail were followed. Forty of these were Grameen women members and 24 were a matched group. A striking contrast was found between the two groups. Forty-six percent of the Grameen families were out of the poverty group, compared to 4% of the control group. Seventy-four percent of the control group were still stuck among the hard-core poor, while only 20% of the Grameen members remained there. Moreover, Grameen children were a little taller and quite a lot heavier than non-Grameen children. (31)

LOANEE DEVELOPMENT PATTERN

Although this has not yet been documented in any comprehensive empirical study, there are strong indications that the women over time probably proceed through a fairly uniform pattern of development as loanees. Several authors have collected case studies that partly or more fully illustrate the same trend. (32) Also this material provides the reader with a large number of examples very similar to that of Asma Kathun. Perhaps it is useful to look at the overall pattern in a simplified manner:

The first stage of a woman's loan taking is characterized by her *strong aversion to risk*. She will reduce risk by taking a small loan of 1 000 to 1 500 taka and by sticking to activities she knows well and feels capable of. She will, moreover, often reduce risk by spreading her investment of the loan monies on more than one activity. She has two major concerns: She wants cash money to improve her family's consumption and she wants to create assets to reduce risk further. Therefore, she will initially both invest in sure immediate cash winners like paddy processing or trading and ensure some capital accumulation in longer term activities like goats or cow fattening. She is likely to repeat this pattern for her next loan.

In the second stage, usually comprising her third and fourth loans, she will ask for bigger loans of 2 000 to 3 000 taka. She will spread her risks as before. She will involve family members in her activities. Her aim is to *consolidate the situation*. She will have reached a steady level of family consumption and she will keep it that way. Instead of expanding consumption, she will lay more emphasis on savings and reduction of future risk through investment in assets for the household or in the land.

The third stage will be characterized by her feeling of a certain achievement. She is backed by some assets. She knows she is capable. Her self-image is enhanced. She is *ready for greater risk-taking*. She will ask for bigger loans, maybe 3 000 to 4 000 taka. She will only slightly raise the level of her family's consumption. She will use some of her savings as venture capital. Although still tending to spread her risk on more than one activity, she will also invest in new means of production, for example, buying a rickshaw for her husband or son or maybe a sewing machine. The family's economy becomes sustainable.

The fourth stage will be characterized by a greater *desire for family comfort*. She has now reached the upper limits of the general loan which is 5 000 taka. The family's consumption is becoming more conspicuous. She takes a house loan. She takes more risk and earns more money but still inclines to spread her risk on several activities. Now in her fifth loan or more, she starts investing in children's education.

The fifth stage is characterized by more *concern for the future*. She will keep on taking maximum general loans. Several family members are likely to be involved in income-generating activities. She may graduate to a family loan and most likely take seasonal loans. She invests in children's education beyond primary level, maybe even having a son or daughter in college. She continues in an entrepreneurial spirit to invest in new or additional means of production and to accumulate assets. She is now 40 to 45 years old and looks forward to being cared for by her children.

At every centre meeting, in every household visit, we asked mothers if they want their children to become Grameen Bank members. All the women answered with a resounding NO! At first this answer may surprise the confirmed Bank supporter, but at second thought it makes sense. The women want their children to reach beyond. As they say: "We do not want our children to always be in debt as we are. Grameen is a Bank for the poor. We want our children to be rich." The economic problematique this view represents is becoming more and more clear to the Grameen leadership and is reflected in its conglomerate growth aiming at connecting the poor to the mainstream economy. If the stages of development a loanee is going through is looked at as a process of gradual economic empowerment, there is no doubt that the women progressively control their situation and take charge of their destiny. Empowerment is not as much the formality of getting access to a human right as it is the personal reality of feeling increasingly capable of mastering one's situation. Yet, there are many constraints to the situation requiring further analysis.

212

THE HORIZONTAL GROWTH SPURT

The rather rapid and steady growth of Grameen Bank proper from the modest action research project in Jobra in 1976 to the present day membership of about 1.5 million people serviced by 1 000 branches is due to an exceptional leadership vision and development of staff and member competence. It is also due to seizing on an inherent, negative social situation in Bangladesh and turning it into an opportunity for a positive organizational response with the potential to reverse it. Very simply stated: Under extreme poverty people are underemployed, leisure has little value. As long as there is surplus labour with little opportunity cost people will respond to clear prospects of economic improvement. Moreover, with high population density, there is a market around the corner for most products. Bangladesh also has the rich resource of academically qualified but unemployed youth who are easily motivated for a cause of this nature. The following pages of charts are self-explanatory. Included as examples are Cumulative growth of membership, Growth in general and collective loan disbursement, Growth in house loan disbursement, Growth in group fund and emergency fund savings.

The tables demonstrate a few very significant features. Grameen Bank has based its expansion in volume almost entirely on growth in female membership, while male membership has remained largely the same. Through its system for savings in group and emergency funds, the Bank is able to continuously strengthen and consolidate its financial position through capital accumulation by its members. The Midterm Review points out a clear lesson: Grameen Bank has been able to replicate its operation in the field at a very high rate of growth. (31) It has successfully raised its capacity to recruit, train and deploy staff members and officers to meet the demands of this expansion while the ratio of employees to members has remained unchanged. The management formula for local operation ranging from branch office organization to centre and group formation has also remained virtually unchanged. Through the successful expansion it has proven itself valid. Repayment rates have remained at a high level throughout and there is little sign of the alienation that can overtake head offices with large, rapidly growing field operations.

The horizontal growth has, in this way, been very efficient since there is no wastage on experimentation. However, a growth spurt of these dimensions would not be entirely free from problems or complications. The ever-ascending growth curve may have a point of culmination by choice or by chance--or a point of flattening out. On its way upwards, the "curve" accumulates potentialities for both success and failure. At this juncture, WHAT NEXT?

213

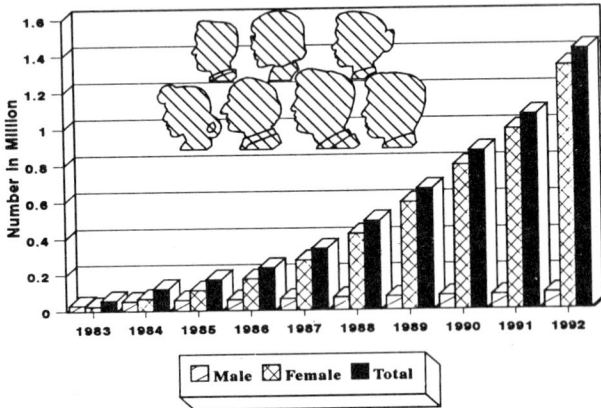

GROWTH OF MEMBERSHIP
(Cumulative)

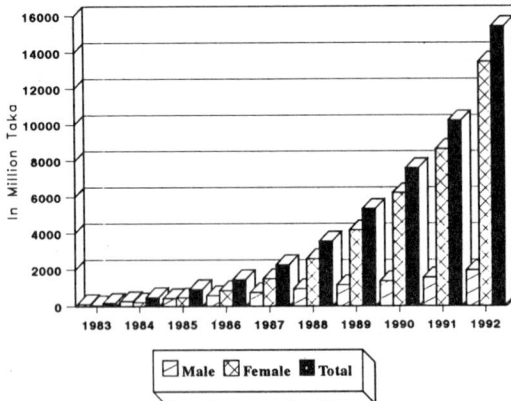

CUMULATIVE LOAN DISBURSEMENT
(General & Collective)

HOUSE LOAN DISBURSEMENT (CUMULATIVE)

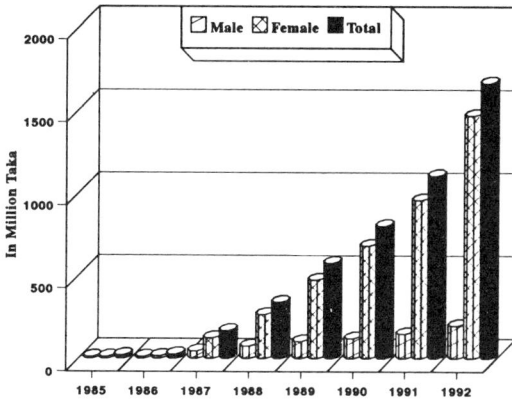

CUMULATIVE SAVINGS
(Group Fund Saving & Balance)

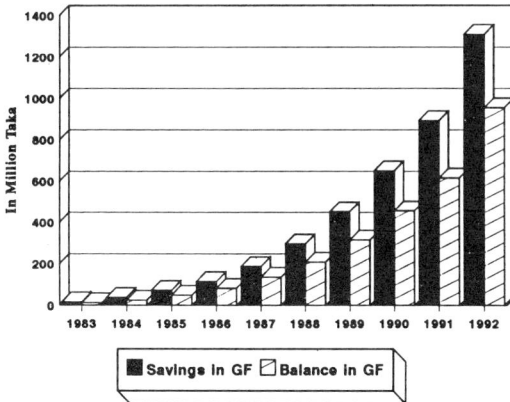

215

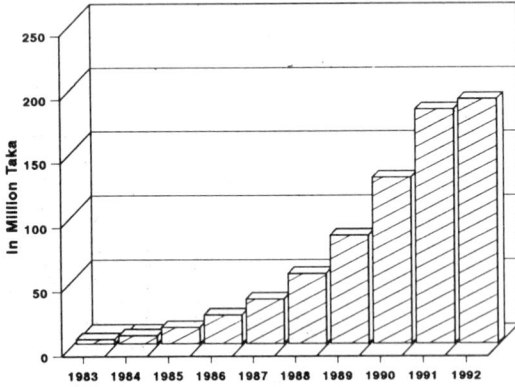
CUMULATIVE SAVINGS
(Emergency Fund)

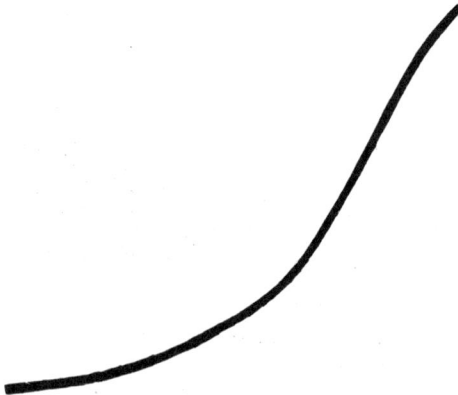
WHAT NEXT ?

216

is an important question. The answer may be found in the organizational symptoms which manifest themselves during this period of horizontal growth.

ORGANIZATIONAL GROWING PAINS

The Midterm Review highlights a number of issues. Although the increase of employees has more or less matched the increase in membership, the expansion has nevertheless exacerbated the increasing cost of salaries. These costs are virtually immutable and set the Bank under pressure to increase revenues and/or productivity. This is not necessarily a drawback; it may even be a spur to further improvement of performance--but it also makes Grameen more vulnerable to external influences. When the Government raised salaries of bank staff by around 25% in July 1991, Grameen had to follow suit with serious consequences for the profitability of its very labour-intensive field operation. The Bank had to respond by increasing its interest rates on general and collective loans to 20% and on house loans to 8%, thereby loading its increased costs on to the members. The increase was effected, however, without an increase in their weekly repayments, since it was compensated for by reduced contributions to the emergency fund. Thus, the problem was solved at the expense of future capital accumulation. It is not so sure that such an operation can be repeated at the next crossroad.

Grameen Bank, which has sustained its management effectiveness during the growth spurt, is now being challenged by the sheer scale of its operations. To some extent this has been compensated for through systematic decentralization. Yet, there is a long way to go before the zonal managers are real managers rather than administrators. The need for management development training emerges as a pressing issue on many levels.

The staff welfare association - Shamiti. Precisely through its rapid expansion with new posts and opportunities becoming available, Grameen has been able to offer incentives and maintain a high level of motivation among staff members. Hard work under difficult circumstances in the field has been rewarded through quick promotions and transfers. But the growth of operations generate staff members' demands for services that are not inherent in the existing administrative set-up. The expansion has been accompanied, therefore, by signs of turbulence in the relations between management and staff. This erupted early in 1991 when a group attempted to take over an office in the headquarters building in order to establish a trade union. The registrar of trade unions and the court declared the attempt illegal and the Bank subsequently dismissed fifteen staff members. After a clearing of the air, the staff welfare association was formed to provide a forum for regular discussion of issues of mutual concern to management and staff. Some of the issues to be worked out in a spirit of understanding are: criteria for promotion and transfers, grading of posting stations on the basis of convenience, revision of benefits and salary scale, career development and opportunities for professional advancement, general welfare and recreation.

The incident clearly shook the management who may have been unaware of the depth of the grievances in the organization. The history of trade unions in Bangladesh is stormy and undisciplined. The presence of such a politicized entity within the Bank could have been extremely disruptive. There is little doubt it would hinder the operation of the Bank's flexible management system and ability to respond to a rapidly changing environment and ultimately affect the Bank's financial performance. Management is now moving swiftly to clear the channels of communication and re-establish a situation of trust. Nevertheless, the issue causes anxiety both inside and outside the Grameen Bank circle. It is likely to be a critical factor in the future. It is not a temporary incident but a problem embedded in the organizational structure requiring total attention. An issue of particular concern is the lack of real progress in the recruitment of female staff. Although the number has doubled, their ratio has remained the same. A development very positive for the future of staff members is the conglomerate growth. The new and expanding organizational entities in the Grameen family are likely to offer aspiring people ever new career and promotion opportunities. Generally the staff members' work situation is being reviewed. Should, for example, peons or secretaries be able to advance to bank workers? What training would that require?

The branch performance. Despite turbulence, it is a comfort that the flight into the future is piloted in a progressive and promising way. Financial projections show that Grameen Bank with 1 000 branches can become a viable and self-sustaining rural credit institution before the end of the decade, able to cover its costs. The Bank should not require donor funds for its general loan activities, although some might still be needed for non-credit expenses and possibly for the long-term housing loans if this activity is to be expanded. In this overall picture, the financial performance of each and every branch is crucial. Grameen Bank has developed an excellent new long-term forecasting model called the Model Branch Model (MBM) which is capable of predicting within 2-5% the Bank's actual performance. Profitability is likely to increase annually. Branch profitability is not objectively determined, however. It is a relative measure of branch performance. Branch profit depends to a significant extent on the fund transfer rate between the branches and head office. The Midterm Review (31) reports the results of an analysis of about 150 profitable and 150 unprofitable branches compared with the MBM projections. It concludes that the single most important factor in determining branch profitability is the outstanding amount of general and collective loans. It concludes also that their growth rate continues to be inadequate to achieve the profit levels anticipated in the MBM. Not enough housing loan funds are available to make up the difference. A steady and predictable growth in savings could theoretically fill the gap, but the increase is likely to be outstripped by rising operating costs. Already in 1988 Mahabub Hossain made an observation in a similar vein. (30) The increase in income would not be high enough to cover the rising costs because of the then taka 5 000 limit on individual loans. He pointed out that the amount of outstanding loans with the borrowers at an average branch reaches a ceiling within a period of two years (then about taka 2 million), but increases very little thereafter.

This situation confronts the bank with essentially three lines of action in its vertical and qualitative expansion:

(a)   Head Office must decide on improving the quality of its bank products, for example by raising the upper limits of its loans and/or by designing and offering a package of loans of larger variety and more adequate to the needs and desires of the members. This requires a change from a demand-driven to a supply-driven operating philosophy.

(b)   Similarly, the Branch Manager and his staff must change their approach from being largely controlled by the local economic environment to managing it in an active manner. They must actively market the Grameen Bank's services to meet the particular needs of the local situation.

(c)   At the same time, both Head Office and Branch must undertake serious and continuous internal cost analyses to rationalize procedures and routines, reorganize operations and generally increase cost-effectiveness. This necessitates the development of more precise and sharper tools to measure branch operating performance. The size of the operation is now such that senior management cannot manage effectively by relying on absolute numbers of gross performance. (31)

With its record of progressive management, it should come as no surprise to the reader that the Grameen Bank is well on the way further upwards.

THE VERTICAL CLIMB
As before when faced with problems, the Bank has responded rapidly with a number of innovations to improve the quality of its services and performance

219

and, as before, it has done so with caution. Changes are tested thoroughly before it is decided to make them generally available in the system. The upper limit for general individual loans was raised to 10 000 taka for collective loans to 30 000 taka. This was done first in the well-tried Dhaka and Tangail zones and, as good results turned up, later in other zones. The family loan with an upper limit of 30 000 taka, and the seasonal credit loan with an upper limit of 3 000 taka were other innovations met with enthusiastic response, especially among older loanees. Such offers keep loanees away from the moneylenders. As explained earlier, these new bank products have a potential for contributing essentially to the profitability of the branches which are now likely to become profitable in a much shorter time. The issue, though, is not as simple as making more money available for people in the form of larger credit. The Bank is fully aware that such advancement must be paralleled by better access to production technology, especially labour-intensive technology that does not demand the acquisition of complex new skills. Leasing of power looms, for example, is considered an interesting proposition in connection with family loans. Hand looms, hand or treadle pumps, threshing machines or shallow tubewells are other examples at varying stages of sophistication discussed earlier. Responding perhaps particularly to the needs of the people in disaster-struck Rangpur, Grameen introduced other types of innovative services already mentioned such as capital recovery loans, food security loans, treadle mill loans and goat loans.

Through Research and Development or under the auspices of SIDE further options are pursued ranging from bee-keeping and sericulture to duck, rabbit or poultry rearing. And the Bank is cognisant of the macrolevel context of its endeavour. Weaving is a traditional craft in Bangladesh, but 300 000 weavers in the country are increasingly unemployed because government allows an import of US$ 50 million of woven products a year! Attempts to influence this absurd situation are underway.

The Bank's consistent look at its products as a package of services comprising both access to credit and access to appropriate technology has a good reason. To get out of poverty the poor must increase their productivity. Mahabub Hossain (30) observed in the conclusion of his study:

"The vertical expansion of the Bank may be constrained by the low level of productivity in many activities that the Bank's credit finances. This is known to be a particularly serious problem for the cottage industry sector, which receives about one-fourth of Grameen Bank loans. It was observed in a previous study that with every repeat loan, the size of the loan increases, but

220

the income increases at a much smaller rate because the rate of utilization of the loan for capital accumulation declines and the rate of return on capital also falls. The same indication is obtained in the present study by the finding that longtime Grameen Bank members spend proportionately less on non-agricultural investment (relative to social investment) than do new members."

Management is aware of this problem and has for this reason encouraged members to reap the benefits of economic scale in collective enterprises. The leadership and collaboration problems of such enterprises have, however, forced the Bank to take another much longer-term tack as explained under the SIDE scheme.

The firefighting programme is the colloquial expression for a focused internal effort aiming to increase cost-effectiveness, profitability and innovation within the Bank. Now the name is changed to *Punar Birnash Karmansuchai* which in English means organizational development or rationalization. The initiative is being carried out by a small unit of 21 experienced senior officers under the management of the Training institute. For this, they receive special training and are then posted throughout Bangaldesh in various zones. There is no real fire yet, but the Bank has identified a series of very specific problem areas for investigation. Also included are areas of general concern to the Bank simply to improve its services to members. Topics have a wide range: The rationalization of paperwork, passbook and accounting procedures, development of deposit banking and general financial independence and profitability of the branch is high on the agenda. Better utilization of the balance group fund deposit for the benefit of the members is another issue. Extra effort is going into increasing the income of members through improvement of appropriate technology and arrangements for leasing of equipment.

The social side of the Bank's work is given greater emphasis: More effective implementation of the *16 Decisions* such as surveying children around the centres to ensure that education reaches all of them, or surveying beggars and the destitute in an endeavour to include them in the centre's work. Development of a health care and medical services system for members and non-members is underway. Improvement of nutritional status through home gardens on homestead land is another possibility.

Each member of the "firefighting" team is assigned a couple of these tasks and sets forth for a two-month stay at a branch office where he will concentrate exclusively on rethinking and discussing with staff how to improve them. On return to the Training Institute, the team members will analyze their findings

ORGANIZATIONAL CHANGES
UNDER DISCUSSION

INCREASE
NUMBER OF GROUPS
FROM 6 TO 8?

AUTHORIZE
CENTRE CHIEF
TO COLLECT
INSTALMENTS?

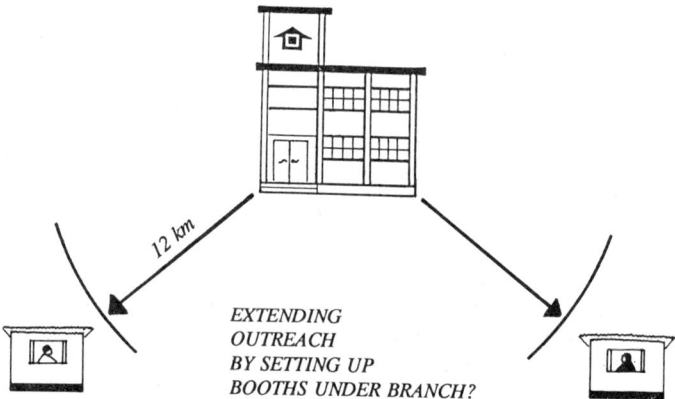

12 km

EXTENDING
OUTREACH
BY SETTING UP
BOOTHS UNDER BRANCH?

and respectively develop their pilot projects for implementation at the branch. In the Bank's characteristic style, each problem area is thoroughly action-researched and potential solutions are tested cautiously in a local context before large-scale decisions are taken.

Oiling the clockwork itself. Even the centre which is such a well-tested and reliable feature of the Bank's operation is now set under scrutiny. A wide variety of potential improvements are considered and questions are raised: Is it possible to increase the number of groups from 6 to 8 in each centre? May the centre chiefs take over some operational duties now done by the bank assistants, for example collection of money? Should one make the seating arrangement in the centre more attractive by introducing a simple type of benches for the group members? Is it possible to change from weekly to fortnightly or monthly payments of instalments? About 12 km. is the maximum operational distance between branch and centre, could a branch reach more outlaying areas in its district by, for example, setting up a booth staffed by a bank assistant?

On the other hand, in some branches the population base is too thin. Will public sentiment allow rationalization by amalgamation of two branch offices? And how will these changes of economic concern affect the Bank's social development programme? And, finally, what to do with those that are not reached at all?

Project for the destitute. Even among the poorest there is stratification. Grameen Bank knows that the local communities harbour poor who are not caught by the safety net of the centres, a lumpenproletariat that are too destitute to handle cash money and incapable of participating in any organized activity with the others. The cause may be an element of social stigmatization but also simply utter deprivation. It is the experience that the Bank's standard approach to credit does not work. The poverty is so abject that people literally "eat their loans". It is quite impossible for people to reserve their cash loan for investment. Concerned about the state of the "outcasts", Grameen is attempting another approach to get people going. It is called the *Nishow Programme* meaning "those who have nothing and cannot be trusted." The issue is twofold: to give people access to resources and to establish a relationship of trust, enabling them to resume contact with the surrounding community. Carried out in three branches, an experiment along these lines now being monitored is built on a tripartite arrangement for producing mats (*motar*) between the Bank, a local trader and the women concerned. The credit is very small, in the range of 200 to 300 taka and only given to a woman in the form of tokens each worth

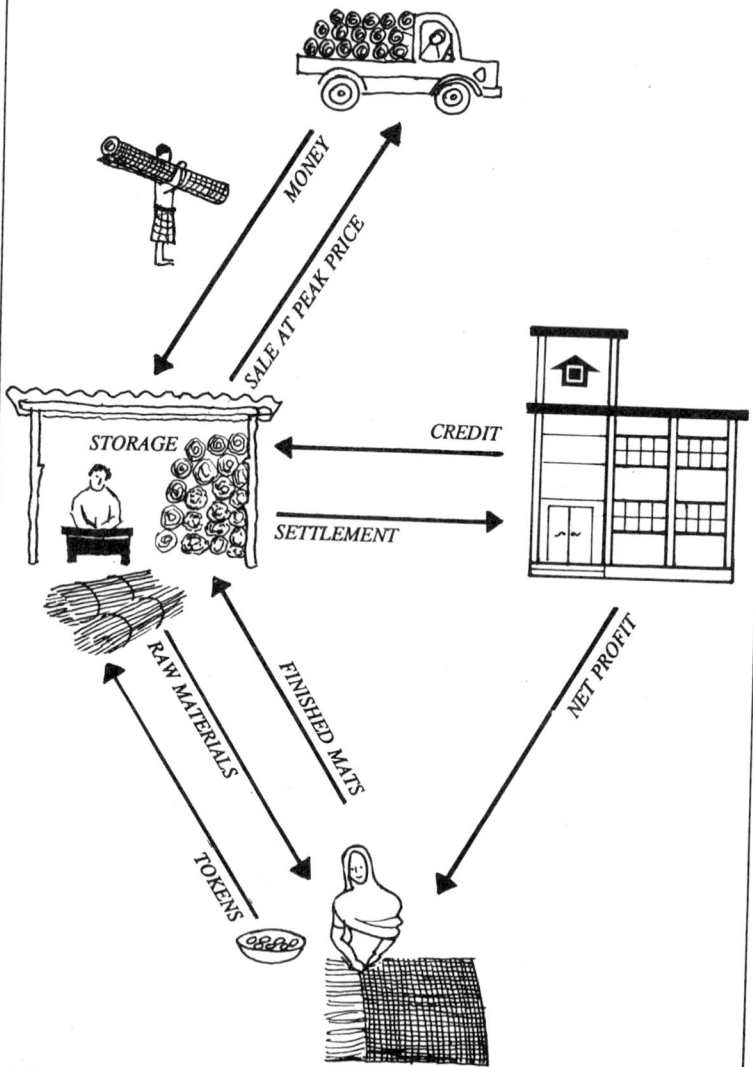

THE NISHOW PROGRAMME - MOTAR EXPERIMENT

MONEY

SALE AT PEAK PRICE

STORAGE

CREDIT

SETTLEMENT

RAW MATERIALS

FINISHED MATS

NET PROFIT

TOKENS

20 taka. By delivering the appropriate number of tokens, a woman gets the quantity of mat-making material she requires from the trader. He has stocked up on these by getting credit from Grameen Bank. When her mats are ready, the woman delivers them to the trader against receipt. The trader stores the mats, together with mats from other women and sells the lot in agreement with the Bank when the market reaches a peak price. Depending on the circumstances, the Bank's arrangement with the trader is on a 50/50 or 75/25 basis. When the transaction is concluded, the accounts are settled and the net profit is accrued proportionately to the women involved. The operation is closely managed and supervised by a bank assistant.

It is as yet uncertain if this micro-experiment will succeed and can be applied on a large scale, but it deserves, indeed, a great deal of respect for its innovativeness. With little hesitation, most organizations would adopt charity as the only approach to this level of ignominious poverty. But in Grameen they insist there is no problem for which a solution cannot be found.

ORGANIZATIONAL LIFE CYCLE
Some students of development processes in private organizations have made observations that may be of interest in the case of Grameen Bank. (33) Organizations go through stages that tend to follow a pattern. An organization's performance can be seen as rising and possibly falling on a time axis. If management shall take the right decisions and implement the right actions to ensure success, it must be capable of recognizing the stage the organization is in at a given time. Growth and expansion may be extended, a peak performance may be sustained or a decline may be turned around.

In the initial stage, someone gets the idea to do something about a problem in the community. It is discussed and generates excitement. The originators fall in love with their idea and start dreaming. They sense a mission and look for people to convert to supporters. This fervour is necessary for the launching of a new organization. If the originators do not generate enough commitment, the idea aborts. If they do, the idea enters the stage of infancy. An organization is born. It is a stage where doing becomes as important as dreaming. Intense activity follows. The organization is screaming for feeding. It is underfunded, understaffed and vulnerable. In the next stage, the *go-go*, the organization has learnt to see and focus. It in fact, sees opportunities everywhere and pursues them with appetite, but it has short attention span and *no* experience from which it can deduce priorities. At this stage the organization may fall in the founder trap. It will not reach the next stage in its development, unless the founder is prepared to relinquish power, to depersonalize policies and begin to establish

225

systems independent of him or herself. This is where strong advisers and a board often provide leadership that builds for the future. At the stage of its *adolescence* the organization takes the time needed to establish an administrative base. More time is spent on meetings for planning and coordination. Accounting procedures, personnel policies, rules and regulations are created. At this point internal contradictions may occur. One group of staff may be devoted to the creation of administrative stability, while another wants to tackle operational challenges and pursue new opportunities. At this point external consultants may be useful to integrate the two forces.

When it comes to its *prime,* an organization has its dream focused into a clearer vision. It is result-oriented and looks at cost-effectiveness and control systems. It sets goals and objectives and meets them. Standards of performance are high and results are predictable. Ideally, organizations would stay in their prime, but in practice this rarely occurs. It will happen only if the organization deliberately plans to do so. Frequently the aspirations of those in power decline. The process of focusing inward commences. Attention is turned to reducing internal conflict and improving staff relations. Leadership and staff seek to enjoy the fruits of yesterday's labour. This signifies both an advance into maturity and the germ of organizational decline. The only remedy is decentralization and creation of new centres of action that can relive the development experience from the beginning. At the point of *maturity,* information overload becomes an increasing problem at head office. The organization is starting to lose the clarity of its vision. The administrative systems are still strong but the sense of urgency is going. New ideas are received with less enthusiasm. Rather than tackling new opportunities people tend to enjoy time spent together. Slowly the result orientation is also disappearing. If such a decline starts, the cure must come from outside, possibly from consultants. A major organizational renewal is required to develop a new sense of mission.

Aristocracy is the next stage. The organizational climate becomes stale if the decline continues. Leadership fears for the organization's future, but does not express it. Don't rock the boat. The organization is fixated in its admiration for its own past. Dress and speech code becomes formalized, communication elusive. No-one challenges leadership decisions. More and more funds are allocated to administrative control systems, human relations and training, rather than to innovation. The organization is on its way into *early bureaucracy.* Sooner or later bad news is going to start hitting--donors refuse funding, media attacks may follow, clients or supporters may band together to protest. Finally, a new Board may decide to change the executive leadership. When this occurs

FREQUENT ORGANIZATIONAL LIFE CYCLE

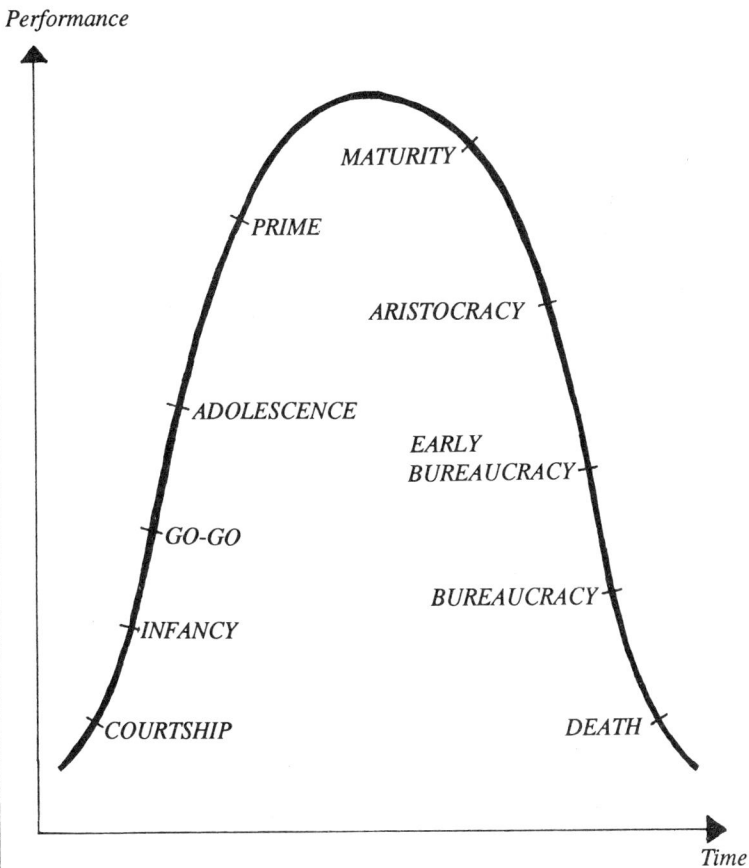

Performance

MATURITY

PRIME

ARISTOCRACY

ADOLESCENCE

EARLY BUREAUCRACY

GO-GO

BUREAUCRACY

INFANCY

COURTSHIP

DEATH

Time

Organizations rise and fall, come and go, but some also survive. The most critical issue for management of organizational development is to identify correctly the current state in the life cycle.

From NGO Management No. 1

the mutual admiration society of aristocrats disintegrates. Paranoia and stabbing in the back sets in. General internal fighting and search for scapegoats ensues. Charges of conspiracies emerge. Coalitions form and energies are devoted to ensuring personal survival. The good people are feared and either fired or leave on their own. Bitter people cease to perform but hang on. If the organization continues to get funding in spite of its abysmal performance, it will move on to the stage of full-fledged *bureaucracy*. The only thing left at this stage is forms, rigid procedures and paperwork. Everything must be put in writing. Access is severely restricted. Nothing gets done. The organizational atmosphere turns to peace and serenity. The battles are over and the staff and leaders who have remained are easy to deal with. They agree on everything, but they just don't do anything. The final stage is organizational *death*, but some bureaucracies never seem to get there. If the basic funding keeps on coming in, they just go on and on.

Many observers of private or public organizations will nod in recognition of this description in NGO Management. The model may be interesting for making judgements about Grameen Bank. There are similarities, but there are also fundamental differences. Where on the curve is it just now? Where will it go from here? Grameen is not a closed organization entity. It has demonstrated a remarkable capacity for organizational learning. It is a people's movement interwoven with the lives of the poor in adversity or aspiration. It is an open system, a transparent formation of people created through integration with its socio-economic environment. Is it just disciplined or has it become bureaucratic? Will its future emerge from its organizational brain of specialists- -or from the mass of poor they want to empower? Is the Bank as yet only an incipient people's movement? Will the poor ultimately be truly empowered? Other questions can also be asked. Will the Grameen family of organizations continue to grow unfettered? Corporate multinational growth is known to succeed, but for how long?

We do not have the answers, but there are three areas of special concern: the future of the members' children, the relationship to the donors, and the relationship to the larger national economy.

GROWTH OF CHILDREN

In its "firefighting" or organizational development efforts, it appears the management in Grameen Bank is paying increasing attention to the issue of children. Yunus is very clear on this point. In an editorial in *Grameen Dialogue* No. 7 under the title, "Thinking Children", he states, "We want the best aspects of life in our generation to pass on to our children, screening out the social deformities, pains of living, diseases and indignities that children are made to suffer through. Our goal should no longer be limited to mere Child Survival, it should be reformulated as "Survival with Dignity". We must rearrange our world of thought, and world of action to ensure this for all children of the world." And in a following lecture on poverty alleviation, "There are two more dimensions of priority. Among the poor we must assign higher priority to women. This is needed both in the interest of expediting development as well as in consideration of their vulnerable position.

Children should get separate importance. Children represent the economic future of the society. They will build the future social structure. Objectives that cannot be materialised today through the efforts of the present generation, may be achieved easily through the next generation if we pay the right kind of attention to children."

This is a clear commitment, but the Bank's analysis of the issue of children has not yet evolved. A clear line of action remains to be defined. True, there are the centre schools and the support to them in the form of school books, but the fact is that only 17 000 out of 50 000 centres have such schools in operation and barely half-a-million books have been distributed. Since it began the substantial amount of 116 million taka has been mobilized through savings by the members in the Children's Welfare Fund, but again the question is: Are these savings effectively utilized to the benefit of the children. Or are the concerns of profitable financial management overriding, or is it simply the Bank and the centre members do not quite know what to do with the money?

The issue of the Bank and its children has some aspects requiring thorough consideration.

The problem of management. As pointed out earlier, the Bank's leadership has, over the years, come to recognize that collective or joint enterprises fail because the members lack essential management and organizing skills. It is also the Bank's experience that adult education courses and training in such skills do not provide the solution. The Bank has chosen, therefore, the longer-term approach of taking over the management itself and involving the members in a process over time through groups and centres. The question is: how long-term will be this process of taking over? There may be need for a parallel approach. Mounting evidence in educational psychology indicates that people's capacity for planning, organizing and managing complex activities originates in early childhood stimulation. Goal-directed action and problem solving--culture as a whole--are normally mediated to the child by mature caregivers, especially by parents. (34)   However, in situations of parental stress, such as extreme poverty, and deprivation, such mediation is limited or does not occur at all. This can be seen as one of the reasons why poverty confronted by the forces of oppression perpetuates itself. Under extreme stress not only material conditions but human relations are subjected to a process of marginalization.

Early childhood education.   There is a strong case for early childhood education with special emphasis on preschools and adult education on the parental role itself. Research on the issue of community participation (35) indicates that processes of participation and empowerment are much longer term than anticipated.   Instead of thinking in project periods of 2 to 5 years, development agencies should be willing to commit themselves to 15 to 20 years. This is the least it takes for such processes to mature and reach sustainability. Grameen Bank's own experience over the last 17 years provides a good demonstration of this.   In such a time perspective, it makes eminent sense to start with the five-year-old children who will become adults in the time required.   Available now are well-tested pedagogical methods available for training in mediation, simple enough to be communicated effectively to persons of very low educational level. (34)   A parallel approach would be required: On the one hand a focus on training of parents, especially mothers through functional adult literacy classes, workshops or centre meetings.   On the other hand a focus on training of preschool/centreschool instructors and teachers.

High rate of return.   Research qualifies that even short, early education programmes over a couple of years can partially offset the negative effects of disadvantage and produce significant educational benefits for some children. (36)   The simple point is that children who have been through an effective preschool do so much better later than children who have not.   It seems as if a good self-image, self-esteem, ability for critical thought--all qualities fundamental for leadership and management--are the greatest gifts caregivers can mediate to a child.   In short it is the personal feeling of agency that counts in the end.   I can do!   I can manage!   If economic models of analysis are applied to education as a social investment, the results are striking.   In development thinking, it has been common to assume a new nation has a great need for academic expertise, an educated elite to manage high technology enterprises.   One would expect that higher education is what counts in this respect. (34)   It is, therefore, surprising to find that leading experts conclude there has been an over-investment in secondary and graduate candidates.   These are idle human resources because of the high unemployment rate and subsequent braindrain to other countries.   These experts urge that national resources be diverted from secondary and higher education to the primary schools. (37)

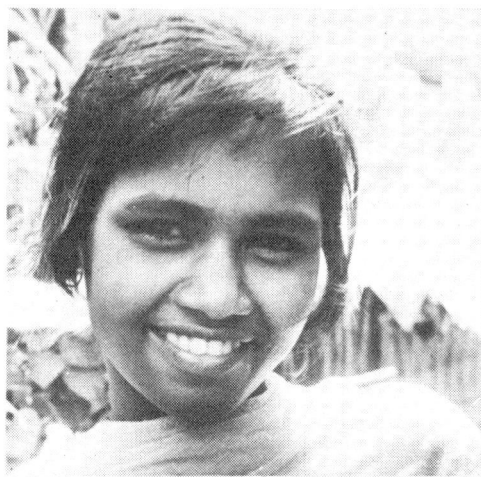

231

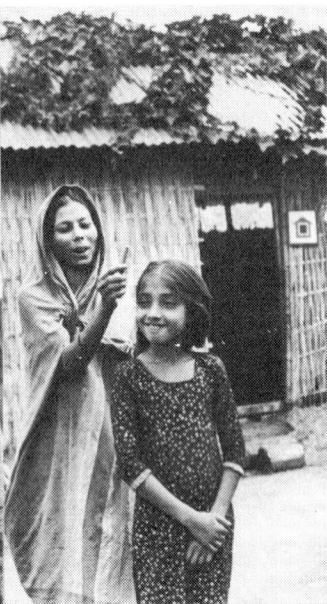

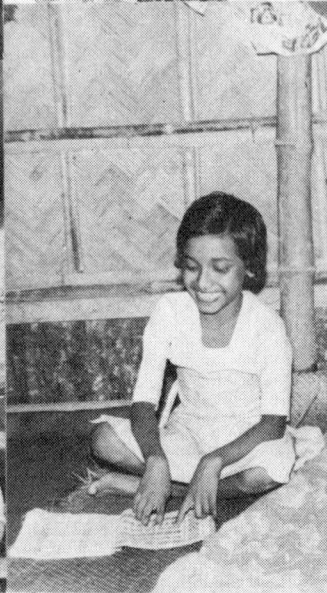

232

Some even go further, suggesting that early childhood education is likely to be the most profitable of all forms of education, according to a World Bank Report. (38) The social rates of return from various investments in education across twenty development and industrialized societies have now been investigated and calculated. While the rates were only from 11 to 13% from higher and secondary education, they were as high as 26% from primary education and as much as 30% from community-based preschool programmes. In other words, in terms of priorities, it is more profitable for society to prepare children to gain a minimum capability in numeracy and literacy.

Likely this problematique is already considered by the Bank's leadership. Such a long-term approach to solving the pressing problem of planning, organizing management and ultimately empowerment of the poor would entail a considerable expansion of the Bank's social development programme. Members would have to be convinced of the need to start more than 30 000 new centre schools. This is in itself a colossal enterprise. Even more demanding would be organizing a comprehensive training system adding thousands of new workshops to the existing schedule. With Grameen's existing organizing talent and capacity, staff certainly could take on such a challenge. The very advantageous link to the Children's Welfare Fund provides a potential for future sustainability. Nevertheless, this can hardly be done without a large infusion of donor funds.

THE DONOR DILEMMA

Grameen Bank's history demonstrates a healthy and successful capacity for organizational development and problem-solving. It has taken into use the most advanced management systems. It has carved a niche for itself in the economy of poverty in Bangladesh where the political environment is not quite stable. Staff relations may tend to be unpredictable. But these are problems the Bank can cope with. The threat is not likely to come from within. There is a greater danger that the donor agencies may destroy the Bank.

The issue is whether donor criteria and premises for continued funding support shall take preference over the responses to people's needs. We do not know the details of what is happening in Grameen's conference room. The analysis is in the situation itself. Donor insight in the deeper problematique of social organizing and participation is scant and stereotype. Predominant in the bilateral or multilateral ideology are such catchwords as self-determination, self -reliance or sustainability. Although the monetarist pressure from international economics advisers is likely to abate after the excesses of the Thatcher/Regan years, there is, and is likely to be for some years to come, donor pressure on the Bank to demonstrate financial viability and profitability. In the short or mid-term such results can be achieved, but in the longer-term, it might be a mistake to yield to that idea. The donor dilemma is also bureaucratic in nature. The procedures for reporting and the amount of financial and substantive reports required is excessive and sometimes not proportionate to the benefits accrued to the Bank. The time of leadership and senior officers can be more fruitfully applied in solving problems with the poor. Grameen Bank is currently without comparison the most interesting and promising large-scale socio-economic experiment on the international development scene. It is a magnificent social achievement. What it requires now is peace to work and opportunity to take decisions in a long-term perspective of the next 15 to 20 years.

In the spirit of the UNDP 1991 Human Development Report, (39) donor agencies should, indeed, be the first to recognize the continuous failure of short-term economic remedies and results to lead to sustainable development. The report points out the need for capital investment in human resources: "The main task is to invest in people, liberating their initiative". In the above long-term perspective and on the basis of current knowledge and experience, if such human resource development shall succeed, it must have a focus on children. In practice this would require a considerable enhancement of Grameen Bank's social development programme.

This is where a serious dilemma becomes apparent. The social development programme is already spread thinly. As mentioned earlier, there is a need to triple the number of centre schools and to improve the quality of the education going on within them. The general seven-day workshop is presently given to selected numbers of centre chiefs only every second year in a branch. Already, under the current pressure of economic performance, the bank workers spend most of their time in the centres on financial matters. Our estimate is that little more than 10% of their time with the members is spent on social development matters.

If the Bank, within the present scope of resources, is pressing further for higher profitability of the branches, such results are likely to be achieved at the expense of the social development programme and its potential long-term effects, especially on the situation of the children. From this perspective several ideas for rationalization need careful scrutiny. Increasing the number

234

of groups in the centre from 6 to 8 will most surely in the short-term increase branch profitability. A similar effect may be achieved by letting the centre chief collect monies instead of the bank worker. Another example is enhancing branch turnover by setting up extra booths. But what are the consequences for the work situation of the bank worker and the wider consequences for the social development programme? Or, rather, what compensatory measures would such rationalization require for the social development programme? In our view, improvement in the quality of life of people's basic needs in industralized countries cannot be attributed to their economic development in isolation, but must be seen in combination with their accompanying social and educational policies and programmes.

A long-term perspective must also be applied to the other organizational development initiatives by the Bank, especially the Krishi Foundation and the Fisheries Foundation. Donor pressure for quick, tangible results can cause great damage. The primary requirement for understanding such organizational learning processes is patience and respect for social and economic complexity. Financial, and not the least moral support, within a timeframe of fifteen to twenty years, is required for these experiments to have a fair chance of succeeding. In this context there is a wider problematique emerging in the literature which may need exploring through more research. Due to our own limitations we attempt to outline some of its major features only.

INTERACTION WITH MAINSTREAM ECONOMY
On several occasions, Yunus has pointed out the need for connecting the production of the poor with the mainstream economy in Bangladesh. There is a dichotomy that has something to do with the urban/rural relationship. Savings from the rural areas through the commercial bank system end up in the cities as capital investment in the industrial sector--and do not benefit the rural areas where the poorest part of the population is grossly underemployed. On the other hand, the industrial sector and especially its producers of secondary products of the cheapest kind benefit from the huge market of 50 million poor with very low but, nevertheless, some purchasing power. At the same time, the poor do not find--maybe with minor exceptions--much of a market among the richer parts of the population for their own products. In addition, billions of US dollars in foreign aid is going into the industrial sector and capital-intensive high-technology projects with no benefit for the poor. Similarly, the upper and middle class of landowners, who, most of the time live in the cities, have benefited from huge amounts of rural credit on which they have defaulted to a tune of 60 to 70%. This situation produces and reinforces continually a dualism in the Bangladesh economy. (32) It is a dichotomy appearing insurmountable.

Economy
of the poorest

ECONOMY
OF THE POOR

ECONOMY
OF THE RICH

Grameen Bank

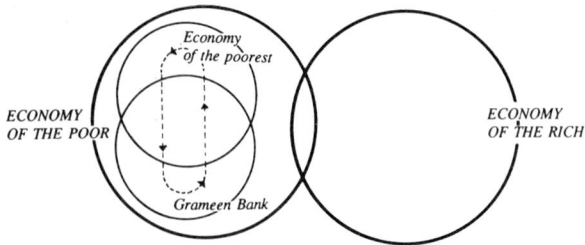

Between the non-formal and formal economy--or as we prefer to label it, the economy of the poor and the economy of the rich, there is very little overlap and interaction. Grameen Bank has created a niche for itself within the economy of the poor. There is a high degree of overlap and economic interaction between the Bank members, the micro-entrepreneurs, and the surrounding section of the other poor that constitute their market. The economy of the poor is characterized by subsistence and extremely low accumulation. The quantity of bank notes and coins circulating is low, leading to a very rapid cash flow. Small monies change hands very quickly. This high velocity circulation has an interesting problematique. (32) It is the very basis for the weekly instalment success of the Bank which yields such high repayment rates, but it also entails limitations. As Kochendörfer-Lucius and Osner point out, the high velocity may have implications for the Bank's savings policies among its members. If large numbers of poor save money and take them out of circulation the velocity may slow down considerably. The consequence of that is that fewer people will have monies passing through their hands during the day.

The high velocity creates the economic illusion that there is money enough for everybody; some money is available for everybody at one point in time or another. But the system leaves no room for large capital accumulation and investment because it ties up a substantial part of the monies circulating in the system. That the Bank's leadership is cognizant of these potential limitations is demonstrated by the organizational developments described earlier. However, further studies are required to understand the economic issues, for example the issue of land tenancy or ownership. In an agricultural economy it is a fairly evident observation that the poorest, given sufficient available capital, will enlarge their asset base by investment in land. The question is: Do they acquire the land from large- or middle-sized landholdings--or just from other poor. In the latter case, the socio-economic stratification is not reduced, but the Grameen poor are enlarging their assets at the expense of other poor? Such issues are of considerable importance for long-term policy decisions in the Bank.

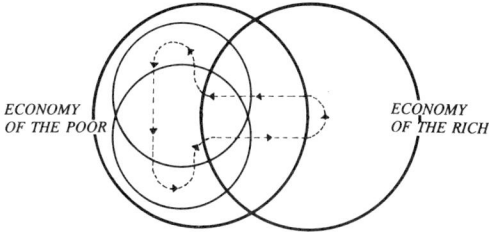

Only when interaction and integration between the two economies are increased, as we attempt to visualize in this diagram, will it be possible for the poor to make more substantial progress. Moreover, the poor need control over and the capability to handle more capital-intensive, high-technology production. Their products must be competitive in the economy of the rich and they must be able to sell increased quantities. This is precisely what the long-term goals are of the Grameen Family of Organizations. And Grameen Bank is cognizant of the need for attracting savings from the lower-velocity richer economy for investment in the economy of the poor. The issue is to break into the economy of the rich and get control of larger resources. This is a new approach to economic and social reform. In a time of ever-faltering development efforts, its demonstration value is indisputable.

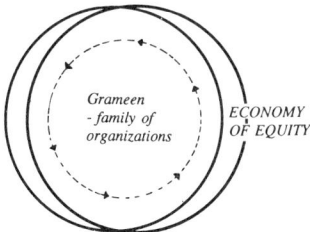

The ultimate goal is a society and a national economy where human rights reign and access to and control of resources is distinguished by equity. This is a

237

balanced social democratic state of affairs which has otherwise been achieved only through subsidies and progressive taxation over 40 to 50 years of parliamentary legislation.

TOWARDS A NEW POLITY?

This is perhaps the point where economic speculation should yield to the considerations of political science: the point where a duck changes to a rabbit in our perception. In our first book about the Bank, "Participation as Process", we suggested that Grameen was more than a Bank. We saw it as a socio-economic formation for people's participation. In this expanded revision, we are adding "Process as Growth". Now, we feel that the Bank has significance far beyond such a formation. It is a people's movement with quite extraordinary implications in terms of its organizational growth in size, capacity and quality.

People's participation is generally the core issue in democracy. More specifically the practice of participation in rural development has been a central theme in the discussion about social and economic change in the countries of the South. (40) While it is much talked about and attempted, participation remains a feeble undertaking in practice. It is very rarely achieved. Several reasons have been proffered. Some maintain that people are too backward, ignorant or intransigent. Others argue that the rural elite constitutes a massive, oppressive power opposed to any form of participation by the people. None of this arguementation holds. Grameen admirably demonstrates that the opposite is the case.

We witness today in many new nations the failing of Statehood. There is increasing doubt about the State as the vehicle of development and human progress. Without an overarching organizational framework, social reality is factionalized in ethnic, clan, political, religious or economic bickering and violence. The poor die or survive whether the State is there or not. The State is not a meaningful quantity in their lives. What Grameen offers people is the opportunity to recreate their social and economic reality in a spirit of meaning and dignity. Grameen succeeds in doing what a State should do--providing an enabling organizational framework, a socio-economic environment conducive to the participation of its people. In this spirit, Grameen is a people's movement profoundly non-political and non-confrontational, achieving its aim through perseverance, sincerity of purpose, quality of performance and capacity for consensus. And, in a sense, the resistance of the rural power structure disintegrates for its lack of the same.

238

In our first book, we raised the tentative question: Is the Grameen socio-economic formation an emerging new approach to forging Statehood? In a recent report analyzing the Bank and its socio-political context, a similar idea is pursued by D. Mauro DiDomenico. He asks two lingering questions: "Will the expansion of political participation among the rural poor and the simultaneous erosion of elite powers that occur in Grameen villages be a source of instability? Or might it pose an alternate foundation on which the institutions of the State can be built?" And he concludes, "The institutions of the modern state, which have so long and so painfully eluded Bangladesh, may ultimately be forged by an organization without formal political ties or ambitions." (41)

WHAT CAN WE LEARN ...
It is important to recognize that Grameen Bank is a product of the Bangladesh economy and a unique organizational culture. It has grown as a response to a situation of extreme poverty and demonstrates the potential of the poor for creative and self-reliant development. All too easily participatory approaches could serve as a pretext for symbolic gestures of responsibility by governments, letting the poor, by and large, cater for themselves while the rest of the economy remains the same. In extolling Grameen Bank's achievements, we should not allow ourselves to be distracted from urgent national issues of social justice and the need for structural transformation. Whatever the country, a Grameen Bank cannot solve the problem of poverty if the prevailing power elite continues its malpractices or a military presence confiscates the lion's share of the national income.

Dispelling the myths. What have we learned? Although the scale of its potential impact is still unknown, Grameen Bank is effectively liquidating several commonly-held assumptions about social and economic development. The first myth is that spontaneous organization in the streets is enough to bring social change. It can overthrow governments, but it has historically never led to the creation of new enabling institutions. Decades of patient organizational development is required.

Another myth purports that macroeconomics offers the valid conceptual framework for development planning and decision-making. Grameen Bank's experience indicates that economists should now concentrate more on microeconomics.

Banking and specifically rural credit banking, is not as complicated as bankers care to believe. Collateral is not a mandatory prerequisite for loans to the poor. Poor people utilize their loans very well and repay according to schedule. It is now a matter of fact that effective procedures for bank transactions with the poor can be established.

It is not true that educated youth in countries of the South are motivated only for lucrative jobs and the easy city life. Very often young people are more concerned about the future of their country than the older generations. Given the opportunity, youth will achieve results and endure hardship out of commitment to alleviate the need around them.

It is not given that the local power structure is invincible. Grameen Bank demonstrates that a participatory process among the poor themselves can disaggregate local power without confronting it.

It is not a pre-condition that people must be conscientized and develop skills before they can enter into a participatory process. The strength people need starts to grow from their stomach. Access to and control of a resource is the first step. All other development follows in the process. Contrary to a cherished development assumption, adult literacy is not an absolute premise for change. It is a myth that the poor are unruly, needing a superior authority to solve their conflicts. Given an appropriate organization framework, the poor are capable of making their own decisions and solving their own conflicts. Grameen Bank brings decision-making back to the people where it belongs. It does not steal people's conflicts nor does it subdue them.

Free elections are not enough. The poor are being bought or manipulated. Organizational development, creation of enabling institutions is the key to an effective, operational democracy and participation of the poorest. Grameen Family of Organizations is a social and economic experiment of historical importance.

Grameen Bank demonstrates for the first time on a large scale that not the individual but the group should be the starting point for development. Social identity is more than individuality. The individual relates only with difficulty to a larger organization, or the State. Therein lies the problems of representative democracy and participation. Through groups and centres, the Grameen Bank formation as a whole reaches a level of accountability that coheres it for large-scale participatory action. Bidhimala can be read in two ways, as a guideline for running a bank and as a constitution for a nation of the poorest.

240

A development bank that turns upside down so many deeply-held beliefs exposes itself to criticism and scepticism. Some argue that Grameen Bank lives off the poor, makes petty capitalists out of them or traps the poor in eternal debt. Others maintain that the bank condemns people to the kind of work and utilization of skills which are not productive because they do not contribute to the national product. The Bank rejoins that the landless poor are oppressed by a monetary economy, so development is more pragmatically initiated with access to credit. To a significant degree, people can learn to manage ever more complex financial transactions and operations. The money is just a medium for people to achieve something else. Besides, the rapacious consumers in industrialized societies are living on instalment plans and credit cards, why should it be morally repugnant when poor people do the same? After all, the vast majority of Grameen Bank loans are paid off in one year.

A survey of development initiatives will reveal very few, if any, which approach the tangible outreach of Grameen Bank's programme. None come to our mind. Grameen Bank has brought concrete changes in people's lives in terms of health, nutrition, status, housing, education, hope and dignity. Statistically, it reaches now 1.5 million members, but in fact it reaches many more. Adult men and women live in families and, as a whole, the families of Grameen Bank members have been lifted from abject levels of poverty. It could be argued that Grameen Bank has affected the daily lives of more than six million people, based on a conservative family size of four.

Trying it somewhere else. Should the Grameen Bank approach be attempted in other countries? Of course it should be replicated; as described under the Grameen Trust several replications are well underway. People with serious intentions to replicate need to be aware, though, of the many technical aspects of banking that are entailed. Immersion studies at the branch level of Grameen Bank itself are necessary. David Gibbons, Sukor Kasim, M. Khalid Shams and Ismael P. Getubig, Jr. provide salient reading in this respect. (42) In our opinion, a replication process begins best with a small, modest action research project just like that in Jobra in August 1976. And those who start it must commit themselves to the autonomy and learning of the process as it evolves. It is an experience very different from what people are accustomed to in ordinary organizations or bureaucracies.

What makes the process work? There are no hard and fast rules for a step-by-step guide to implement Grameen Bank projects. In the spirit of Grameen Bank, we prefer to steer the attention to the personal attitudes and norms of behaviour so vibrantly alive among its leaders, staff and members: commitment to people, commitment to the eradication of poverty, belief in hard work, honesty, integrity, accountability, openness and confidence, learning from mistakes, responsiveness, supervision and discipline and creativity. To start a Grameen Bank there is one overriding question to ask: What is necessary to create a social and organizational environment which allows the people involved to feel and act with the above attitudes?

Others may see it otherwise. Personally, we see in Grameen Bank's work an example of true social democracy. It gives the individual opportunity for initiative and enterprise, but it also subjects that same person to strong social accountability. All industrialized countries have a lesson to learn from this experience. Scandinavian countries are no exception. Dwindling solidarity and social accountability are the fundamental issues facing the modern welfare state.

BEYOND THE APPROACH ...

An analysis of the Grameen Bank approach by itself is insufficient for an understanding of its success. As well, it is important to be aware of some of the predominant socio-economic features likely to have conditioned the approach. Two major factors of influence are population density and the degree of labour division among the landless poor in Bangladesh.

Population density. According to the Bangladesh Bureau of Statistics, the country's population was 104 million in 1991. With its small area of 55 598 square miles including all the rivers, the resulting population density of Bangladesh is extremely high, 1 870 people per square mile. Even the most densely populated countries in Africa such as Egypt, Ethiopia or Nigeria have only a fraction of this population density. This factor has implications for two important aspects of the Bank's work: communication and transport. Although transportation and access to the villages in Bangladesh are difficult at certain times of the year, it is possible for the bank workers to carry through their regular schedule of morning centre meetings and afternoon training and supervision. As walking is the most common means of transport with bicycles becoming more and more common, the costs are obviously low. The elaborate accounting, reporting and supervising procedures are undoubtedly a main reason for the effectiveness of Grameen Bank. At the same time, these are also highly labour intensive and costly. It would need to be assessed if or how such a high intensity of processing and supervision could be sustained in rural areas with a relatively scattered population. Would it be cost-effective? In other words, is there a threshold of population density below which the approach as it is practiced by Grameen Bank is inoperable?

The factor of local distances might be decisive for the extent of people's participation in centre activities. In general, women and men who are subsistence farmers have a work routine which limits their time and women have the extra work load of fetching water and fuel as well as labour-intensive food preparation. People can only walk so far for a meeting. In themselves, these factors do not deter replication, but are a reminder of the importance of population density for economic profitability. In areas of Africa where the population is clustered densely, a replication will have good chances to succeed. Pragmatically, the issue is to choose such areas of which there are many. For Africa, the concern is to meet its different conditions of poverty with the same challenge that inspired Grameen. As demonstrated by the Recovery Programme in Rangpur, Grameen now provides us with an even greater number of strategies from its own experience which replicators can draw on fruitfully.

Labour division. The landless poor in Bangladesh constitute a huge market unto themselves. It is not given that a high population density should always be considered a liability. Aside from their labour contribution in agricultural production, the poor provide a multitude of goods and services to meet an ever present demand among themselves. However capricious, an exploitative economic system also ensures a demand for their work and services. The wealthier land-owning class need labour, even if the pay they offer is far from just. Grameen Bank lists several hundred different activities members finance with their loans. We are asking if such a high degree of labour division is a prerequisite for the type of credit programme the Bank has evolved.

Population density and the refined division of labour do have implications for meeting personnel requirements, the scope of the market and the type and number of business activities generated. How important these factors are, will come to light through the experience of the replications themselves. Certainly the staff of Grameen Bank would reply: Trust the innovativeness of people, trust their assessment of the market, trust the potential of socially-generated solutions and respond to these.

In so many of the branch offices we visited, the bank workers had made beautifully ornamented wall posters out of the following passage by Muhammad Yunus. Losing its elegance in translation, but not the meaning, it reads, "We are all teachers and we must not behave otherwise. Ours is a creative work and we must always bear that in mind."

244

REFERENCES

1 FUGLESANG, Andreas. 1982. *About Understanding--Ideas and Observations on Cross-cultural Communication.* Uppsala, Sweden: The Dag Hammarskjöld Foundation.

2 FUGLESANG, Andreas. 1984. *The Myth of People's Ignorance.* Development Dialogue No. 1/2. Uppsala, Sweden: The Dag Hammarskjöld Foundation.

3 QUDDUS, Md. Abdul. 1984. *Food Habits in Bangladesh: Changing Patterns and Diversities.* Kotbari, Comilla: Bangladesh Academy for Rural Development.

4 BANGLADESH RURAL ADVANCEMENT COMMITTEE (BRAC). 1984. *Peasant Perceptions--Famine, Credit Needs, Sanitation.* Rural Studies Series, Volume 1.

5 WESTERGAARD, Kirsten. 1983. *Rural Pauperization: Its Impact on the Economic Role and Status of Rural Women in Bangladesh.* In HUQ, J. et al. eds. *Women in Bangladesh: Some Socio-economic Issues.* Seminar Papers, Volume 1.

6 BARI, Fazlul. 1974. *An Innovator in a Traditional Environment.* Kotbari, Comilla: Bangladesh Academy for Rural Development.

7 HALIM, Abdul and Md. Shahidul Islam. 1988. *Women In Homestead Agricultural Production.* The Journal of Rural Development, Volume XVIII, No. 2. Kotbari, Comilla: Bangladesh Academy for Rural Development.

8   HANNAN, H. Ferdouse. 1988. *Resources Untapped : An Exploration into Women's Role in Homestead Agricultural Production System.* Kotbari, Comilla: Bangladesh Academy for Rural Development.

9   ISLAM, Mahmuda. 1980. *Folk Medicine and Rural Women in Bangladesh.* Dhaka: Women for Women.

10   ISLAM, Shamima and Jakia Begum. 1984. *Women: Victims of Violence 1975-1984.* Dhaka: Centre for Women and Development.

11   SHARIFULLA, K.A. 1991. *Floods: Recurrent Natural Disasters in Bangladesh.* The Journal of Rural Development, Volume XXI, No. 2, Kotbari, Comilla: Bangladesh Academy for Rural Development.

12   NEWSWEEK. *People Power.* Special Report 21 December 1992.

13   KORTEN, David. 1980. *Community Organizations and Rural Development: A Learning Process Approach.* Public Administration Review 40.

14   GRAMEEN BANK. 1990. *The Preparation Report for Grameen Agricultural Project (1990-93).* Main Report, Volume 1. Dhaka: Grameen Bank.

15   YUNUS, Muhammad. Ed. June 1984. *Jorimon of Beltoil Village and Others: In Search of a Future.* Dhaka: Grameen Bank.

16   INTERNATIONAL FUND FOR AGRICULTURAL DEVELOPMENT (IFAD). Sept. 1984. *Bangladesh Grameen Bank Project Staff Appraisal Report.* Rome: IFAD.

17. RAHMAN, Rushidan Islam. July 1986. *Impact of Grameen Bank on the Situation of Poor Rural Women.* Working Paper No. 1, Grameen Bank Evaluation Project. Dhaka: Bangladesh Institute of Development Studies.

18   RAHMAN, Atiur. July 1986. *Impact of Grameen Bank Intervention on the Rural Power Structure.* Working Paper No. 2, Grameen Bank Evaluation Project. Dhaka: Bangladesh Institute of Development Studies.

19   RAHMAN, Atiur. July 1986. *Consciousness Raising Efforts of Grameen Bank*. Working Paper No. 3, Grameen Bank Evaluation Project. Dhaka: Bangladesh Institute of Development Studies.

20   GREER, Germaine. 1985. *Sex and Destiny: The Politics of Human Fertility*. London: Picador.

21   HOSSAIN, Mahabub. 1988. *Tax Burden on Agriculture: The Bangladesh Case*. The Journal of Rural Development, Volume XVIII, No. 2. Kotbari, Comilla: Bangladesh Academy for Rural Development.

22   HUSAIN, A.T.M. Alaf. 1985. *Share-cropping System in Four Villages of Bogra District*. Bogra: Rural Development Academy.

23   BARI, Fazlul. 1974. *An Innovator in a Traditional Environment*. Kotbari, Comilla: Bangladesh Academy for Rural Development.

24   *Memorandum and Articles of Association of Grameen Krishi Foundation, The Company's Act, 1913.*

25   CHOWDHURY, Md. Masudul Hoq and Abdul Kalam Azad. 1991. *Pond Fish Production in Bangladesh, Problems and Prospects*. The Journal of Rural Development, Volume XXI, No. 1. Kotbari, Comilla: Bangladesh Academy for Rural Development.

26   WATANABE, Tatsuya. 1992. *Reviving Water Resources with the Landless : GB's Fisheries Project*. Grameen Dialogue No. 12. Dhaka: Grameen Trust.

27   GRAMEEN BANK. 1990. *Progress Report on Joysagar Fish Farm (JFF) (July 1988 - June 1990)*. Dhaka: Grameen Bank.

28   GRAMEEN TRUST. 1992. *Semi-Annual Report, January to June 1992*. Dhaka: Grameen Trust.

      Memorandum of Association and Memorandum of Articles of Grameen Trust, The Company's Act, 1913.

29   GHAI, Dharam. 1984. *An Evaluation of the Grameen Bank Project*. Dhaka: Grameen Bank.

247

30   HOSSAIN, Mahabub. 1988. *Credit for Alleviation of Rural Poverty : The Grameen Bank in Bangladesh.* Dhaka: International Food Policy Research Institute and Bangladesh Institute of Development Studies.

31   *Grameen Bank Phase III, Project Midterm Review Mission Final Report,* June 1992.

      TODD, Helen. 1993. *More Taka, More Power: Grameen Women in Tangail: Ten Years On.* Article from Cashpor's Newsletter, *Faxnet,* Kuala Lumpur, Malaysia, May 1993.

32   KOCHENDORFER-LUCIUS, Gudrun and Karl Osner. 1992. *Development Has Got a Face: Life Stories of Thirteen Women in Bangladesh on People's Economy.* Interpretation of Life Stories. Dhaka: Grameen Bank.

      SHEHABUDDIN, Rahnuma. 1991. *Empowering Rural Women: The Impact of Grameen Bank in Bangladesh.* Dhaka: Grameen Bank.

      RAY, Jayanta Kumar. 1987. *To Chase a Miracle: A Study of the Grameen Bank of Bangladesh.* Dhaka: University Press Limited.

33   HOLMES, Al. 1987. *Managing the Non-Profit Organizations.* NGO Management, No. 1. Winnipeg, Canada: MIM.

34   HUNDEIDE, Karsten. 1989. *Development and the Relevance of Early Education.* Bergen: Centre for Development Studies/University of Bergen. Colombo: Redd Barna - Sri Lanka.

      FUGLESANG, Andreas and Dale Chandler. Eds. 1991. *Early Childhood Development.* Lessons Learnt No. 2. Oslo: Redd Barna.

      FUGLESANG, Andreas and Dale Chandler. Eds. 1992. *Children's Rights Through Community Caring. A collection of resource materials for staff training.* Harare: Redd Barna Regional Office Africa.

35   FUGLESANG, Andreas and Dale Chandler. 1985. *Search for Process. Reports from a project on Methods and Media in Community Participation.* Vol. I - a report; Vol. II - a collection of case studies; Vol. III - a selected bibliography. Unpublished reports of The Dag Hammarskjöld Foundation, Uppsala, Sweden.

248

36   KELLAGHAN, Thomas and Betty Jane Greaney. 1993. *The Educational Development of Students following Participation in a Preschool Programme in a Disadvantaged Area in Ireland.* The Hague, Netherlands: Bernhard van Leer Foundation.

37   BARKER, W. 1987. *Early Childhood Care and Education: The Challenge.* Occasional Paper No. 1. The Hague, Netherlands: Bernhard van Leer Foundation.

38   WORLD BANK. 1980. *Education Sector Policy Paper.* Washington DC: World Bank.

39   UNITED NATIONS DEVELOPMENT PROGRAMME (UNDP). 1991. *Human Development Report.* Oxford University Press.

40   OAKLEY, Peter. et al. 1991. *Projects with People: The practice of participation in rural development.* Geneva: International Labour Office.

41   MAURO DiDOMENICO, David. 1992. *Reaching the Poor in Bangladesh, Reform, Resistance and Quiescence: The Grameen Bank Experience.* A Thesis, Harvard College.

42   GIBBONS, David S. and Sukor Kasim. 1990. *Banking on the Rural Poor.* Penang: Centre for Policy Research, University Sains Malaysia. Kuala Lumpur: Asian and Pacific Development Center.

      GIBBONS, David S. Ed. 1992. *The Grameen Reader: Training Materials for the International Replication of the Grameen Bank Financial System for Reduction of Rural Poverty.* Dhaka: Grameen Bank.

      SHAMS, Khalid M. 1992. *Designing Effective Credit Delivery System for the Poor: The Grameen Bank Experience.* Dhaka: Grameen Bank.

      GETUBIG, Jr., Ismael P. and M. Khalid Shams. Eds. 1991. *Reaching Out Effectively: Improving the Design, Management and Implementation of Poverty Alleviation Programmes.* Kuala Lumpur: Asian and Pacific Development Centre.

REFERENCES FROM THE WRITINGS OF MUHAMMAD YUNUS
Quotations from the work of Professor Muhammad Yunus are taken from the following literature.

YUNUS, Muhammad. 1992. *Grameen Bank: Experiences and Reflections.* Presented at the Consultation on the Economic Advancement of Rural Women in Asia and the Pacific held in Kuala Lumpur, Malaysia on 15-21 September, 1991. Dhaka: Grameen Bank.

YUNUS, Muhammad. 1991. *Peace is Freedom from Poverty.* Speech delivered at the Thirtieth Anniversay Celebration of the Returned Peace Corps Volunteers at Washington DC, USA, on August 3, 1991. Dhaka: Grameen Bank.

INTERVIEW with Muhammad Yunus. 1991. *The Grameen Bank.* CBC IDEAS Transcripts, 5 March 1991.

YUNUS, Muhammad. 1989. *Grameen Bank: Organization and Operation.* In LEVITSKY, Jacob. Ed. *Microenterprises in Developing Countries. Papers and Proceedings of an International Conference.* London: Intermediate Technology Publications.

YUNUS, Muhammad. 1989. *Strategy for the Decade of the Nineties.* Presented at the Regional Meeting of UNICEF at Agra, India on September 7-8, 1989. Dhaka: Grameen Bank.

YUNUS, Muhammad. 1987. *Credit for Self-employment: A Fundamental Human Right.* Dhaka: Grameen Bank.

GENERAL REFERENCES
ALINSKY, Saul. 1972. *Reveille for Radicals.* New York: Vintage Books, Random House.
ALINSKY, Saul. 1972. *Rules for Radicals: A Pragmatic Primer for Realistic Radicals.* New York: Vintage Books, Random House.
CALAVAN, Kay et al. 1989. *The Grameen Bank Project (A): Who are the poor and how can they best be helped?* In MANN, Charles K. Merilee S. Grandle and Parker Shipton, Eds. *Seeking Solutions: Framework and Cases for Small Enterprise Development Programs.* Connecticut: Kumarian Press, Inc.
COUNTS, Alexander M. Ed. 1990. *Grameen Bank Training Guide.* (English edition). Dhaka: Grameen Bank.
FREIRE, Paulo. 1970. *Pedagogy of the Oppressed.* New York: Seabury Press.

GRAMEEN BANK. *Annual Report 1991*. Dhaka: Grameen Bank.

GRAMEEN BANK. 1990. *Forms and Formats of Grameen Bank*. Dhaka: Grameen Bank.

GRAMEEN BANK and GRAMEEN TRUST. 1992. *Report on the Third Grameen International Dialogue Programme April 18 - 29, 1992*. Dhaka: Grameen Trust.

HUQ, Muzammel and Maheen Sultan. 1991. *"Informality" in Development: The Poor as Entrepreneurs in Bangladesh*. In CHICKERING, A. Lawrence and Mohamed Salahdine, Eds., *The Silent Revolution: The Informal Sector in Five Asian and Near Eastern Countries*. San Francisco: International Centre for Economic Growth.

ISLAM, Nazrul, Amirul Islam Chowdhury and Khadem Ali. 1989. *Evaluation of the Grameen Bank's Rural Housing Programme*. Dhaka: Grameen Bank.

ANNEXES:

THE RECKONING
...One does not, should not, doubt the self-corrective capacity of
democracy. The difficulty with this assumption will be evident. We
now have democracy--a democracy of the contented and the
comfortable. The comfortable monopolize or largely monopolize
the political franchise; the uncomfortable and the distressed of the
poor urban and rural slums and those who identify with their bad
fortune do not have candidates who represent their needs and so
they do not vote. As has been emphasized, the democracy of
contentment is the policy of the untroubled short run....
JOHN KENNETH GALBRAITH
IN "THE CULTURE OF CONTENTMENT"

253

BANGLADESH
GRAMEEN BANK DISTRICTS IN 1992

LEGEND

INTERNATIONAL BOUNDARY —— · ——
DISTRICT BOUNDARY — — —
RIVER
GRAMEEN DISTRICTS

PANCHAGARH

THAKURGAON
NILPHAMARI
LALMONIRHAT
DINAJPUR
KURIGRAM
RANGPUR

GAIBANDHA
JAIPURHAT
SHERPUR
NAOGAON
BOGRA
JAMALPUR
NETRAKONA
SUNAMGANJ
SYLHET
NAWABGANJ
MYMENSINGH
RAJSHAHI
NATORE
SIRAJGANJ
KISHOREGANJ
HOBIGANJ
MOULVI BAZAR
TANGAIL
GAZIPUR
PABNA
Padma
NARSINGDI
KUSHTIA
DHAKA
BRAHMANBARIA
MEHERPUR
RAJBARI
MANIKGANJ
NARAYANGANJ
I N D I A
CHUADANGA
JHENAIDAH
FARIDPUR
MUNSHIGANJ
MAGURA
COMILLA
KHAGRACHARI
HILLTRACTS
MADARIPUR
NARAIL
CHANDPUR
JESSORE
GOPALGANJ
SHARIATPUR
I N D I A
FENI
KHULNA
BARISAL
LAKSHMIPUR
SATKHIRA
PIROJPUR
NOAKHALI
RANGAMATI
HILLTRACTS
BAGERHAT
JHALAKATI
BHOLA
PATUAKHALI
CHITTAGONG
BARGUNA
BANDARBAN
HILLTRACTS
COX'S BAZAR

B A Y   O F   B E N G A L

```
10  0  10 20 30  40 MILES
├──┼──┼──┼──┼──┤
10  0  20   40   60 Km
```

BURMA

ANNEX 1

ENGLISH VERSION OF BIDHIMALA (Constitution)

Bye-laws of the GRAMEEN BANK PROJECT

Project Director: Professor Muhammad Yunus

1.0 Grameen Bank Project

1.1 The objective of Grameen Bank Project is to introduce and institutionalize a non-traditional banking system in rural areas which would provide credit facilities under special terms and conditions. This project attempts to serve those rural people who are not covered by the traditional banking system. The success of this project entirely depends on the sincere efforts to follow the rules and regulations prescribed below:

2.0 Group

2.1 This project will provide credit facilities to the rural landless people through the formation of a particular organizational structure.

3.0 Formation of Groups

3.1 Only the landless poor will be eligible to form a group. Any member from a family (i.e. a household unit) owning less than 0.4 acre of cultivable land will be considered to be a landless poor person.

3.2 A group shall be formed with five members.

3.3 All the members of the group must be inhabitants of the same village.

3.4 A group shall be formed with persons who are like-minded, are in a similar economic condition and enjoy mutual trust and confidence.

3.5 There shall not be more than one member from the same household in any one group. If more than one person from the same household intend to become members of the landless groups, they can do so by becoming members of different groups.

3.6   It is not desirable to form a group with close relatives (eg: father, brother, uncle, father-in-law etc).

3.7   There shall be a Chairman and a Secretary in each group. They shall be elected by the group members. Election will be held at the time when a group is formed and subsequently in the month of **Chaitra** (last month of Bangla calendar year) every year. Chairmen and Secretaries elected in the month of **Chaitra** will assume their offices from the first of **Baishak**.

Duties and Responsibilities of the Members

3.8   The Chairman and the Secretary of a group will maintain constant contact with the Landless Association and the loan-giving Bank on behalf of the group. The Chairmen and the Secretaries of the groups will be responsible for recommending credit requirement of the individual members, ensuring proper utilisation of the credit and repayment of loans.

3.9   All the members of the group shall remain present in the weekly meeting of the group.

3.10   At the weekly meeting, each member of the group must deposit at least one taka as his savings. This amount which is collected as his weekly savings shall be deposited in the group's own account with the Bank.

3.11   In the weekly meeting the Chairman will maintain discipline, collect weekly dues from the individual members and deposit it to the representative of the Bank.

3.12   Every member of the group must be fully aware of his responsibilities as a member and of the rules and regulations governing the activities of the group. Every member must endeavour to maintain discipline within the group and to observe the rules and regulations of the bank. All members shall always keep vigilance over each other regarding the proper use of bank credit and regular payment of instalment. They shall also make sure that every member attends the weekly meetings regularly.

4.0   Loan Disbursement and Repayment Procedure

4.1   The lending bank will recognize a group only after being satisfied with the eligibility of its members and after observing in several successive weekly meetings their eagerness to maintain group discipline.

4.2   The bank will consider loan applications from the members of the recognized groups, for different economic activities. Group membership alone will not entitle a member to get bank loans. The members, as their turn comes, will be considered qualified for loans from the bank only if they full abide by the rules and regulations of the bank.

4.3   Receiving loans by the remaining members in subsequent turns shall depend on regular payment of instalments by the members who already received loans, and strict observance of rules and regulations by all group members.

4.4   All loans taken from the Bank shall generally be repayable in weekly instalments.

a)   In cases where the utilisation of a loan generates opportunity for daily or weekly incomes, the loan shall have to be paid off in weekly instalments.

b)   In cases where utilisation of a loan does not create opportunity for daily or weekly incomes but generates a large income in a lump after the expiry of a certain period of time, a "token instalment" shall be paid every week.

The remaining amount shall be paid in one single instalment immediately after the receipt of the lump income.

Failure to pay this token weekly instalment shall be considered as a breach of discipline as in cases of non-repayment of "regular" instalments.

Group Fund

4.5   a) Five percent of the loan amount shall be deducted as contribution to the Group Fund. This amount shall generally be known as "group tax" or "group savings". This money shall be deposited in the group's own account. The member from whose loan this amount is deducted shall have no personal right or claim over it.   This deducted money as a whole shall be treated as a fund belonging to the group. All members shall have equal rights to this fund.

Withdrawals from this fund shall be made under joint signatures of the group Chairman, Secretary and the Field Manager. While withdrawing money from this account, the group Chairman and the Secretary shall have to be present in person at the bank.

If any member of the group intends to leave the group voluntarily or is expelled at any time, he shall not get any share of this money.

b) The combined fund of group savings and weekly individual savings shall be known as "Group Fund". Up to a maximum of 50% of the total amount accumulated in the Group Fund may be borrowed and invested by the group members jointly or in partnership with another group and/or taken by individual group members as loans for any purpose with the approval of all the members.

c) In taking individual loans from the Group Fund, a special meeting of the group members in the presence of the bank worker shall be necessary. Money from the Group Fund may be withdrawn only on the basis of unanimous decision of that meeting. This meeting shall also decide the term, repayment procedures etc of the loan.

d) Five percent of the loan money shall be deducted as "group tax" at the time of disbursement of loans from the Group Fund.

e) Each group shall fix its own rate of interest on loans from the Group Fund (the group may also advance loans without charging any interest, if it so desires). The rate so fixed shall apply to all loans. In other words, the rate of interest fixed for Group Fund loans shall, in no circumstances, vary from individual to individual.

f) The group shall be fully responsible for the recovery of the loans given from the Group Fund. It may, however, be specially mentioned that if this loan money is not repaid in due time according to its terms and conditions, it shall be considered by the bank as breach of discipline of the group.

g) When a member leaves the group, he will be entitled to a refund of the entire amount of his personal savings deposited in the Group Fund at the rate of one taka per week. This personal savings, however, cannot be withdrawn for any other reason except this one.

h) If any member of the group does not repay bank loans willingly or unwillingly, the loan has to be repaid in full from the Group Fund deposits.

i) If any loan taken from the Group Fund remains unrepaid even after the expiry of the agreed time limit, no new loan shall be advanced from the Fund.

j) If all the members of any group leave the group willingly or if the members do not keep the group in operation, the group savings of that particular group shall be deposited in the Emergency Fund of the Association.

4.6   All the loanees shall pay interest on all loans taken from the bank at the rate fixed by the bank.

4.7   Emergency Fund

After payment of the total interest accrued on any bank loan, an amount equal to one fourth that amount shall be deposited in a special fund of the centre. This special fund created through compulsory contributions shall be known as the Emergency Fund.

Money accumulated in the Emergency Fund of the centre shall be spent for arranging insurances of different types for the members eg: cattle insurance, crop insurance, life insurance, etc. The money from the Emergency Fund shall be spent on such programmes only on the basis of decisions taken by the centre.

The Emergency Fund shall be operated under the joint signatures of the centre chief, deputy centre chief and the branch manager.

4.8   Loans taken from the bank shall be repaid generally in weekly instalments according to the terms and conditions of the loan.

4.9   Loan money shall be utilised within one week of the receipt of the loan inactivities for which it has been taken. Those who will fail to utilise the money within one week must keep it deposited in the bank until opportunity for its proper utilisation comes. Any sort of deviation from this shall be considered as serious breach of discipline.

4.10   All properties/materials purchased with the loan money shall be regarded as properties of the bank until the loan is repaid in full. Until the loan is paid back, the bank workers will, from time to time, inspect these materials/properties and the loanees must extend full cooperation to them in their work.

4.11   Credit facilities offered by the bank to the members shall primarily depend on the regular attendance of all group members in the weekly meetings, their sense of discipline and regularity in payment of loan instalments. Failure of members to attend weekly meetings in time, absence from meetings, underpayment of loan instalments, non-payment etc shall disqualify the group for bank facilities.

5.0 Joining the Group

5.1 Any person, qualified as per provisions of these regulations, may become a member of a particular group at any time subject to the consent of all the members of that group (if the number of members of the group is below ten).

6.0 Fines

If a member of a group is found indulging in activity subversive of discipline (such as absence from weekly meetings, irregularity in payment of instalments, failure to repay loans of the Group Fund, etc) the remaining members may, by unanimous decision, impose a fine on him. The money so received shall be deposited in the Group Fund.

7.0 Leaving the Group

7.1 A member who has no outstanding liability with the bank may leave the group voluntarily at any time. While leaving the group, he shall be allowed to take back the entire amount of his personal savings.

7.2 If a member, who has outstanding bank loans, desires to leave the group, he must repay the entire bank loan before he leaves the group.

7.3 If any member leaves the group without paying off his bank loans, the group shall be responsible for repayment of the loan of the member concerned. If the members dissolve the group without repaying bank loans, the Association shall be liable to pay off all the outstanding loans.

7.4 If the membership of any group is reduced to less than 5 due to desertion by one or more of its members, the group concerned must fulfil the condition of minimum membership (i.e. five) within three months by enrolling new members.

If the required number of new members cannot be enrolled with the prescribed time-limit, the incomplete group has to merge itself with some other group. Alternatively, two or more incomplete groups may unite to form a complete group.

8.0 Expulsion

8.1 The group members may, by unanimous decision, expel any member of the group for breach of discipline (such as long absence from weekly meetings, unwillingness to pay instalment etc). If any expelled member owes any money to the bank, it must be realised before his expulsion, else the group concerned shall be liable to pay the amount involved.

8.2 a) The Landless Association may declare a group dissolved for activities detrimental to discipline (such as absence from weekly meetings, non-payment of instalments, failure to abide by rules and regulations, etc).

The Executive Committee of the Association, the Centre Chief, or the Chairman of any group may move a proposal in the General Assembly of the Association for the dissolution of a group. If the dissolution proposal is passed by the General Assembly, the group concerned shall stand defunct and the Association shall inform the bank accordingly.

b) The responsibility for repayment of bank loans, if any, of the dissolved group, shall rest on the Association.

c) The savings of the defunct group shall go to the Emergency Fund of the Association.

9.0 Compulsory Resignation from Membership

9.1 If the total quantity of land owned by the family of any member during the tenure of his membership of the Landless Association exceeds 0.4 acre or the value of the assets owned by his family exceeds the amount prefixed by the bank, he shall be compelled to resign from his membership of the Association.

10.0 Meeting-Centre

10.1 Any place in the village where weekly group meetings are held shall be known as a "meeting-centre".

10.2 Each meeting-centre shall have a "Centre Chief". The group Chairmen of all the groups in the centre shall elect a Centre Chief and a "Deputy Centre Chief" from among themselves. The "Centre Chief" and the "Deputy Centre Chief" shall be elected in the month of **Asharh** every year. They shall assume their offices on the first day of **Shraban.**

261

10.3 The overall responsibility of conducting weekly meetings shall rest on the "Centre Chief". In his absence, the "Deputy Centre Chief", shall perform this responsibility.

10.4 As part of conducting the meeting, the Centre Chief shall ensure attendance of the group members at the meetings, payment of instalments and overall discipline and order. He shall help the bank worker present at the meeting in receiving instalments and deposits and explaining bank rules.

10.5 If any Centre Chief absents himself from half or more of the weekly meetings held during any three consecutive months, the post of the Centre Chief shall be deemed to have fallen vacant and a new Centre Chief shall be elected in his place.

10.6 If the Centre Chief becomes a "difficult loanee" at any time (i.e. if he does not pay his instalments for ten consecutive weeks or remains absent from the weekly meetings for ten consecutive weeks or if he has not fully repaid his loan in 52 weeks), he shall be disqualified for the post of Centre Chief and the post of the Centre Chief shall be deemed to have fallen vacant. In such cases, a new Centre Chief shall be elected to replace him.

11.0 Interpretation, Amendment etc. of the Bye-Laws

11.1 In case of any ambiguity in these bye-laws the interpretation given by the Project Director of the Grameen Bank Project shall be final.

11.2 The Project Director shall have the power to change and amend these rules and regulations.

11.3 The Project Director shall have the power to give ruling in all cases not covered by these rules and regulations. These rulings shall have the force of a bye-law.

ANNEX 2

EXTRACT of the FIRST PAGE of the GRAMEEN BANK ORDINANCE

GOVERNMENT OF THE PEOPLE'S REPUBLIC OF BANGLADESH

MINISTRY OF LAW AND LAND REFORMS

Law and Parliamentary Affairs Division

NOTIFICATION

Dhaka, the 4th September, 1983

No. 482 - Pub. The following Ordinance made by the Chief Martial Law Administrator of the People's Republic of Bangladesh, on the 1st September, 1983, is hereby published for general information:

THE GRAMEEN BANK ORDINANCE, 1983

Ordinance No. XLVI of 1983

An

ORDINANCE

to provide for the establishment of the Grameen Bank

WHEREAS it is expedient to establish a Grameen Bank to provide credit facilities and other services to landless persons in the rural areas and to provide for matters connected therewith or incidental thereto;

NOW, THEREFORE, in pursuance of the Proclamation of the 24th March, 1982, and in exercise of all powers enabling him in that behalf, the Chief Martial Law Administrator is pleased to make and promulgate the following Ordinance:

1. **Short title and extent.** (1) This Ordinance may be called the Grameen Bank Ordinance, 1983.

Published in the Bangladesh Gazette, Extraordinary, dated the 4th September, 1983.

Price: 30 Paisa

Available in full on request from Grameen Bank, Dhaka

263

GB HEAD OFFICE

ORGANIZATIONAL CHART

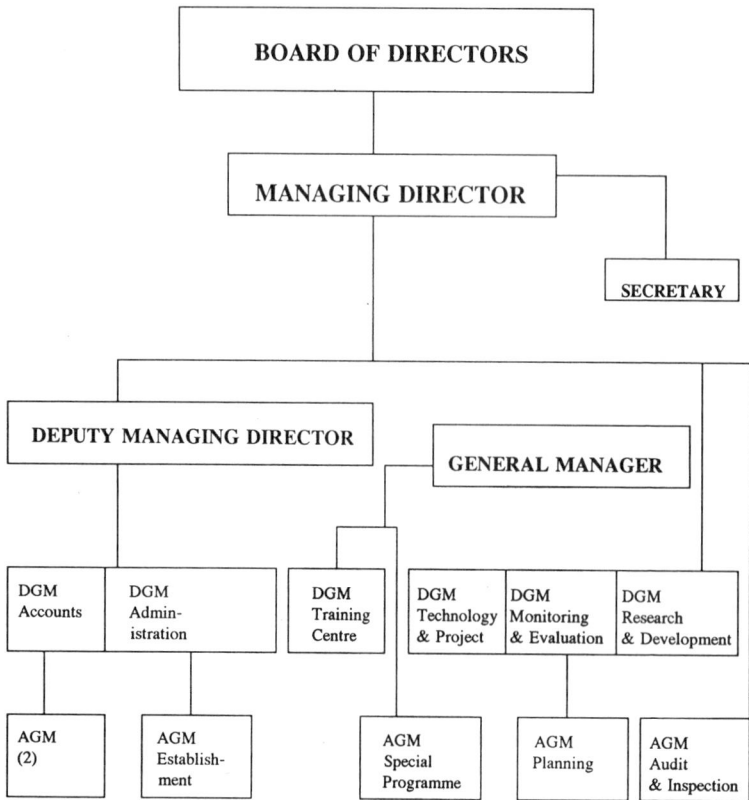

```
                    ┌──────────────────────────────┐
                    │      BOARD OF DIRECTORS       │
                    └──────────────────────────────┘
                                   │
                    ┌──────────────────────────────┐
                    │      MANAGING DIRECTOR        │
                    └──────────────────────────────┘
                                                    ┌──────────────┐
                                                    │  SECRETARY   │
                                                    └──────────────┘
```

| DEPUTY MANAGING DIRECTOR | | GENERAL MANAGER | | | |

| DGM Accounts | DGM Administration | DGM Training Centre | DGM Technology & Project | DGM Monitoring & Evaluation | DGM Research & Development |

| AGM (2) | AGM Establishment | | AGM Special Programme | AGM Planning | AGM Audit & Inspection |

LIST OF PERIODICAL STATEMENTS
PREPARED BY THE
MONITORING AND EVALUATION DEPARTMENT

A. Weekly:

1. Loanee attendance in weekly meetings including instalment & deposit payments by the loanees.
2. Staff attendance statement (Head Office).
3. The loan operation of the branches under different Zones including fund position.
4. The loan operation of the branches under different Area Offices including fund positions (of every Tuesday)

B. Monthly:

5. Zone-wise repayment index (general loan).
6. Bottom 10 Branches' repayment index (general loan).
7. Zone-wise repayment index (collective/joint venture).
8. Bottom 10 Branches' repayment index (collective/joint venture).
9. Zone-wise Group Fund statement.
10. Area-wise Group Fund statement.
11. Zone-wise Expenditure of fuel, repair & others for vehicles.
12. Area-wise Expenditure of fuel for vehicles.
13. Statement on TA/DA of Zonal Office employees.
14. Statement on TA/DA of area office employees.
15. Zone-wise telephone bills analysis.
16. Area-wise telephone bills analysis.
17. Summary of Narrative Statement of Monitoring & Evaluation Units of Zonal Offices.
18. Analytical Statement on leave of Head Office employees.
19. Expenditure of fuel for vehicles (Head Office).
20. Analytical statement on Overtime bill for Head Office employees.
21. Analytical statement of Head Office telephone bills.
22. Zone-wise consolidated cumulative statement on loan disbursement, number of loanees & branches, savings, etc.
23. Monthly zone-wise statistical statement of branches.
24. Zone-wise cumulative consolidated comparative statement on disbursement of loans, number of members, branches, etc.

25. Monthly branch-wise comparative statement of disbursement of loans, savings and new members, etc.
26. Cumulative comparative statistical statement on the total number of defaulting loanees & the amount defaulted at the end of 52 weeks.
27. Cumulative statistical statement on housing loan disbursement & recovery.
28. Area-wise statement on the number of 104 weeks loanees.
29. Zone-wise statement on side loan.
30. Zone-wise cumulative statistical statement on savings and share purchase.
31. Cumulative statistical statement on individual loanees and instalment.
32. Zone-wise cumulative statement on centre schools and other special programmes.
33. Cumulative statistical statement on total disbursement of collective loans.
34. Zone-wise cumulative statement on irregular loanees of all branches.
35. Area-wise statement on the number of default loanees not repaying the loans within 52 weeks showing simultaneously the areas free from the defaulting loanee.
36. Branch-wise statement on overdue loanee (above three Lakh).
37. Cumulative trend percentage of outstanding.
38. Zone-wise statement on Group Fund loan with 36% repayment.
39. Statement on defaulted loans beyond 52 weeks (amount per head in descending order).
40. Area-wise statistical statement on different programmes.
41. Cumulative comparative statistical statement showing increase/decrease of default loanees beyond one year.
42. Statement on top 10 branches in descending order showing the amount of defaulted loans and loanees beyond 52 weeks.
43. Zone-wise statement on Emergency Fund & Group Fund.
44. Statistical statement on overdue collective loanees.
45. Monthly statement on expenditure of Monitoring & Evaluation Department.
46. Zone-wise statement on recovery programme for 52 weeks exceeding loans.
47. Zone-wise statement on monthly deposit mobilisation progress under deposit banking scheme.
48. Monthly statement on expenditure of Monitoring & Evaluation Units at Zonal Offices.

49. Area-wise comparative statement on recovery programme of 52 weeks exceeding loanees and its actual achievement.
50. Area-wise statement on Bank Worker utilization.
51. Area-wise comparative statement on Plan-wise Outstanding Loan and Actual Outstanding Loan.
52. Monthly statement on daily expenditure of Head Office.
53. Statement on Capital expenditure from the statement of daily expenditure.
54. Statement on current expenditure from daily expenditure.
55. Statement on advance and adjustment of daily expenditure.
56. Monthly graphical statement on loan disbursement, repayment and outstanding.
57. Statement on frequency distribution of loan disbursement and loan outstanding.
58. Monthly and cumulative statement on item-wise loan disbursement.
59. Statement on item-wise expenses for construction under construction section.
60. Statement on staff position.
61. Zone-wise cumulative statement on outstanding position.
62. Area-wise cumulative comparative statement (in order of outstanding per branch) on disbursement of loans, number of members, branches, etc.
63. Zone-wise narrative special statement on defaultee (exceeding 52 weeks) loans.
64. Statement on top 10 branches in descending order showing the amount of defaulted collective loans.
65. Area-wise statistical statement on overdue (different category) amount of loans.
66. Area-wise statement on centre chiefs replacement.
67. Analytical statement on attendance of Head Office employees.
68. Area-wise comparative statement on expenditure.
69. Zone-wise comparative statement on expenditure.
70. Area-wise comparative statement on budgeted expenditure and actual expenditure.
71. Zone-wise comparative statement on budgeted expenditure and actual expenditure.
72. Branch-wise statement on budgeted expenditure and actual expenditure.

C. Quarterly:

73. Statement on Bank workers/Bank assistant utilization.
74. Zone-wise operation trend analysis.
75. Zone-wise cumulative operational result of all branches.
76. Quarterly comparative statement on disbursement, repayment, savings, new members & Centre, etc.
77. Zone-wise statement on special programmes.
78. Area-wise statement on special programmes.
79. Quarterly statement on housing loan.
80. Zone-wise statement showing the comparative position of repayment of principal loan by the loanees within a given time but failed to repay the interest & emergency dues within a period specified by the bank management.
81. Area-wise statement showing the comparative position of repayment of principal loan by the loanees within a given time but failed to repay the interest & emergency dues within a period specified by the bank management.
82. Statement on loan disbursement & loan repayment behaviour.
83. Comparative statement on plan-wise loan disbursement & actual disbursement.
84. Comparative statement on plan-wise group formation and actual group formation.
85. Comparative statement on plan-wise group formation & actual group formation.
86. Comparative statement on plan-wise organisation of centre school and actual achievement.

D. Half-yearly:

87. A complete picture of Grameen Bank's profit/loss during June closing.

E. Yearly:

88. Statement on group chairman replacement/election.
89. Preparation of annual report '86.
90. Publication of book on item-wise code number.
91. Statement on year-wise progress.

F.   Special statements:

92.   Analytical statement on expenditure of Audit Section.
93.   Zone-wise statement on printing stationery & work-aid expenditure.
94.   Statement on printing stationery and office stationery expenditure of Department & Section at Head Office.
95.   Summary of narrative statement on housing loans.
96.   Preparation of Four Year Plan (1989 - 1992).
97.   Preparation of Third Year Plan (1993 - 1995).
98.   Preparation of Annual Work Plan & Budget.
99.   Analytical statement of income expenditure of Head Office from June Closing & Annual Closing.
100.   June Closing & Annual Closing Analysis:
       (a)   Zone-wise analysis of Area Office expenditure from total income of branches.
       (b)   Statement on Profit/Loss (According to loss per branches in descending order).
101.   June Closing Annual Closing analysis:
       (a)   Income expenditure ratio of branches.
       (b)   Important information of 5 profitable branches during June Closing of 1986.
       (c)   Some information on expenditure of top 10 branches.
       (d)   Important information on bottom 10 loss incurring branches.
       (e)   A Statement showing the increase in loss with respect to the three years old branches comparing the relative positions during June & December Closing.
       (f)   The information on the branches which have reduced the loss during June Closing by more than 50% of the yearly closing.
       (g)   Statement on net profit/loss in June Closing/Annual Closing.
102.   Preparation of the Bank Budget (for Ministry and the Board).
103.   Preparation of the Grant/Aid budget for the bank (Monitoring & Evaluation Department, R & D and Tr. & Sp. Depts).
104.   Preparation of Five Years Plan (1984 - 1988).
105.   Preparation of Five Years Plan (1989 - 1993).
106.   Analysis of June Closing & yearly closing : Analysis of income/expenditure of Zonal Offices.
107.   Preparation of Annual Budget of Zonal Offices.
108.   The Zone-wise Yearly recovery programme of the defaultee loanees beyond 52 weeks.

109. The zone-wise yearly recovery programme of the defaulted loans beyond 52 weeks.
110. Preparation of Annual Budget of the Area Offices.
111. Report on Construction of Training Institute Complex and Branch Office buildings.
112. Year-wise Progress, 1976-1987.
113. Year-wise statement on year ending outstanding position.

DUTIES and RESPONSIBILITIES of a GROUP CHAIRPERSON

(Bidhimala specifies most of these responsibilities. However, as the Bank enlarges its sphere of activities, new duties are added. Here they are enumerated from our interviews with bank staff and members.)

1. She/he will arrive on time for the weekly meetings with the other four members of the group.

2. She/he will keep discipline in the group and be sure the group is in its proper row in the centre meeting.

3. She/he collects the group's passbooks (with instalment in it), then gives them to the Centre Chief. After the payment is made, she/he returns them to the members.

4. On behalf of the group, the Group Chairperson requests personally or in writing for their respective loans.

5. At least once a week, she/he will supervise how the members are utilising their loans.

6. Within a week after a loan is received, the Group Chairperson is obliged to see if the loanee is utilising the loan. If the loan utilization is perfect, then the Group Chairperson will given her/his signature on the appropriate form and give it to the Centre Chief.

7. She/he is responsible for collecting the instalments and maintaining the Group Fund account.

8. She/he abides by the Centre Chief, discussing all problems and matters of concern to the Group with the Centre Chief, entering into an exchange of views from both sides.

9. She/he will supervise whether or not the members are practising the 16 Decisions such as using pit latrines and producing vegetables.

10. She/he will buy the Bank's share in time.

11. She/he keeps in her possession all types of accounts and the pass book of the Group Fund.

ANNEX 6

DUTIES and RESPONSIBILITIES of a CENTRE CHIEF (Bidhimala specifies most of these responsibilities. However, as the Bank enlarges its sphere of activities, new duties are added. Here they are enumerated from our interviews with bank staff and members.)

1. For weekly meetings, she/he will arrange in advance that the centre house is clean and there are proper arrangements for sitting.

2. She/he will request the Group Chairpersons to ensure that all members form in rows according to groups.

3. She/he will formally open and close the meeting. If a member arrives late, then the Centre Chief will not allow the member to participate in the meeting. Upon approval of all members, a fine will be requested.

4. The Centre Chief will collect pass books, instalment books from the Group Chairpersons and deliver them to the Bank Worker, returning them later to the Group Chairpersons.

5. She/he will handle the attendance register and check if the members are signing it properly.

6. After consulting with the Group Chairpersons, the Centre Chief proposes loans for members.

7. At least once a week, with the help of the Group Chairpersons, she/he will supervise how members are utilising their loans.

8. Within a week after a loan is distributed, the Centre Chief will check to see if the loanee is utilising the loan. If satisfied, the Centre Chief will sign the appropriate form and return it to the Bank Worker.

9. She/he will have responsibility for the centre's Emergency Fund, Special Fund, Current Fund etc and will keep in her possession other centre books.

10. She/he will keep all the centre's accounts.

11. She/he will take care of the centre school and children's welfare activities.

12. She/he must investigate if the members are practising the 16 Decisions.

13. She/he will try to encourage and improve the centre's joint activities.

14. She/he will keep a good working relationship with Bank staff.

15. After one year, the Centre Chief will hand over the centre's responsibilities to the newly elected Centre Chief.

16. With the help of other members, she/he will solve the centre's problems.

17. If any member dies, then the Centre Chief will arrange for the money from the Emergency Fund with the consent of the other members.

ANNEX 7

TRAINING MANUAL FOR WOMEN'S WORKSHOPS

Taken from Atiur Rahman's study, *Consciousness Raising Efforts of Grameen Bank* (19, pp. 57-70), this manual serves as a guide for the Social Development Officers (i.e. Programme Assistants) who are responsible for the 7-day workshops for women.

Objectives of the Workshop

a. Exchange of ideas and experiences among the participants.
b. To inform the participants about the principles and rules of the <u>Grameen</u> Bank.
c. To create awareness about the importance of family planning, health and sanitation among the participants so that they can take effective measures in these regards.
d. To give the participants knowledge about nutrition and preservation of food.
e. To impart knowledge about the steps to take care of children, pregnant women and to prevent child diseases/mortality.
f. To inform about the necessity and means to grow more vegetables and plant various trees.
g. To inform the women leaders (centre-chiefs) of their role, responsibilities and duties in a comprehensive way.
h. To inform about various new ventures undertaken and experiences gained by different social problems.
i. To impart a sense of perseverance, and confidence among the participants so that they can make their groups, centres strong.

Training Programme

A. A comprehensive training programme has been formulated for the participants of the workshops. The following points and aspects are highlighted and given importance during the training sessions:

1. Introduction of the participants among themselves.
2. Objective of the training programme.
3. Methodology of materialising the <u>Grameen</u> Bank objectives.
4. Procedure and criteria to form groups.
5. Rules and criteria for utilising and managing the group fund.

274

6. Rules and criteria for utilising the emergency fund.
7. Difference between the emergency fund and the group fund.
8. Preparation of draft loan proposal and fixation of the amounts of loan for the loanees.
9. Utilisation of supervision of loans.   Procedure to supervise loan utilisation.
10. Rules for filling up the loan contract.
11. Aims and objectives of the formation of centres.
12. Responsibilities and duties of the group leaders/centre chiefs.
13. Various aspects of collective enterprises.
14. Need for cleanliness.
15. Poultry and livestock culture.
16. Cultivation and vegetables.
17. Tree plantation and the preservation of the plants.
18. Child care and child education.
19. Maternity.
20. Various child diseases and prevention of these diseases.
21. Measures to take care of pregnant women.
22. Nutritious food stuff and preservation of food.
23. Usefulness of a small family.
24. Prevention of diarrhoea.
25. Drinking tubewell and boiled water.
26. Cooking procedures.
27. Preparation and doses of oral saline.
28. Elimination of dowry.
29. Role of centres in resolving the conflicts and other problems of the members.
30. Implementation of the '16 Decisions'.
31. How to ensure "Visit your fellow member everyday" scheme of Grameen Bank.
32. Reading from Uddog.
33. Visiting groups and centres and the areas under them.
34. Discussion on matters related to the group.
35. Session to satisfy questions and trial of centre affairs.
36. Exhibition of relevant charts, posters, nutrition cards, etc.
37. Adopting resolutions in the workshop and announcing them to the participants.
38. Brief cultural functions.
39. Various aspects of housing loan.
40. Nursery programme.
41. Purchase of Grameen Bank shares.

B.   Training programme should be discussed in the class on schedule time. Groups and Centres should also be visited properly. (A programme is enclosed herewith in a latter sub-section).

C.   Each participant will discuss a particular topic or aspect. For that matter a specific and systematic routine should be followed in the class.

D.   Zonal Managers, Area Managers, Programme Officers and Assistant Programme Officers will take classes.

E.   The Branch Managers and the Bank Staff will also have to take classes.

F.   Available local resource persons may also be approached to take classes on specific topics.

G.   APOs will conduct the classes according to the routines. They must keep the information about who will take class and when.

H.   Every trainer must be aware of the given time period for his/her class. They should not finish their lectures in a hurried manner.

I.   The participants must be shown the posters, charts, nutrition cards and photographs in due time and all these should be explained to them.

J.   The trainers should discuss topics in a simple language so that the participants can easily understand them and can participate in the discussions.   Some of the topics to be discussed in the workshop programme are given below with some clearly defined points which should be covered:

Collective enterprises

The participants should be given a clear conception about collective enterprises. Stories of successes in collective enterprises in different branches and centres should be cited as illustrations.   Besides, the following points should be discussed elaborately.

1.   Principles of taking up collective enterprises.
2.   Special savings.
3.   Collective enterprises by female members.
4.   Commercial and economic aspects of collective enterprises.

5. Method of keeping accounts for incomes and expenditures.
6. Potential activities for collective enterprises.

Child care

1. Normal and ideal food
2. Breast feeding
3. Prepared food
4. Appropriate age of children for taking prepared food
5. Excess food for children from the age of four months
6. Classification of food items
7. Frequency of meals
8. Preventives against various diseases (Immunisations)
9. Cutting nails and hair of children regularly
10. Measuring nutritional status of the child (e.g. food intake, height/weight)
11. Bath and meal at proper time

Food and care for pregnant women

1. Additional food for pregnant women
2. To drink more water
3. To eat adequate vegetables and fruits
4. To eat fish regularly
5. To eat protected and hygienic food stuff
6. Consulting local doctors whenever need be
7. Adequate physical exercise in the form of walking
8. To keep oneself joyful

Small family

1. Ills of bearing too many children (bad health, economic poverty, lack of education, malnutrition, food crisis, lack of peace in the family)
2. Happiness due to few children (better education, health, economic solvency, peace in the family)
3. Definition of planned family
4. Adoption of different birth control measures.

Various child diseases and preventive measures
Diseases

1. Worms
2. Lack of proper growth
3. Night blindness
4. Measles
5. Goitre (due to deficiency of iodine)
6. Tetanus
7. Diarrhoea
8. Dysentery
9. Whooping Cough
10. Dental disease

Preventive measures

1. Not to walk bare-footed in dirty places, to drink tubewell water, to take food with a clean hand.
2. To take fresh and leafy vegetables and fruits
3. To take clean food in time and in the right quantity
4. To keep clean
5. Not to take a bath in the river
6. Immunizing against diseases
7. Cutting the umbilical cords of the newborn baby with a blade washed in boiled water after the delivery
8. Using antiseptic medicine (Savlon) as and when needed
9. To take oral saline as soon as a diarrhoeal problem is diagnosed. Saline must be prepared in a clean pot.
10. To eat small fish
11. To consult doctors when necessary
12. To clean teeth and take water after taking meals (especially by children)

Cooking procedures

1. Vegetables should be washed before cutting.
2. Curries should be kept covered while cooking.
3. Vegetables and other things should not be hard boiled.
4. The liquid left over of the boiled rice should not be wasted, but should be taken.
5. Cooked food must be kept covered in a clean atmosphere.

6. Dirty water should not be used in cooking.
7. Plates, spoons etc, should be washed with clean water before using.

Method of preparing and taking saline

1. A unit of saline is prepared with half a seer of tap/tubewell water, a little quantity of salt and a tablespoon full of sugar.
2. If tap or tubewell water is not available, pond water should be boiled first and then filtered for using it to prepare saline.
3. The water of those tubewells/taps also should be boiled if the ground is not pucca.
4. The saline remains effective for six hours after its preparation.
5. Hands must be washed with soap before preparing saline.
6. Boiled rice (delicate), papaya, banana, water of green coconut, may be taken by the patient immediately after taking saline.

Cleanliness

1. Houses, yards and the adjacent places must be kept clean always.
2. To take bath and keep clothes clean regularly
3. To keep children clean
4. Cooking pots, kitchens must be kept clean.
5. Latrines should be hygienic.
6. Hands must be washed with soap or ashes after attending nature's call.
7. The clothes, bedding materials etc of the patients must not be washed in the ponds or rivers generally where people take baths. These should be washed in an isolated place with lifted water.
8. Dust and garbage should be kept in pits.
9. The clothes and the bedding materials of diarrhoea patients should be washed with boiled water.
10. Children must not be allowed to respond to nature's call hither and thither.

Elimination of dowry

1. Dowry is a social vice. It must be eliminated.
2. Every Grameen Bank centre must be declared 'dowry-free'
3. No Grameen Bank group member will receive dowry for his/her son's marriage and will not offer it for his/her daughter's marriage.
4. All Grameen Bank group members will be encouraged for arranging marriages without dowry.

Conflicts, problems, solutions

1. Grameen Bank group members themselves will solve their problems and conflict, without any intervention from outside.
2. They should also help solve problems and conflicts of the other group members in and around the centre.

Procedures to be followed for visiting centres, groups and areas under them

1. The visit should be made on the fourth and fifth day of the week.
2. A total of seven teams will visit the centres.
3. Each team will have a leader who will work as the guide. Generally, the centre-chief should be the leader. The other four members will come from different centres.
4. The team leader will lead the team to a certain centre in the morning according to a specific routine. She/he will lead the visiting members to the houses of all the local group members and acquaint them (visiting members) with the local ones. She/he will also inform them of the purpose of their visit.
5. The visiting team must establish a cordial relationship with the group member, discuss with them the matters related to their children, husband, family and their well being.
6. The team will also inquire into the holding of the meetings at the centre, the condition of the centre-premise, repayment of instalments, special savings, collective enterprises, etc.
7. The team will also inquire into whether economic activities undertaken by the group members are profitable, how these were being run, whether they face problems in repaying the instalments?
8. The team will talk about the cleanliness of the house premises, cultivation of vegetables, plantation of various trees.
9. They will investigate whether the group members have actually built and use hygienic latrines (pit-latrines).
10. The team will also look into whether the members drink tubewell and if not, see for themselves the sources of water.
11. Whether measures have been taken to keep the family small.
12. Whether group members can prepare oral saline.
13. The team will also take interest in the education of the children of the group members.

Discussion on group activities

1. Thirty five participants will be divided into seven teams. Each team will separately discuss about their group activities by sitting in a circular form.
2. Each team will discuss the problems of the centres of its members. They will also work out the possibilities and prospects of their centres.
3. Each team will submit a report of its discussions in the workshop session.

Resolutions/decisions taken in the workshop

a) On the last day of the workshop, all the participants will take part in taking decisions on certain/necessary issues.
b) The APOs will note down the decision in black and white and will also document the final decisions.
c) The decisions will have to be announced/read out in the workshop session. Advice or suggestions will be provided to the participants to materialise the decisions in every participant's centre.
d) A copy of the decisions will have to be submitted to the branch manager.
e) All the branch officers and other employees will have to be present in the session while the decisions are announced.
f) The zonal office as well as the headquarter also must be provided with one copy of the decisions.
g) The centre-chiefs will be instructed to follow up whether the decisions taken in the session are materialised in their centres.

Cultural function

The workshop will be rounded off with holding a brief cultural function for the relaxation of the participants.